Utterly Immoral

Robert Keable and his scandalous novel

Simon Keable-Elliott

Matador
Unit E2 Airfield Business Park,
Harrison Road, Market Harborough,
Leicestershire. LE16 7UL
Tel: 0116 2792299
Email: books@troubador.co.uk
Web: www.troubador.co.uk/matador
Twitter: @matadorbooks

ISBN 978 1803134 857

British Library Cataloguing in Publication Data.
A catalogue record for this book is available from the British Library.

Front cover image: Robert and Jolie Keable on beach in front of Gauguin's house, 1923
Back cover image: SANLC labourers in France 1917 {©Imperial War Museum (Q 7827)}

Printed and bound in the UK by TJ Books LTD, Padstow, Cornwall
Typeset in 11pt Minion Pro by Troubador Publishing Ltd, Leicester, UK

Matador is an imprint of Troubador Publishing Ltd

Thanks so much!

[signature]

Utterly
Immoral

Robert Keable and his scandalous novel

To Cathy
with love

CONTENTS

Contents

IMAGES

ACKNOWLEDGEMENTS

This book could not have been written without the research on Robert Keable by three authors to whom I owe a huge debt of thanks. Dr James Douglas (1922–2003), editor or writer of twenty books including the *New Bible Dictionary*, carried out his research in the 1950s and 1960s, corresponding with many of Keable's friends and associates. Before he died, he generously passed all his research on to my father and me. Dr Hugh Cecil (1941–2020), author and military historian, wrote a chapter on Keable in his book *The Flower of Battle* and was looking to expand this into a full biography working with Tim Couzens (1944–2016), the South African author and literary historian. Cecil and Couzens researched Keable's life, travelling together to Tahiti, Basutoland and elsewhere before Couzens died suddenly and Cecil became ill. Before he died, Cecil kindly gave me all his research papers on Keable, along with his blessing for my endeavours. Couzens's widow, Diana, also generously offered me her husband's papers and encouraged me to write this book.

I have been researching Keable's life for a number of years and have been helped by so many. I would like to thank the archivists at Dulwich College, Whitgift School, the Royal School, Bath, and Magdalene College, who answered my enquiries with such patience; Pam Buck for her father William Buck's letter about his early life; Brian Willan, Bob Edgar and Peter Limb for their help and suggestions about Keable's time in Basutoland and with the SANLC; Roger, Juliet and Lee Moy Gowen for making me feel so welcome in Tahiti, for allowing me to stay in Robert Keable's house and for so kindly renovating Keable's grave in Uranie Cemetery in Tahiti; Nancy Hall Rutgers, Homer Morgan, Vivienne Millet and Jimmy Nordhoff for allowing me to interview them in Tahiti.

I would like to thank everyone at my publishers, too many to mention by name, for all their help and advice. I would also like to thank my family: my father, who patiently answered my many questions about the parents he never had the chance to get to know; my children, India, Jessie and Jack, who allowed me to indulge in my Robbie obsession for so long, and Jessie for designing the book cover; but most of all to my wife, Cathy, for all her support, guidance and patience while I did my research, and her invaluable help in turning my rough draft into this final book.

If anyone, having read this book, is interested in finding out more about Robert Keable then please visit my website www.robertkeable.co.uk.

CHAPTER 1

SIMON CALLED PETER IN ENGLAND

In 1919, Robert Keable, a London-born Anglican priest working in Basutoland, took a three-week holiday, staying in an isolated hut up on the veld overlooked by the Drakensberg – the dragon's mountains. He spent the days writing his first novel – *Simon Called Peter* – unaware of the storm he would later unleash.

The novel was, in its day, as notorious as books like *Lady Chatterley's Lover*, *Lolita* and *Fifty Shades of Grey*. It became a bestseller in America and across the English-speaking world. When published, it was seen by some as pornographic; by others as besmirching the role of military chaplains and ordinary soldiers who valiantly fought in the First World War. Others, still, argued it was a brave book that shone a light on life behind the lines and showed the torment of a chaplain unable to console his troops. And some saw it as a glorious love story. F Scott Fitzgerald considered it a 'piece of trash' and 'utterly immoral' and had Nick Carraway read and mock it in *The Great Gatsby*.

Few readers today would be offended by *Simon Called Peter*'s plot, but it is not hard to see why, when it was published, many claimed to be shocked and scandalised. The book was written within a year of the ending of the First World War – a war in which 8.5 million soldiers died, including 750,000 British and 100,000 American. Although set in France, there is no fighting, there are no cases of heroism, no scenes showing the horrors of war. Instead, there are detailed descriptions of parties, heavy drinking, visits to brothels and time spent by an unmarried couple in a hotel suite. The novel was written plainly, in the third person, with no attempt to criticise or justify the behaviour of any of the characters, and no obvious consequence for what, in those days, was seen as improper behaviour.

Robert Keable at the time of writing Simon Called Peter

At first, one can hardly imagine a man less likely to write a scandalous novel than Robert Keable: a studious, young Christian man with a first-class honour's degree from Cambridge; a successful priest and missionary serving in Africa; a chaplain working in France during the war. But there is far more to Keable's life than the writing of *Simon Called Peter*, and he surprised, shocked and scandalised people throughout his life – at Cambridge, in Zanzibar, in Basutoland, during the war, back home in England and finally in Tahiti. There is so much more to the life of Keable than the scandal that followed the publication of *Simon Called Peter*; but that is how he became, briefly, famous, so that is where I shall begin.

*

In October 1918, Robert Keable returned to Basutoland – then a British protectorate and now known as Lesotho – having served in France with the South African Native Labour Corps (SANLC). He returned to the parish he had been appointed to back in January 1915 and was soon busy supporting the men who had travelled with him to France, visiting the outstations in his vast parish and dealing with the consequences of the Spanish flu epidemic which had swept through Basutoland.

For his holiday, Keable set himself up in a hut, alone, an hour's horse ride away from the nearest town – and that with only three houses. Around the hut, the clean veld wind blew constantly, and through the main window he had an amazing view of the barren landscape and the flat, bare mountain outcrops. Every day, he settled down to write, completing one chapter a day until the novel was finished. Although the setting of the novel – in France and England – could not have been more different from the view from his hut, Keable later wrote that during the war he had 'seen vivid things and it chanced that he was able to write vividly'.

The novel tells the story of a newly engaged young priest, Peter Graham, who gives up his job in his Westminster parish to travel to France, as a military chaplain. Stationed behind the lines in the busy port town of Le Havre, Peter has little work to do. He finds nearly everyone he meets is uninterested in religion and more concerned about having a good time. He initially disapproves of the drunken parties and the prostitutes he sees on every street corner. However, he makes friends with Julie, an unconventional South African nurse who starts to make him question his prudery. After an acquaintance is killed in an aeroplane attack on their train, Peter re-evaluates his life and decides to spend his free time supporting the local drunks and prostitutes. After visiting a prostitute named Louise, a few times, he demands that she sleep with him. Peter's fiancée, Hilda, breaks off their engagement and a few weeks later he meets up again with Julie at a raucous New Year's Eve party and invites her to spend part of her leave with him in London. After a weekend together in a hotel suite, Peter visits Westminster Cathedral and realises he is torn between his love for Julie and his calling. Julie persuades him to give her up and return to his job in France.

Novel written, Keable began to approach publishers, beginning with two, Christophers and Nisbet & Co, who had already published other, non-fiction, work by him. They, along with seven others, rejected the book.

The tenth firm Keable sent the manuscript to was Constable & Co. The publishing house had been founded in Edinburgh in 1795 but its great days – when it published first Sir Walter Scott's *Waverley* novels and, almost seventy-five years later, Bram Stoker's *Dracula* and George Bernard Shaw's *Man and*

Superman – were long gone. Having moved down to London in 1910, the company – after the war – was trying to rebuild its reputation.

It was Michael Sadler who decided to publish *Simon Called Peter*. He had worked for Constable & Co before the war as an editor and had only recently rejoined as a director and was soon to become chairman of the company. During the war, he was employed at the War Intelligence Department and afterwards served as a delegate to the 1919 Paris Peace Conference. He briefly joined the Secretariat of the newly formed League of Nations, helping to organise the League's Department of Publishing and Printing.

Sadler later wrote that he liked the book's honesty and thought it was too important a novel not to publish. But he also said he felt his firm's decision to publish was a brave one. By 1920, he believed the public were 'no longer hysterical' about the war but that 'there persisted… enough prejudice and enough of folly to make the publication of *Simon Called Peter* a definitely risky business'.

One risk was that the press, and more importantly the public, would be so upset by the book that no one would buy it. The greater risk lay with either a prosecution or a book ban. At the end of the war, the emergency powers of the Defence of the Realm Act were repealed so books were neither censored nor checked before publication. However, after publication, writers, publishers, booksellers and even customers could still be prosecuted for obscenity. And the vague understanding of what made a book obscene – 'the tendency… to deprave and corrupt those whose minds are open to such immoral influences, and into whose hands a publication of this sort may fall' – still dated back to Chief Justice Cockburn's phrasing from a trial in 1868.

Reading the novel today, it seems unbelievable that *Simon Called Peter* could be seen as obscene. However, Sadler was concerned about three passages: when the priest first visits a brothel; when he sleeps with Louise, the prostitute; and the detailed final section describing his time in the hotel room with the nurse, Julie.

An example of what could have happened to *Simon Called Peter* happened to James Joyce's *Ulysses* the following year. In December 1922, a copy of that novel, imported from Paris, was seized by customs because of what was deemed an obscene passage. The Director of Public Prosecutions, Sir Archibald H Bodkin, supported the seizure, declaring, after reading about forty pages of the book, that it contained 'a great deal of unmitigated filth and obscenity'. The Home Office then used the *1876 Customs Consolidation*

Act, which banned the import of 'indecent or obscene' material, to order the forfeiture and destruction of all imported copies. A ban on the book meant it wasn't then legally published in England until 1936.

The language in *Simon Called Peter* is much more restrained than in *Ulysses*, but Sadler was concerned. The last thing his firm wanted was for the book to be deemed obscene and for a destruction order to be granted. That would have meant either a full-scale ban or the need to remove any offending passages. The latter would have resulted in the book being withdrawn, re-edited, reset and reprinted – an expensive process.

Initially, Sadler planned to publish the novel in January 1921, and he had given the go-ahead for the novel to be printed in full before he panicked over the suitability of some of the content. He wrote to Keable explaining that he heard about another novel, *Martha and Mary* by Olive Mary Salter, which had been hit by last-minute problems. Its publisher, Collins, was having to make major alterations. He added that, following 'strong representation from a reliable quarter', he decided they would have to rewrite a small section of *Simon Called Peter*. Fortunately, although the book had been printed, the sections hadn't yet been sewn together and stuck down. Sadler suggested they should make changes to, and reprint, a couple of pages, which they could then swap over.

The passage that worried Sadler was when Peter was tricked by his friend Pennell into visiting a brothel. Under the pretence of following Pennell's girlfriend home, Peter is led up into the brothel, where Pennell's girl, Lulu, and another prostitute (unnamed in the book) are waiting for them. While Pennell kisses and cuddles Lulu, the other prostitute manages to get Peter to kiss her. Later – on the next page – Pennell and Lulu leave the room and the prostitute quickly locks the door and drops the key down the neck of her dress. As Sadler explained:

> we must make three slight verbal excisions on pages 220 and 221 of Simon Called Peter. We propose to reprint these two pages so that there disappears from the bottom of page 220 the sentence beginning 'The tip of a warm tongue' and from the page 221 the words, 'now you must undress me to find it' and 'between her breasts'.
>
> Honestly, I don't think the loss of these words makes any difference to the effect of the scene, but we have good evidence that ordinary brutish man is offended by these particular passages.

Keable was more amused than upset by the changes. He later wrote that the book's publication was delayed for a month:

> because it was felt that whereas the booksellers might display a book containing a certain passage which referred to a woman's bosom, they would not do so if it contained a plural synonym.

Keable was desperate to see the novel published. He had returned to England, with a wife he no longer loved, and with no job and no income. Constable, which was the first company to give its authors an advance against royalties (back in 1813), hadn't felt able to pay him any money upfront for *Simon Called Peter* since, as they later admitted, they only expected to sell about 3,000 copies. Keable, too, was not expecting many sales; he just hoped it would kick-start a career as a novelist, and he had already completed a second, very different, novel. He was busy trying to get other non-fiction books and articles published, but for very little money. By the spring of 1921, he was completely broke.

Books were, of course, marketed very differently in 1921, with no radio, TV or internet and so no opportunity for live interviews with authors. Constable was the first publisher to advertise using billboards on the Underground, which they started doing that year, but newspapers and magazines were still seen as the best source of advertising. As today, publishers aimed to get a good review out of a paper and then use quotes in small adverts.

Constable saw the book cover as a miniature poster and commissioned top artists to produce designs. Aubrey Hammond, who quickly became a firm friend of Keable, probably designed the cover of the first editions, priced at 8s/6d, with Forster and Blampied designing covers for later popular editions selling for 3s/6d. I have failed to track down a copy or picture of the original cover by Hammond, but Blampied's 1922 cover has the scantily dressed nurse, Julie, smiling coquettishly, her arm raised invitingly towards the reader. Forster's later cover shows Julie in a yellow dress drinking champagne in a restaurant, while the reflection in the mirror behind her is of Peter, complete with dog collar and military jacket, staring lovingly at her.

The initial price of 8s/6d was the equivalent of about £21 today, so not dissimilar to the price of a hardback novel now. Constable waited two years before publishing the popular edition at 3s/6d. The higher price was unaffordable for many workers in 1921, so Constable, in their first newspaper advertisements for *Simon Called Peter*, posted a week before publication, carried the comment, 'Do not fail to ask your library for this, the most astonishing love story in modern fiction. A novel men will read'. Sadler also knew that, once libraries started lending the book, an obscenity charge against it was less likely.

Simon Called Peter *cover*

Eventually, the book was launched on 1st May 1921. Keable explained in a letter to a friend that 'when it finally appeared, the main portion of the English Press cried to heaven against it, and a smaller section clamoured for disciplinary action'. Fortunately for Constable, despite the fierce critical reaction, there were no serious attempts to ban or censor the novel in England – unlike in America.

Keable expected the religious press to be upset by the novel, but he was still taken aback by the review in the *Church Times*, the main weekly paper for members of the Anglican Church. The paper had reviewed favourably many of Keable's previous non-fiction books, but not this one. The review was headed: 'A Very Disagreeable Novel'.

It wasn't a long review, but the reviewer made it clear he didn't like the plot: 'Mr. Keable's book is the story of unattractive and sordid vice on the part of clergyman', and ended by writing: 'Mr Keable no longer belongs to our communion, but we cannot think he would willingly give such pain and offence to Anglicans as this book is bound to give'.

Keable avidly read all the reviews and, once he was in London, frequently visited Sadler's office to see the latest cuttings. Many of the reviews were short and scathing, and as he read more and more from around the country, he must have felt under siege.

The Guardian: 'Not only is the theme unpleasant but its working out is infinitely nasty... if Mr Keable has not written an actually immoral book he had certainly produced a very offensive one'.

Yorkshire Observer: 'the sorriest medley of licentiousness it has been one's unhappy fate to meet between covers for long enough... He takes the reader behind the seamiest scenes and describes lax things with a fullness that is frankly nauseating'.

Sheffield Daily Telegraph: 'Was the war an orgy of lust as well as of blood, mud and hate...? The book dwells tenderly, lovingly on lust'.

Pall Mall Gazette: 'The plain truth of the matter is, Mr. Keable's hero is a bounder, and his broad-mindedness is but a euphemism for slackness of character, and his unwholesome love affair, told with uncompromising realism in its "bedroom scene" seemed to us, for all the cleverness of its relation, most unsavoury reading, and a regrettable lapse on the part of a highly competent literary man'.

Eastbourne Chronicle: 'If they did not know how untrue it was, thousands of readers might gather the impression that life of our officers in France was one long round of drinking and immorality... The character of Peter Graham is a libel, an infamous libel, on those brave, painstaking, sympathetic fellows, the padres, who were often a comfort to the living and always a solace to the dying'.

British Weekly: 'The book reeks of drink and lust... The awful thing about this book is the manner in which religion and lust are combined'.

Glasgow Herald: 'He blackens unduly the soldier's moral character'.

The Sphere: 'It is not a story of war, but of incidents in the life of a young curate who served as a captain-chaplain… They leave me cold'.

The Woman's Leader: 'The book is offensive, especially the end, where indecency is mixed with sentiment'.

The Spectator: 'The book is very well written, and obviously has a serious intention… It is, however, marred by a tendency to revel in the descriptions of the passionate, episodes in which Peter is engaged'.

The Observer: 'There is no reason why the book should not be very popular, but we think Mr. Keable will live to wish he had burnt it'.

Sadler struggled to find positive articles to show Keable but he managed to source a few helpful quotes. *The Sketch* reviewer called it a 'human and humanising experience', and the *Dundee Advertiser* critic spoke of the 'queer jumble of heaven and hell. The novel is tremendously human and shows great literary power'.

Keable was very upset by the constant stream of critical comment, both the personal attacks and – what he considered to be – ill-informed criticisms of his novel. Almost immediately he wrote to a few newspapers to complain, including the *Yorkshire Observer*, *British Weekly* and *Church Times* and to their credit they published his response. In a long letter to the editor of the *British Weekly* he wrote:

If your reviewer is correct, a writer of a steady series of devotional and religious books has, in the midst of them, suddenly put his name to a pornographic [novel] of the worst type.

Keable wasn't alone in thinking he was in the middle of a storm. On 19th May, Sadler wrote to publisher John Macrae in America, saying *Simon Called Peter* had started 'a violent controversy here between the religious and puritan critics and those of the other party'. In their original adverts, Constable made no mention of Keable's previous life or work, partly because they hadn't published any of his books themselves, and partly because they didn't want to add to the controversy. However, faced with the onslaught of criticism of *Simon Called Peter*, Sadler realised he had to act and published a four-page leaflet entitled *Concerning the Novel Simon Called Peter*. The front page contained complimentary quotes from the press praising Keable's literary output before his first novel. *The Times Literary Supplement* talked of a missionary priest who had a 'love and care in the choice of words'. *The Guardian* explained Keable was 'well-known as the author of several devotional books'. Most of the rest of the leaflet juxtaposed the negative comments of the critics alongside responses from Keable explaining how mistaken the critics were. This allowed Constable to advertise in June that:

> To meet demands from many quarters a leaflet has been prepared tabulating the case for and against this tremendous novel of faith, love and war.

It was unfortunate for Keable that by the time *Simon Called Peter* was published he had no money, and he was forced to take a job as a supply teacher at the well-known independent school in south London, Dulwich College. He began work on Monday, 16th May, just two and a half weeks after publication. This meant moving down to London and leaving his wife in their rented cottage in Cambridge.

In London, Keable quickly discovered that he had been ostracised by many of his own family and friends. His relatives were upset both by the very unchristian portrayal of the priest and by what they believed was the besmirching of the memory of his younger brother, Henry, who had died during the war. Keable's parents refused to read the book, and even thirty years later a family friend wrote about 'the very unpleasant book'.

Nearly all of Keable's old friends and acquaintances from his days as a trainee priest at the Cambridge Clergy Training School also cut him off. When Dr Douglas – the author and biographer who researched Keable's life in the late 1950s and early 1960s – contacted many of them, no one admitted to keeping in contact with him after *Simon Called Peter* was published, although one admitted bumping into him in France a few years later. Many refused to discuss their feelings about the book. Keable's closest friend at the Training School, Rev L Whitcombe, who had a room on the same staircase, wrote: 'I have thought what I could say in answer to your letter, and I have decided that I would rather say nothing at all'.

Keable tried to downplay the reaction of his fellow priests. He claimed that he had received an amusing letter from a parson praising the work unreservedly, and that the only outrage he faced came from a bishop who crossed the road to avoid him, and from a clergyman who declined to meet him for dinner because he had taken the book out of the library by mistake – having seen the scriptural title – and had then caught his daughter reading the book wrapped up in the *Church Times*.

Thanks to Constable's promotion, and word of mouth, *Simon Called Peter* sold well from the start, and the book was reprinted eleven times in its first year. It is impossible to know how it did compared to other novels of the day, as the practice of producing bestseller lists in England only began in the 1970s – in contrast to America, which had had bestseller lists since the 1890s.

As Keable was starting a teaching job days after the publication of his novel, it would have been understandable if he had tried to keep a very low profile. But far from it. His new friend Sadler introduced him to his friends and contacts and soon Keable was receiving invitations to parties and dinners across London. He learnt at a theatrical dinner that his novel 'was being talked about' and was happy to dine out on his newly found celebrity. Much as happens today, when writers or actors or social media stars are discovered, everyone wanted a piece of him. He described the experience of those two months as being 'lionised in town'. His old school friend, Basil Dean – the actor and director who made his name as one of the founders of ENSA (the Entertainments National Service Association) – invited him to a performance of Clemence Dane's *A Bill of Divorcement*, which he had produced and directed, and soon nearly every producer in town wanted him to be seen at their latest productions. In July alone he was offered sixteen free boxes at London theatres.

Dulwich College were clearly embarrassed to find they had employed a teacher who was courting so much publicity. He has now been removed from all records of the school. A search by their archivist could find no mention of him in any staff list, governors' minutes or account books for the period. She concluded he did not work there. Other evidence proves otherwise. Teaching at Dulwich is mentioned in his obituaries. A letter survives in which Keable explains to his writer friend Arthur Grimble that he earnt £100 for teaching there in the summer term. There are also other letters written at the time on college-headed notepaper. And the recently released 1921 census states he was, at the time of the census, employed by the school while boarding at 14 Park Street, Dulwich.

It was not only Dulwich College that tried to hide its association with Keable. He was certainly made *persona non grata* by Church authorities.

A good example came a couple of years later when a new, revised and re-edited version of Keable's book *Darkness or Light* was published under the name of Canon Geoffrey Dale. Although the first five chapters of this edition were Keable's original ones – 'republished by permission of the author' – significantly Keable's name was not mentioned anywhere in the new edition.

For Keable, perhaps the most important episode in *Simon Called Peter* was when his priest visited Westminster Cathedral, at the end of the novel. There, in a Roman Catholic church, the priest gradually began to regain his faith in God. The message was clear – his Church, the Church of England, had failed him, but there was the possibility he could find God's love in the Roman Catholic Church.

When Keable wrote to the *Church Times* about their review, he insisted on making it clear that, if his book was the 'fruit' of any religion, it was Anglicanism not Catholicism. He wrote: 'The novel was written, accepted by Messrs. Constable, and prepared for press, while I was still an Anglican'.

Chapter 2

Keable's religious upbringing

Keable's religious education was begun by his father. Robert H Keable had run a successful business as a tallow melter and candle-maker in Battersea before deciding in his late forties to train as a priest. He was described as a thoroughgoing evangelical of the old school, which today would be considered very Low Church. He saw himself as part of the traditional Church of England which, throughout the early and mid-nineteenth century, stood up against ritualism and all forms of Catholicism.

At the beginning of the nineteenth century, Roman Catholicism was an all-but-banned religion. Only in 1829, with the Catholic Relief Act, were Catholics allowed any sort of parity in law. But, while Roman Catholics gradually saw an increase in their rights, there remained a complete ban on Catholic practices within the Church of England. John Newman did try to introduce ritualism in the 1830s but he, and some of his followers, eventually converted to Roman Catholicism and left the Church. Others, later known as members of the Oxford movement, tried to continue with some of the Catholic practices, including the 'Six Points' of ritualism, which most Anglicans considered unacceptable. It seems odd today, but these unacceptable activities were celebrating Holy Communion from the eastwards position; mixing holy wine and holy water in a chalice openly during the church service; serving unleavened bread during the Eucharist; placing candles on the altar; wearing silk vestments; and using incense.

In 1874, when Keable's father was twenty-two, the attack on Anglo-Catholic practices intensified with the passing in Parliament of a private member's bill introduced by the then Archbishop of Canterbury, Dr Tait. *The Public Worship Regulation Act* – which aimed to put down ritualism – led to a new court being set up to hear cases. Quite a few clergymen were bought before the court and, in total, over time, five were given prison sentences for contempt. The case of Sidney Faithorn Green, Vicar of St John's Miles Platting, proved the most contentious. He ultimately served a sentence of one year, seven months, for numerous offences which included all of the 'Six Points' as well as using the sign of the cross towards the congregation, unlawfully displaying a large brass cross and also displaying a *baldacchino* (a canopy over the altar).

With the death of Dr Tait, and the release of Sidney Faithorn Green in 1882, the repression of members of the Oxford movement began to be relaxed, but even six years later, with Edward Benson as Archbishop of Canterbury, there was a prosecution against the Bishop of Lincoln, Dr Edward King, who was found guilty of making the sign of the cross at the absolution and the blessing. It was only in 1906, following a Royal Commission, that a halt was finally called to prosecutions, although the *Public Worship Regulation Act* itself was not formally repealed until 1965.

Throughout his life, Robert H Keable held a deep suspicion of Catholics and Anglo-Catholics and maintained a dislike of all forms of ritualism. He had been sponsored and supported through his training by the then Bishop of Rochester, Randall Davidson. Randall Davidson had been Archbishop Dr Tait's chaplain and private secretary and he took the lead on the archbishop's behalf, with the introduction of the *Public Worship Regulation Act*. Randall Davidson, himself, became Archbishop of Canterbury in 1902, and in ceremonies held in Canterbury Cathedral he made Robert H Keable a deacon in 1903 and ordained him as a priest the following year. Robert H Keable was the only priest in that session to be ordained who had not been to university.

In Keable's semi-autobiographical novel *Peradventure* (his third novel, published in 1922), the protagonist, Paul Kestern, has an argument with his father about placing flowers on the altar at Christmas, which his father considered sacrilegious. Keable described Mr Kestern, a priest based on his father, as having:

> very kindly eyes, a forehead which would have made for intellectuality
> if his ever-narrowing outlook on life had given it a chance, and a weak
> chin hidden by a short-beard and moustache.

The 'ever-narrowing outlook' was an evangelical one. An outlook which placed personal piety and the authority of the scriptures at the centre of his life. Parishioners in his last parish of Pavenham, Bedfordshire, suggested Robert H Keable was a good man with a sense of humour and much human kindness, but inclined to be fussy in the parish about little things.

His wife, Keable's mother, was, if anything, more zealous. Her reputation in the parish, according to Dr J W Linnell, who lived in Pavenham, was 'of one who believed that the best way to bring home a waundering sheep is by worrying it to death'. Her well-meaning efforts often proved embarrassing. Dr Linnell told of meeting a woman in the village who had just escaped from Mrs Keable who said, 'Oh dear, Doctor, I do so much hate being worked amongst.'

Her grandson remembered staying with her when he was eight. Her companion, his Aunt Grace, taught him a card game for one – patience – one Saturday afternoon. Waking next morning to a sleeping house, the boy went downstairs and started to play more rounds. When his grandmother found him, she exploded, saying that only the Devil played cards on the Sabbath. He was sent to his room for the whole day – receiving lunch on a tray.

So, home life in Croydon, where Robert H Keable became a parish priest, was very puritanical, which Keable described as a 'pleasant, simple, kindly routine'. There was a church service every day and twice on Sundays, as well as prayers and time for reflection or serious reading every evening. It was a routine that ensured everyone was busy. Perhaps tellingly, Keable wrote that 'one never did nothing' at home. There was no alcohol, no fancy cooking and no frivolous activities – Keable never went to the theatre while he lived at home.

Keable had scarlet fever when he was eight and was in bed for twenty-one weeks. What better use of the time than to read the Bible? After this, he had problems with his kidneys for at least another year and a half, which returned twenty years later. Once recovered, Keable threw himself into the life of the church. From a young age, he helped out at the Sunday school, and by the time he was fifteen he was out and about in Croydon preaching the Gospel. His father's library was full of evangelical theology, with yards of commentaries and sermons, and the young Keable devoured them.

In 1901, Keable and his brother Henry started at Whitgift Grammar School. Keable loved his time at Whitgift, joining in many after-school activities. He was secretary of the Debating Society, a member of the school's committee on natural history and a sergeant in the school cadet corps. He was a good marksman, shooting at Bisley – in the school competition – and getting the best score for his house in the annual shooting match.

It was at Whitgift that Keable first began to develop his talents as a writer and to show his interest in history. He wrote a number of stories and poems for the school magazine, which he eventually edited for a year. In 1905, he won two 'Eastty' medals, one for his poem 'An Incident at Bannockburn' and the second for his essay 'The First Tangerines' – a history of the Queen's Regiment.

His nickname at school was Kibbles and he had a few good friends, although he seems to have only kept in touch with Basil Dean after he left school. Dean remembered Keable as a 'son of a Nonconformist minister, tallish, red-haired and quick-tempered', adding that at school 'he was already giving signs of the temperament that was to lead him away from the beaten track of his contemporaries'.

The teacher who had the most influence on Keable was Mr Frazer, an English teacher who was also active in the school cadet force. He would encourage Keable to read out his essays aloud and would sometimes quote from them in lessons. He also invited Keable and others to his room for tea, where they sought information on books and fired questions at him. Dean described his own, and Keable's, attitude as 'hero-worship in an advanced form'. Frazer, who left Whitgift in 1909 to become headmaster of Batley Grammar, wrote Keable's obituary in the Whitgift school magazine. He stated Keable was 'well loved' at school, 'companionable' and 'not lacking in ardour'. Referencing an aspect of Keable's evangelicalism, he added: 'to himself [he] was perhaps too conscionable and this at times led to moments of austerity'.

Keable's almost unquenchable intellectual curiosity did not prevent him from fully accepting his father's brand of Christianity, and the Protestant work ethic suited him. He led two very different lives – at home and at school – but was comfortable with both.

He left Whitgift with a scholarship to Magdalene College, Cambridge, to study history – his favourite subject. He had already decided he would follow his father into the priesthood, but neither he nor his father saw the need for him to study theology. They both believed that a good understanding of the Bible, and in particular of the Gospels, was all the training needed to become a priest.

By the time Keable arrived at university, he was a thin, knock-kneed young man. Roughly five foot ten, he had a weak chin and wiry, coarse red hair with a tendency to curl up at the front, and pince-nez, perched on the bridge of his nose – he wore glasses all his life. He never dressed very smartly, usually favouring a Norfolk jacket and a rather tight-fitting pair of checked patterned trousers. So, he was not a handsome man, but he was a strong character, and a friend at the time said that most people found he 'possessed strong personal magnetism'.

His strength of character came out when he spoke. He had the confidence of youth, backed up by an impressive intellect. Even at Cambridge he was respected and to some extent feared for his ability to be deadly in an argument. Being both witty and clever, he could run rings round many. Keable enjoyed a good argument and was perhaps insensitive to the hurt he could cause when driving home his advantage. While an undergraduate, he had many arguments with his parents which greatly distressed them and all who saw the consequences. Ben, his cousin, unflatteringly suggested Keable was chameleon-like, capable if the fancy took him of reflecting the mind, belief and vocabulary of anyone he was talking to or chose to impress.

At university, Keable carried on the double life he had experienced at home in Croydon. He threw himself into college life, studying hard but finding time to join societies and to row, winning a place in the college's second boat. But he also quietly continued with his religious life, joining the Inter-Collegiate Christian Union and preaching in the open air. He became a member of the Children's Special Service Mission – now called the Scripture Union. At the end of his second year, he joined a beach mission at Port Erin on the Isle of Man. There, each day, he and a group of others built a pulpit out of sand, held a service with jolly hymns and a short address, and then organised activities for the children. There were walks for the girls, sports for the boys, excursions and picnics. Over the week, other events were organised, including special services for the children in the hope of hooking them into accepting Christ into their lives. Keable loved the whole experience, joining in all the games and activities with boyish enthusiasm.

He also attended the Keswick convention, an annual meeting of evangelical Christians. He described the experience in his novel *Peradventure* – attending many meetings to listen to a Church of England bishop, a Baptist layman, a Methodist missionary and an Adventist – 'who volunteered the details and date of the Second Coming of Christ', as well as a dirty, very ragged and unkempt prophet – who denounced modern Christianity in the cause of

'Humanitarian Deism' – and a prominent evangelical woman – whose subject was 'The Personal Devil'. At one meeting that stretched out late into the night, some of the attendees spoke in tongues.

Keable was clearly intrigued by the different types of religious experience on offer and, once he got back to Cambridge, he decided to visit every church in the area.

Until he went to university, Keable had never met or socialised with Catholics or Anglo-Catholics. But that was all to change when he met two of the Benson brothers, sons of the former Archbishop of Canterbury, Edward White Benson.

AC Benson, RH Benson and EF Benson, 1907

There is no evidence Keable ever met EF Benson, the socialite and successful author of the *Mapp and Lucia* novels, but he knew AC and RH Benson well.

AC Benson was, like his brothers, a prolific writer – now perhaps most famous for writing the lyrics to *Land of Hope and Glory*. He had taught at Eton for many years before returning to Cambridge and joining Magdalene College in 1903 as a fellow, to teach English literature. When Keable arrived, there were fewer than ninety undergraduates at the college, which meant everyone knew everyone. AC Benson, who later became master of Magdalene, described Keable as a friend and former pupil in his introduction to Keable's

City of Dawn. Keable was often invited up to AC Benson's room to discuss his writing, and it was there that he first met Monsignor RH Benson.

RH Benson had followed his father into the Anglican Church, getting ordained in 1895, but then shocked his family by becoming a Roman Catholic priest in 1904. He worked as a chaplain in Cambridge. Despite the sixteen-year age gap, Keable and RH Benson became good friends. RH Benson was a very appealing character, with a pleasing stutter and boyish eagerness, and the two of them were drawn together by intellectual conversation. In the holidays, Keable often stayed at his house in Hare Street, and many reported that RH Benson worked hard on trying to convince Keable to convert to Catholicism. In Keable's touching five-page tribute to RH Benson, written after his death in 1914, he described their conversations:

> [he] had the knack of putting Catholic truths simply and illuminatingly... and of illustrating them from homely incidents in his own life that made them abundantly clear.

Following his church visits and many conversations with RH Benson, Keable began to lose his evangelical instincts and was clearly tempted by Roman Catholicism. Keable's Christian friends noticed a difference in him. Rev James later wrote that Keable spoke of Catholicism instead of Protestantism, and he started to genuflect in chapel and cross himself – 'practices then unknown amongst us'. Keable also became fascinated by necromancy and spiritualism, which also had always interested RH Benson.

Keable's behaviour was, of course, an almost treasonable offence in the eyes of his parents. In *Peradventure*, Paul's father writes letters vigorously denouncing any relationship with a papist. His view was that: 'Rome was the great Babylon, the Scarlet Woman, Anti-Christ; it had lied, tricked, tortured and sold its Master all down the centuries', and he added: 'I would sooner see a son of mine dead... than a Roman Catholic'. Keable was exaggerating his father's view, but Robert H Keable was certainly concerned. A friend, AV Atkinson, remembers Keable's father arriving at Cambridge to point out to him the error of his son's ways:

> It was a painful experience for them both, but I never asked [Keable] what happened, feeling that to do so... would have been faintly indecent.

Keable thoroughly enjoyed his time at Magdalene. He was an earnest and intense young man, never happier than when engaged in deep discussion. A good university friend was Arthur Grimble – who later wrote *A Pattern of Islands*. The two of them would stay up late discussing literature, poetry and philosophy, puffing away on their pipes. Keable set up the Pepysian Society – after the diarist who had been an undergraduate at the college – where members would read out original verse and prose.

Keable wrote poems himself and a few were published in 1913 in a collection chosen by Aelfrida Tillyart under the title *The Cambridge Poet Anthology 1900–1913*. AC Benson introduced Keable to another, rather more successful, poet who also featured in the collection: Rupert Brooke. Brooke was an undergraduate at the same time as Keable but way out of Keable's league: ridiculously handsome, president of the Fabian Society and one of the Cambridge Apostles – a secret society with very exclusive membership. Years later, when in Tahiti, Keable searched for traces of Brooke, who had visited the island before the First World War. Although there is no evidence that they ever spoke of it, Keable's other connection with Brooke was through his friend and publisher Sadler. Nigel Jones, in his biography of Brooke, revealed that, as young men at Rugby School, Brooke and Sadler had had an affair.

There is no indication that Keable was romantically linked to anyone at Cambridge. He certainly didn't seem to be interested in girls at that time. In *Peradventure*, he wrote of his alter-ego Paul (while at university):

> He had no sister, and his girl friends were mainly a family of cousins
> so closely interested in each other, that, although they were friendly
> enough and admitted him to the family circle on long summer
> holidays together, he was not really intimate with any one of them.
> Nor had he wanted any girl in his life.

Keable could have been romantically linked to a man at Cambridge, since many of his friends were either repressed or openly gay, despite the law of the day, but there is no evidence. A Cambridge friend of his later wrote that Keable was 'much in favour of celibacy of the Clergy in his undergraduate days', and he had to sign up to celibacy when he joined the Universities' Mission to Central Africa (UMCA) in 1912.

Incidentally, the rule on celibacy hadn't come into existence until twenty-five years after the UMCA had been founded. It was claimed that the climate and conditions of life were unsuitable for married people and their children, although the more likely reason was that wives and children were seen as a financial burden on the mission, and, without dependents, priests were able to be more easily moved from one place to another.

Keable always had fond memories of his time at Magdalene and was proud of his success. He was the first Magdalene student ever to get a first-class honours degree in the history tripos – a degree which had been offered at Cambridge since 1873. He left a large sum of money in his will to set up a scholarship for students from Whitgift wishing to study at the college.

He didn't leave Cambridge after he got his degree. He just moved across the river and down the road from Magdalene to the Cambridge Clergy Training School (now known as Westcott House), starting his course in September 1908. It is likely his father, concerned by his attraction to Roman Catholicism, encouraged him to get going with his training.

Keable could have gone to a more Anglo-Catholic training college – St Stephen's House in Oxford had been founded by members of the Oxford Movement – but, by choosing to remain in Cambridge, he ensured his training wasn't too evangelical. Brooke Foss Westcott, who founded the Training School in 1881, had been unhappy by the way the Church of England was factionalised and wanted to offer training that was open to ordinands from all backgrounds and traditions.

Keable decided to keep his head down for two years and prepare himself for the priesthood, but even during his training he continued to have doubts. As his friend Ivan Manor remembered:

> He was curiously emotional and very attracted to Rome. He would spend, I think, long periods brooding and I remember him coming down to breakfast one morning with the remark 'I nearly went over last night.'

BTB Smith, vice principal of the Training School, who described Keable as 'that lovable man', suggested he was 'outstanding among the men at Westcott'. He acknowledged that Keable was influenced by the two Bensons – AC and RH – but doubted he seriously contemplated following RH Benson to Rome.

Keable's reputation for brilliance was shown by a letter Rev E Sharpe wrote to Dr Douglas in the early 1960s. When asked about Keable, he replied:

You have fulfilled a prophecy which I have long come to expect to
be fulfilled, to wit that my chief claim to fame would be that I was at
Westcott House with Keable.

The ordinands at Westcott wrote limericks about each other at the time and
Keable's was:

Brother Keable, I've more than a notion,
Lives a life of monastic devotion,
He chiefly surpasses,
In rubbing of brasses,
And ritualistic emotion.

Keable was finally ordained as a deacon by the Bishop of Ripon on Sunday,
25th September 1910, and he took a job in Bradford. A friend, Rev Blythe,
wrote, 'It always seemed strange to me that he went as a curate to such a very
evangelical parish as Bradford Parish Church'.

Again, his father encouraged him to work in the large inner-city,
northern Low Church parish, perhaps in the hope he would put aside his
Anglo-Catholic sentiments. It didn't really work. Although AC Benson
noted in his diary that Keable was 'working wonders as evangelical rector',
he added that Keable was still considering 'going over' and becoming a
Roman Catholic. He thought Keable's view was 'utterly ludicrous and
meaningless' to him, but admitted that 'one cannot argue with a man in
this frame of mind anymore than we can argue with a drunkard who has a
whisky bottle inside a broken door'.

For a year, Keable threw himself, life and soul, into the work of the parish
and the surrounding area. He was the driving force behind a mission to Bury
which was launched that year and, although only a young curate in a new
parish, he quickly gained a reputation as a fine preacher. He often preached
in what is now Bradford Cathedral, and he was still remembered twenty years
later, as shown by a letter to the *Yorkshire Post*, published in 1931:

Sir, I had occasion recently to break my railway journey at Bradford,
and having time to spare, I wandered round the Cathedral. I looked
in vain for any memorial of Robert Keable, one of Bradford's most
illustrious sons. Before the Great War, when I was a curate at St

Barnabas', Heaton, I can well remember large numbers of Bradford folk crowding their Parish Church, and eagerly listening to his many helpful pulpit instructions.

The letter writer went on to suggest that 'the time is now surely opportune for some form of permanent memorial in the church, which was his first and only curacy, the Cathedral Church of the Diocese of Bradford'.

The idea that he should be deemed an illustrious son of Bradford would have amused Keable. But he would have been pleased to be remembered for his pulpit instructions.

When Keable preached at Magdalene, AC Benson – a hard man to please – said his sermon was 'rather moving', although he added it lacked 'in breadth of sympathy'. The then undergraduate – later Marshal of the Royal Air Force – Lord Tedder was also impressed, writing in a letter to his parents:

> We had Keable (late of Whitgift) to preach in the college chapel for the Universities' Mission in Central Africa on Sunday morning. He is a very fine preacher; his sermon was by far the best (which I am afraid is not saying much) we have had in the chapel since I have been up. He preached the university sermon for the mission the same night – rather an honour. He has got a good post as director of some clerical college in Zanzibar to which he goes out this Christmas. I think he will make a name for himself.

So, after a year as a curate in Bradford, Keable took the plunge and headed off to Zanzibar, southern Africa, appointed as a mission priest to the Universities' Mission in Central Africa (UMCA), as well as a tutor and vice principal of St Andrew's College.

CHAPTER 3

SIMON CALLED PETER IN AMERICA

In September 1922, four months after the publication of *Simon Called Peter*, Keable was forced to take another teaching job, this time at Dunstable Grammar School. He had still not earned any money from the sales of his novel, even though it was selling well and royalties were accruing.

Constable had the rights to sell the novel in Great Britain, Ireland and throughout the British colonies, but not in America. So, while Keable was safely ensconced in Dunstable, teaching history and English, John Macrae, at publishers EP Dutton, was pushing to get *Simon Called Peter* published in America.

EP Dutton began as a book shop in Boston, Massachusetts, in 1852, before relocating to New York in 1869, where it expanded first into book importing, and later publishing. Macrae joined the company in 1885 as a nineteen-year-old office boy and rose through the ranks. By 1921, he was vice president of the company, and soon to become president.

He was the typical Virginian businessman. Gentle, courteous, very correct in his dress and manners. He was also handsome, with a fine chiselled face and well-trimmed beard. He spoke quietly and hesitantly, which one journalist suggested made her want to be assertive and abrupt even when she agreed with him. But, despite first impressions, he was a strong character, never reticent about expressing his opinion, and a natural born salesman. Unlike Michael Sadler at Constable, who hadn't published anything by Keable until *Simon Called Peter*, Macrae had followed Keable's writing career for many years. Before there was any mention of a novel, he had imported three of Keable's non-fiction works into America – *The Loneliness of Christ, A City of Dawn* and *The Drift of Pinions* – and then published *Standing By*. And he went on to publish *Pilgrim Papers* towards the end of 1921. He later admitted he had made no money out of these books but had seen Keable's potential as a writer.

He was sent a copy of *Simon Called Peter* to read before it was published in England. One could imagine why he would have hated it. Macrae's twenty-year-old son had served in France with the American forces from 1917 and had recently joined his father working for the firm. Macrae could have seen the book, which focused on the seamier side of life behind the lines, as an insult to all those who served. However, rather surprisingly, he liked it. And as a salesman he saw the potential, at last, of making some money out of Keable's writing.

That said, even though Constable had decided to go ahead and publish in England, Macrae knew he was taking a big risk. As in England, there was no pre-publication book censorship in the States, and publishers were expected to self-censor, knowing that anyone could be prosecuted and punished by the courts for the publication, sale or transportation of an inappropriate book. Since the 1896 US Supreme Court case *Swearinger v United States*, a successful prosecution could lead to a book being banned if it contained 'anything of a lewd, lascivious, and obscene tendency calculated to corrupt and debauch the mind and morals of those into whose hands it might fall'.

Macrae was very proud of the fact that he paid independent readers to assess would-be novels before publishing them, a practice that was not common in publishing at that time. He suggested to a journalist in October 1920 that newspaper critics 'came into the game too late to greatly make or mar a book', because he believed his 'radicals', as he called the readers he used to evaluate a book, were much better at predicting the success of a novel than the newspaper critics.

The radical readers from whom he sought advice for *Simon Called Peter* must have given him cause for concern. One of the reviewers, LW, wrote:

I don't know why such stories as this have to be written. It is enough that they are lived. But some fools can't let flowers grow; they must pick them... There is something criminal about a man who can write up a very, very private episode like this... How men can pin, as they pin a butterfly to a board, their innermost, most sacred thoughts and emotions and rather most secret acts, pin these wings outstretched to public gaze in a vibrating, quivering passionate tale is more than I can see!

And he continued:

There is a place to stop. The ancient Greek dramatists knew where that place was. The actual stabbing was done off stage. Over the secretest love scenes a veil was drawn. So it should be. But with Keable, it must all be told, though I cannot help admit – told sincerely, told even pathetically. Still, I see this is my attitude. Others may want to watch the knife enter the flesh. Others may care to sit between twin beds, or even climb into the bath.

And LW's final verdict:

In spite of the fact that externally the book is not badly written, I do not think it is worth celebrating, though it may sell to a public … ten million boys died in France while this was going on. All the material in the world for a story, clean material, and a man must use this.

GMA, another reader, found the book 'very unusual and sincere' and admitted:

This is a very hard book to criticize. The American public, which is far more puritanical than British with respect to such matters as the clergy taking a drink of whiskey when they need it or dining in a hotel of doubtful reputation in the society of ladies whose reputation is of by no means doubtful, would probably condemn it unheard and unread, and it must be confessed that there is enough in it to shock the conventional in this respect. On the other hand, the book is written with absolute sincerity and the truthfulness of a diary.

These differing views must have created an interesting discussion in Dutton's boardroom, but Macrae managed to persuade the directors to go ahead.

Taking advice from Sadler, Macrae also commissioned Keable to write a new preface to the American edition in part to justify his book. In it, Keable argued that:

> to lift the veil on life behind the lines in time of war is a thankless task. The stay-at-homes will not believe, and particularly they whose smug respectability and conventional religion has been put to no such fiery trial. Moreover, they will do more than disbelievers; they will say the story is not fit to be told. Nor is it. But then it should never have been lived.

Keable also wanted to counter criticism that the priest, who had behaved so badly, was not only unpunished but also intended to return to his living as a chaplain. Keable claimed his story was unfinished:

> The last page has been left blank. It has been left blank for a reason, because the curtain falls not on the conclusion of the lives of those who stopped upon the boards, but at a psychological moment in their story.

Simon Called Peter, priced at $2, was not cheap – actually, despite fluctuating exchange rates, always more expensive than in England ($2 was worth about 10s/5d in 1922). Throughout his life, Macrae challenged cut-price selling and he never allowed his novels to be featured in book club deals. Readers had to either buy the book at full price or borrow it from a library. This perhaps explains why *Simon Called Peter* sold so many more copies in America than the UK or Australia, where Constable allowed book clubs to stock the novel.

When Constable first launched *Simon Called Peter* in England, they decided not to mention Keable's former career. Dutton, however, were happy to promote the novel as one written by a priest, mentioning his devotional writings in many of the early adverts. This was despite the fact Keable had by then given up the priesthood and by then considered himself an atheist.

John Macrae Junior, Macrae's son, was head of marketing and took a cautious approach when advertising the novel in January 1922. The intention was to make it clear that Keable was a serious writer whose first novel deserved to be taken seriously, even if some would not like the content. The very first newspaper advert for *Simon Called Peter*, published on 14th January 1922, pointed out that Keable was also the author of *Standing By* and *Pilgrim Papers* and explained:

> The fine spirituality, and the keen, understanding observation shown in all Mr. Keable's books will win many readers to this surprising novel, which has been described as 'the most beautiful, and the most outspoken love story in modern fiction'. Yet it is certain to meet with heated criticism. We shall be glad to receive the opinions of those who have the experience which qualifies them to judge of its significance.

The cautious approach appears to have paid dividends. Many of the American newspaper critics took the novel much more seriously than had the British critics. For example, the *New York Tribune* reviewer compared it to John Dos Passos's *Three Soldiers,* a very influential and unsentimental American novel about the war which F Scott Fitzgerald called the 'first war book by an American which is worthy of serious notice'. The reviewer wrote:

> However puzzling and inadequate the end, Simon Called Peter is a novel far out of the ordinary and ranks with Three Soldiers in presenting a startling picture of the effect of war in stripping men and women to the essentials. It is not a pretty picture. We do not advise those who wish to cling to their illusions about religion or man to read it.

Other newspapers also struck a respectful and serious note.

New York Herald: 'The chief value of the novel consists in its vivid demonstration of the moral decay and pollution that accompanies warfare. If it did no more than show the deterioration in Peter's character, it would be well worth reading at least by those who insist that warfare develops moral virtues. As a piece of realism it is commended for presenting a graphic and undoubtedly veracious picture of actual conditions'.

Richmond Times-Dispatch: 'I think it is one of the books which has got to be read. It is gay and amusing, much of it, and Julie is a fascinating witch, but after all it is a serious book written by a serious man, who is describing conditions which he knows existed'.

Evening Public Ledger: 'The theme of this powerfully conceived and artistically presented novel is that of an English war-padre who goes among publicans and sinners to find God and his own soul. ... Yet it is not a work of realism, in the technical, or even sordid, sense. In tone and temper, *Simon Called Peter* is romantic'.

Beside these thoughtful, and generally supportive, reviews, there were others that railed against the novel. A publication of the *Church Socialist League* described the novel as 'A filthy book, disgraceful to author and publisher'.

The *Kansas City* reviewer reported:

There is no honour in being the author of a book like Simon Called Peter. A reviewer would ignore a book of this sort if he followed his own inclinations. But Simon Called Peter has for several weeks been one of the six best sellers in various parts of the country. Therefore it becomes the reviewer's duty to affix the leprosy label... Pray what sort of logic is this that argues because a filthy experience has been lived it must be served up at the library table?

Thanks to the reviews, as well as word of mouth, *Simon Called Peter* began to sell across the country. John Macrae Junior's newspaper adverts concentrated on the story, extolling the characterisation of Julie as 'Vivid, alluring womanhood' and 'Alluring as the very devil'.

As the book's publisher, Macrae took it upon himself to deal with letters of complaint. One particularly unhappy man was Rev CF Humpreys of Mantolocking in New Jersey, who wrote:

The writers of the notice advertising the book will continue to make it attractive and 'catchy' with the result that the average reader will read and be polluted, being led to believe that an ideal of 'highbrow' morality is being absorbed but actually getting only the degradation of facts which are unfortunately true... The thing that made me explode was the fact that Keable used all his charm and gift of pen on the conditions that we all know so well as the plague-spot of France and the war, to make it seem that the evil was a normal development to the average person coming into contact with it. He wrote a panegyric dedication to an unclean woman with a harlot's soul… The temptation to use sincerity insincerely and evil vilely is always present.

In reply, Macrae wrote, 'Nothing would induce me to publish a book which was to me immoral', and he offered a strong defence.

Simon Called Peter became increasingly well known in America, and the press started to include small references to it in their gossip columns. The *Moline Dispatch* quoted a librarian who said: 'We've renamed it *Simon called Putrid*,' while another newspaper offered up one side of a conversation heard in Watson's café:

'Have you read the new book *Simon Called Peter* yet?'…
'Well, don't do it, it's simply shocking.' …
'Oh, any bookstore.'

Another offered a parody of the poem *Casabianca*:

The girl stood on the burning deck
    She uttered not a shriek;
She didn't even feel it burn
    For she had read *The Sheik*.
We know a girl whose name is _____
    We think she could beat her,
She never knew when the house burned down –
    She was reading *Simon Called Peter*.

As the book gained in notoriety, so attempts began to ban it.

The New York Society for the Suppression of Vice was set up in 1873. Its mission was to monitor compliance with state laws and work with courts to prosecute offenders. It also campaigned to tighten up laws against immoral conduct. From 1915, it was led by the lawyer John S Sumner, who had taken over from the founder, Anthony Comstock. 1922 was a busy year for Sumner and his organisation. In January, it had seized and burnt 7,000 copies of magazines in Greenwich Village which were tainted with 'sex suggestions and sex jokes'. In May, it had successfully prosecuted, and seen jailed, the explorer Professor LD Covington for selling indecent 'sporty' pictures. In June, it managed another successful prosecution which saw Victor Shinkin fined $1,000 for reproducing an article called 'Turbidness' in his Russian newspaper, which had previously been copied from the Moscow-based newspaper, *Pravda*. In July, it began the prosecution of two booksellers for selling the first-century work of fiction *Satyricon*, and the following month they prosecuted a third bookseller for stocking works such as Sigmund Freud's *A Young Girl's Diary*, *Casanova's Homecoming* by Arthur Schnitzler and DH Lawrence's *Women in Love*.

In August, Sumner launched a campaign to 'unsex' literature in America by ensuring that manuscripts were censored before publication. On 10th August, Sumner used a speech to the Catholic Club to discuss the 'avalanche of immoral books being brought from abroad' and for the first time referred to *Simon Called Peter*. Nothing may have come of the call to ban Keable's book if it hadn't been for the huge publicity around a double murder case.

In September 1922, the bodies of a man and woman, throats cut and bullet wounds to the head, were found in a field near New Brunswick, New Jersey. Torn-up love letters had been placed between the bodies, and the man's calling card was left by his feet. The two were thirty-four-year-old Eleanor Mills, a married woman with two young children, and Rev Edward Hall, a forty-one-year-old Episcopalian minister – also married. The murder, subsequent investigation and later trial received huge coverage, with every nugget examined in detail by the press. It quickly became clear that the two had been having an illicit love affair for some time before they were murdered. One 'fact' which hit the newspapers was that Hall had given both *Simon Called Peter* and Keable's second novel, *The Mother of All Living*, to Eleanor Mills, and both books were subsequently found by her bedside.

For weeks following the discovery of the murdered pair, the story dominated the news. The content of the love letters between Mills and Hall was gradually revealed. In her last letter to her lover, written the day before she died, Mills discussed the fact that Keable was also a priest, who understood that true spiritual connections needed to be expressed physically. Journalists jumped to the conclusion that *Simon Called Peter* was the inspiration behind their love affair and, possibly, even the cause of their murder.

Slain Rector and Choir Singer Found Illicit Love Prototypes In Novel "Simon Called Peter"

Excerpts From Mrs. Mills's Passionate Love Letters to Pastor Hall Prove They Considered Love for Each Other More Compelling Than Love of God.

By Marguerite Mooers Marshall.

"You darling! I believe I'd rather have you than—than God!" "I love you; you know I love you. I love you far, far more than anyone else. I won't give you up, even to God!" Were these impassioned cries

of Peter Graham, clergyman-hero of Robert Keable's book, "Simon Called Peter"—the challenge the inspiration to the remarkable erotic relationship between the Rev. Edward Hall, rector of the Church of St. John the Evangelist in New Brunswick, N. J., and Mrs. Eleanor Mills, his attractive young choir leader?

Since the dead and mutilated bodies of these two were found lying side by side, the outlines of their passionate love affair have been emerging more and more clearly from the mists of suspicion and gossip which clung around them, and the picture is completed by the publication of their feverish correspondence. However long the mystery of the manner of their death may persist, he mystery of their forbidden love is one no longer.

ROBERT KEABLE

What were its mainsprings? How did they justify it to each other? It is the habit

New York Evening World *article, 19th October 1922*

In an article in the *New York Evening World* titled 'Slain rector and choir singer found illicit love prototypes in novel *Simon Called Peter*', Marguerite Mooers Marshall asked:

Were these impassioned cries of Peter Graham, clergyman hero of Robert Keable's book *Simon Called Peter* – the challenge, the inspiration to the remarkable erotic relationship between the Rev Edward Hall, rector of the Church of St John the Evangelist in New Brunnswick, N J and Mrs. Eleanor Mills, his attractive young choir leader?

She went on to quote from one of Mills' letters to Hall: 'This man Keable certainly knows people's hearts', and Marshall continued:

Keable's clerical hero called his Julie by her first name within a quarter of an hour of the time when they first met in France. When they parted, she gave him two kisses. Peter, despite his cloth, and Julie, were both what the unregenerate would characterise as fast workers.

Following the coverage of the double murder, John Sumner leapt onto the bandwagon and immediately attempted to prosecute a bookseller for stocking *Simon Called Peter*. He claimed in a New York court that: 'It is the kind of book that certain men present with a smug expression in the hope that it will open up a field of conversation which is ordinarily forbidden.' The chief magistrate rejected the case but did say: 'It is quite true it is a nasty book and particularly objectionable because written by a clergyman.'

Following this and other articles, the Boston Watch and Ward Society decided to try and get *Simon Called Peter* banned in Boston, also via a prosecution. They chose Edith Law, a librarian in Arlington, six miles northeast of Boston, and accused her of loaning out obscene literature to the boys and girls of Arlington High School. Although Edith Law insisted that she had never lent the book to anyone under twenty-one, she was still found guilty of stocking the 'obscene book' by the Cambridge District Court and fined $100. The judge ultimately suspended the fine but warned that Law would go to prison if she ever repeated the offence. The following year, the Boston Modern Bookshop chose to stock the novel, and its owner, Morris Honigbaum, was also fined $100. So, *Simon Called Peter* joined the list of 'banned-in-Boston' books.

The *New York Times* journalist, and book reviewer, Louise Maunsell Field had fun reporting all of this and concluded (not with total accuracy):

Mr Keable comes from South Africa, a country traditionally hot and excitable, at least in literature. His books deal rather freely with phenomena which are not exactly news to most of the reading public, but may have some novelty in the clerical eye freshly turned on the profane world... Being a clergyman, Mr Keable knows that the one sure seller is pornography with a moral purpose.

It so happened that his latest book attracted the attention of a wayward Jersey clergyman and the lady who was in love with him... unless Mr. Sumner heads him off, the Reverend Mr. Keable will probably gain many thousands more readers, because two of his readers were found under the apple tree with their throats cut.

Field was right to suggest the publicity of the case helped Keable sell more books, although *Simon Called Peter* had already sold well before the double murders. Back in April, within three months of publication, it was listed as one of the ten bestselling novels across America by Baker and Taylor, alongside EM Hull's *The Sheik* and Scott Fitzgerald's second novel *The Beautiful and the Damned*. *Simon Called Peter* was to remain in the top ten for the rest of the year, before coming fifth in the *Publishers Weekly* list of bestsellers for 1922. An article in the *New York Times* in 1933 went even further, naming *Simon Called Peter* the bestselling book of 1922.

Chapter 4

Keable in Africa

At Cambridge and while in Bradford, Keable had worked hard to raise both the profile of, and money for, the Universities' Mission to Central Africa (UMCA). It owed its existence to David Livingstone, who in the late 1850s, having written his book *Missionary Travels in South Africa*, toured England pleading for new missions. Taking up Livingstone's call, Charles Frederick Mackenzie was made leader of the UMCA at the Great Zambesi Meeting in 1859. The plan, to establish an English village in Africa, was quickly supported by four universities: Oxford, Cambridge, Dublin and Durham.

The attempt to set up the village, at Magomero, in what is now southern Malawi, was a disaster and within a year malaria had killed the Bishop and most of the missionaries. Bishop Tozer, who took over the mission, decided to relocate to Zanzibar – a small island (just forty-eight miles long and twenty-two miles wide) off the south-eastern coast of Africa.

Zanzibar originally developed as a centre of wealth through the trade of slaves and spices in the nineteenth century, with the Sultan keen to encourage foreign traders to settle. That meant there was already a French mission in town and a good smattering of Christians – Catholics from America, Lutherans from Germany and Presbyterians from Scotland. Instead of building a village, Bishop Tozer rented from the Sultan a large white stone building, with open cloisters on the first floor. The Sultan gave the Bishop five slave boys, and two of the missionaries became their teachers. Slowly, school numbers rose, thanks mainly to rescuing slaves from slave ships. Once the school was up and running, the Bishop sought a site for a missionary college and St Andrew's College, where Keable later worked, was built.

When, in December 1911, Keable disembarked, the capital – Stone Town – was perhaps the most multicultural city in Africa, with, as today, the majority of the population Muslim. In his book *City of Dawn*, Keable describes picking his way through the narrow streets, passing a Swahili woman dressed in blue, as was the latest fashion; an Arab in traditional dress; a Hindi woman in a long brick-red veil with silver at her feet and ankles; a European in a suit; and an African man in a loincloth.

Keable felt much more at home in the church in Zanzibar than in Bradford. The UMCA had always been an Anglo-Catholic organisation, and Frank Weston, who had been Bishop of Zanzibar since 1908, was one of the leading Anglo-Catholic figures of the day. A friend from his Zanzibar days wrote later that:

> [Keable] was in some ways a curiously complex creature; how could it be otherwise with one who had been brought up in the strictest sect of Fundamentalism, but whose mind was entirely Modernist, while his heart was completely Catholic?

Weston too had been bought up as an Evangelist, so, to a certain extent, Keable was on a similar journey to him. Another friend suggested it had been Keable's desire to work as the Bishop's chaplain that led him to Zanzibar and, once there, he very much attached himself to the coat tails of the Bishop. 'We kept him from Rome, as we promised,' wrote Bishop Weston, quoted by Hugh Cecil in *The Flower of Battle*, which includes an account of Keable's life. Although Cecil suggests that Keable and Weston did not get on while they were in Zanzibar together, there is no evidence to suggest that is true. Later, Weston complained about sections of Keable's book *City of Dawn* and about an article Keable wrote in 1918 on the training of African priests, but these were both published after Keable had already left the mission. While in Zanzibar, Weston and Keable seem to have got on fine. In *City of Dawn*, he quotes admiringly someone who complements the 'friendly courtesy, theological learning and broad-mindedness' of the Bishop.

According to AC Benson, Keable claimed Weston behaved like a pope, which from Keable was probably a compliment. As an African bishop, he had real power and total authority in terms of faith and morals. Keable

Frank Weston, Bishop of Zanzibar

described him as 'humourous, active, amiable' and as 'a man who really is such an individualist, with a Catholic theory and no instinct for obedience'. AC Benson suggested Frank Weston:

> will not join the Church of Rome though he is a pure Roman, because it would interfere with his individualism. That is the sort of man who stays in the Anglican Church because it has no discipline. He would be miserable as a Roman because he wants to take his own line untrammelled.

At the mission school, Keable was given a fair degree of autonomy so did not suffer under the authoritarian hand of the Bishop, and, when it came to the almighty row over the Kikuyu incident in 1914, he stood by his bishop.

*

The thin, bespectacled twenty-four-year-old who arrived in this cultural melting pot was little changed from the eager student at Whitgift and

Cambridge. Everyone who knew him – even in later life – described him as boyish, with unbounded energy, ready to rush off on an adventure. Whenever not working, he got on his bike and set off to explore the island, always taking his trusty camera with him. When he travelled across to the African mainland, he visited villages, went searching for mud-built mosques and even climbed Kilimanjaro – not an easy trek in those days.

He was also boyish in the sense that he seemed to lack a filter. He was happy to talk about anything, to anyone. His friend at the time described him as:

> a truly charming companion, with the simple sincerity of a child, always ready to admit us all to his mind and to his heart, with a child's contempt for the grown-up quality which we call 'tact', a child's amused delight in shocking his elders, a child's love of mischief, and a child's wide-eyed interest in things and people, which made boredom impossible in his company.

Keable never really seemed to behave as one might expect a young priest to behave. Perhaps because he never took himself too seriously, but it could also be that he was oblivious to the views of others. For example, in *City of Dawn*, he describes cycling through the countryside with his camera and trying 'to snap a couple of maidens who, in primal nakedness, were splashing the water of their bath at one another', but they were too quick and covered up. Notwithstanding the fact a priest should not be trying to photograph naked women, what surprises me is his willingness to recount the incident.

It was Keable's ability to fit in and make friends with nearly everyone which impressed people on the island. A missionary with him in Zanzibar wrote later: 'he possessed an unusual power of becoming all things to all men', and pointed out that 'he was admitted to the Arab Club; was welcomed as an honoured guest at the country villas of the rich Indian merchants; and was no less popular a visitor at the homes of Europeans'.

Although Keable came to the island as a newly ordained priest, the main part of his job was as a teacher. The school was badly understaffed and Keable was free to teach how and what he wanted. He taught all subjects but particularly enjoyed teaching history, though not in the traditional way, such as looking at a particular period or giving an account of a leading person and the events they were involved in. The temptation would have been to teach

Portuguese fort in Zanzibar, 1913

English history, but he wanted the lessons to be relevant to the students – by concentrating on the history of Zanzibar – and fun. He quickly realised the students had no idea of chronology, so decided instead of working forwards he would start in the present and work backwards. He began his first lesson by showing the boys a rupee and discussing why the King of England was on it. From there, he re-enacted the shortest war in history, the forty-five-minute Anglo-Zanzibar war, which followed the Heligoland-Zanzibar deal of 1890. One boy played the role of captain of a German man-o-war, while he played that of the Consul-General, to help explain how Zanzibar had become a protectorate. He then set the boys the task of finding the oldest building in the town (which was the Portuguese fort) and went searching for old postage stamps, swords and pictures to serve as props for his lessons. All very different from the chalk-and-talk lessons of the day.

Beside his main lessons, he gave private tuition to four boys who wanted to learn Latin who he described as a Parsee, a Hindi, a Spanish-Eurasian and a Goanese; and he also taught history and English to a couple of wealthy young men in their twenties.

As soon as he arrived in Zanzibar, Keable decided to set up a scout group. He had first discovered scouting while a curate in Bradford. The movement had grown very quickly in Edwardian Britain. Lord Baden Powell had run the first boys' camp on Brownsea Island in August 1907 and started to sell his handbook *Scouting for Boys* a few months later. By the end of 1908, almost one hundred scout groups had been set up around the country and 11,000 boys attended a scout rally in Crystal Palace in September 1909. When Keable arrived in Bradford, the organisation was flourishing. When Rev James visited Keable there, he noted:

finding [Keable] fully interested in his work and immersed in the boy-scout movement, then in its infancy. We went for a long walk... I observed that whenever we passed small boys, he gave the scout sign.

In Zanzibar, Keable started by training eighteen boys near his house to become officers, even before he obtained uniforms. The boys' skills were very different from those of the scouts he had known in Bradford. For example, they were brilliant at camping and living out in the bush but struggled with learning how to use a compass. Still, they loved doing drill and he quickly trained them as his officers.

He had no intention of doing things by halves and managed to raise enough money to order uniforms from Gamage's, the department store in High Holborn, London, which had quickly become the main store for scouts' equipment. Photographs from book *African Scout Stories* reveal the boys to be well equipped, wearing long shorts, shirts (complete with scout badges), scarves and hats, and a number with sturdy boots and bugles.

Keable introduced scouting to the island and, by the time he left, more than seventy boys were involved, though he claimed if he had had more uniforms, he could easily have recruited 180 more. The key merit for Keable of the Scout movement was the opportunity to bring together children of different cultures and religions. An article in a Buckinghamshire newspaper in July 1913 explained:

An interesting account of his troop has been sent home by Mr Robert Keable from Zanzibar. He has five patrols, the Lions and the Bulls, who are all Swahili boys with a touch of Arab blood in them; the Woodpigeons, an Indian patrol, the Rooks, whom he describes as a 'Greek-cum-Eurasian-cum-Parsee-cum-Goan' patrol and the Rattlesnakes who are more Arab than Swahili.

In spite of the very cosmopolitan lineage of his troop, they all seem to 'shake down' well together; but what is especially pleasing is the way the boys take to the Scout Law. 'Imagine,' says Mr. Keable, 'A line of Mohammedian boys reciting with Christians that they must fear God and honour the King and the Sultan.'

His obituary in the *Church Times* discussed the significance of this:

Perhaps the best bit of work he did in Zanzibar, certainly the work in which he most delighted, was that which he did for his Troop of Scouts, the first in the Protectorate. Probably no one other than Keable would have thought at that time of including Arabs, Africans and Indians; Christians, Moslems and heathen; in one Troop; certainly no one other than he could have made the Troop so successful, or have infused, as he did, such a spirit of comradeship into so mixed a company.

Boy scout in Zanzibar, 1913

It was in Zanzibar that Keable began to write books for publication. His enthusiasm for scouting led him to write a children's book – *The Adventures of Paul Kangai* – about a slave boy who became a scout, published in 1918. He also co-wrote *African Scout Stories*, with Edward Sedding, who took over the running of the scouts after the war. He had a small collection of his poems published in 1914 under the title *Songs of the Narrow Way*, with proceeds going to the Universities' Mission. The *Church Times* praised the many good poems and suggested 'those who support the Mission will find its spirit very truly presented'. Two years earlier, his history of the Universities' Mission, *Darkness or Light*, had been published, written for study circles of friends of the Universities' Mission. A fellow priest in Zanzibar later claimed that the book 'was a fascinating account of the UMCA which I venture to believe reflected the true Robert Keable far better than the novels which afterwards received so much public attention'.

Every month, Keable wrote a letter to friends about his experiences in Zanzibar, which he had specially printed. This, he later turned into *The City of Dawn* – part travelogue, part spiritual reflections – which was published in 1915. The *Church Times* praised Keable's 'two great gifts of the imaginative artist: the eye to see, and the gift of words to describe'. A reviewer in the *Liverpool Post* praised the:

brilliant description, brilliant delineation of character. And over all is the glamour of the blue sky and the rolling sea, and gorgeous colours of Africa... more arresting still is the influence of quiet reflections which search the heart and make one long to do something to hasten the spiritual dawn.

Keable's time in Zanzibar coincided with the Kikuyu incident. In June 1913, two African bishops, William Peel, the Bishop of Mombasa, and John Willis, the Bishop of Uganda, attended an interdenominational conference with other Anglicans, Methodists and Presbyterians in Kikuyu, Kenya. The bishops suggested a closer union with other Protestant churches was the way forward in Africa since they were concerned that missionaries in Africa were losing ground to both Islam and, perhaps more worryingly, Catholicism. Bishop Weston, and Keable, did not agree. In open letters, Weston accused the two bishops of being heretics and demanded that they be tried for heresy. The first open letter, *Ecclesia Anglicana: For What Does She Stand?*, led to a pamphlet war. Among others, the Bishop of Durham responded with an open letter, *Quo Tendimus? The Issue of Kiruyu*; a sermon; an article in the *Edinburgh Review* and six letters to *The Times*. *The Times* declared in a leader that, far from being heretics, the two bishops had organised the most important conference 'to the life of *Ecclesia Anglicana* since the Reformation'. The Bishop of Mombasa, emboldened by this, then announced he would refuse communion to Anglicans from the Zanzibar diocese because their ritualistic practices displeased him.

Bishop Weston was recalled to England to make his case, and Keable travelled with him. For a while, it felt as though the uncomfortable compromise, achieved back in 1906, between the wings of the Anglican Church was going to be blown apart again. Anglo-Catholics were very concerned that the Archbishop of Canterbury – Randall Davidson (the man who had ordained Keable's father) – was the judge and jury on this case, especially as they had been the only group to challenge his appointment in 1902. Ultimately, however, there was no trial for the perceived heresy, and Randall Davidson issued a statement which concluded the matter in a typically muddled compromise, which probably upset both sides but, importantly, prevented a schism.

Keable was twenty-six when he arrived back in London in February 1914. He was in England both to support the Bishop and to again raise money for the work of the UMCA. There have been suggestions that he was invalided out of Zanzibar and returned to England to recover. He did suffer from bouts of malaria all his life, so he may have first contracted the disease in Zanzibar. However, there is no evidence that he was ill for long, and throughout the spring and summer he was busy travelling up and down England preaching.

That summer, Archduke Franz Ferdinand was assassinated in Sarajevo and less than forty days later Great Britain declared war on Germany. The war meant Keable was unable to return to Zanzibar. Although the island was a British protectorate, it was only a few miles away from German East Africa, and all the mainland work of the Universities' Mission was carried out in German territory. As soon as the war began, everyone from the diocese who was working on the mainland was arrested and interned, including many of the students and some of the staff from St Andrew's College.

Without a job, Keable was keen to enrol as an army chaplain and join the soldiers heading to France. He was not alone. The War Office Chaplains' Department was 'overwhelmed in the first few weeks by the rush of men volunteering to serve as chaplains, regardless of age and fitness'. Reportedly, there were more than 1,200 names on the Chaplain-General's waiting list in 1914. Before the war, very few chaplains served with the professional army and only sixty-five chaplains embarked with the British Expeditionary Force in August 1914. By the end of the war, there were almost 2,000 Church of England chaplains, and about the same number of other denominations.

Bishop Taylor Smith had been the Chaplain-General of HM Forces since 1901. He was an evangelical who trained at St John's Highbury, north London, and served as a priest in Upper Norwood, south London, before becoming Canon Missioner and then Bishop of Sierra Leone. After a few years as Queen Victoria's honorary chaplain, he was appointed as the army's chaplain-general. He took charge of the appointment process for all Anglicans applying to be chaplains in the British Army, and he developed a reputation for appointing only like-minded men. The Bishop carried out the majority of the selection interviews personally. His favourite question was: 'What would you say to a man who was fatally wounded but conscious and [had] only ten minutes to live?' Anglo-Catholics who answered, 'Hear his confession and give him absolution' were rejected. Those who replied, 'Give him a cigarette and take any last message he may have for his family' were much more likely to be appointed.

Lord Halifax, an Anglo-Catholic, wrote first to Lord Kitchener and then to the Chaplain-General himself to complain about the failure to appoint any High Churchmen.

Intriguingly, a *New York Times* article from 1922 suggested that Keable twice tried to join up in 1914, but each time he was rejected on the grounds of physical unfitness. However, as a member of the UMCA, and as a supporter of Frank Weston, Keable was never going to be selected.

Junior clergy like Keable, acknowledging the pro-war stance of their churches, felt under acute pressure to be seen to be doing their bit. Some joined the army as regular soldiers despite the Archbishop of Canterbury having said in September 1914 that being a combatant was incompatible with being a priest. Keable decided not to do that and instead was left to choose between two job offers in very different parishes. Gresford Jones, who had been Rural Dean of Bradford when Keable was a curate, and who was appointed Archdeacon in Sheffield in 1914, offered him the first job – a parish in Sheffield. AC Benson wrote at the time:

[Keable] told me very tentatively of his offer and was surprised and pleased that I warmly advised acceptance of it. It is what he wants – a sphere just to try his own theory. He will find it won't work with everyone – and he will realise that one can't have an all-embracing theory of religion.

A few years later, AC Benson recorded in his diary a conversation with Gresford Jones ('a nice… ugly man'): 'He had an affection for Keable and thought he had some genius'. Keable was worried that Gresford Jones would not allow him to have as much freedom as he wanted in Sheffield, and an old friend (E Thorne) who heard Keable preach in Birmingham, and had him to stay at the time, said that he was desperate to return to Africa. So, in the end, Keable decided to accept the other job as a vicar in Basutoland.

Though landlocked, encircled by three provinces of the Union of South Africa – Free State, Cape and Natal – Basutoland (renamed the Kingdom of Lesotho following independence in 1966) was never part of South Africa. Although Dutch settlers did have designs on the territory during the nineteenth century, it was the British who managed to claim Basutoland, initially as a British territory in 1869 and later, following a rebellion or 'Gun War' in 1880, as a crown colony. The western third of the country, where the bulk of the population live, is between five and six thousand feet above sea level. The rest of the country forms part of the Drakensberg range of mountains and reaches a height of 11,000 feet. When Keable arrived, the majority of the population, of just over 350,000, were Basotho, an ethnic group that has lived in that region for over 1,500 years. There were fewer than 1,000 white settlers.

Keable was to be based in Hlotse, a town founded in 1876 by the missionary John Widdicombe, although he would have responsibility for the whole district of Leribe (one of the colony's ten districts). According to the 1875 census, there were 31,434 residents in Leribe, of whom just forty-three were literate.

By the time Keable arrived, Hlotse had grown into a small town. Kathleen Molteno, who visited the town with her sister soon after the end of the First World War, described it as:

a beautifully situated camp planted with trees, chiefly pines, willows and wattles and everywhere peach trees in blossom growing wild. There are quite a lot of houses there, mostly with very nice gardens, a fine hospital, a church, Courthouse, schools and a library. The nearest railway station is Ficksburg, which we could see against a mountain about 12 miles distant.

The Bishop of Bloemfontein, who appointed Keable, was delighted to have finally found a replacement for John Widdicombe, who had retired in 1906. For the previous eight years, Archdeacon Balfour had covered the church but he was now sixty-eight and initially relieved when Keable was appointed.

The Bishop was based more than 130 miles from Hlotse in the Union of South Africa so really left Keable to get on with his job. What is clear from letters from contemporaries of Keable at Cambridge is that he liked to be in charge. A friend said: 'he was always against anything, unless he was the authority'. His predecessor had been told to 'keep aloof from politics… not to write letters of a public or political import… and to abstain entirely from controversy unless attacked', but Keable did not take much notice of that advice.

For Keable, this was a wonderful opportunity to grow the church. It must have helped that, having learnt Swahili and a couple of other Bantu languages in Zanzibar, it did not take him long to learn Sesotho, the main language. He was quick to take charge. He explained later, in his book *Standing By*, that he was responsible 'not merely for marriages but for matches, not merely for Sundays but for sundries'. He went on to write:

In my parish I am a bit of a farmer, doctor, lawgiver, schoolmaster and choir trainer, architect and all but magistrate, as well as priest. Even when other people undertake these duties, I cannot stand by and watch them do it.

Keable decided his first task was to introduce his High Church approach to the people of his parish. His parishioners weren't totally unaware of the Anglo-Catholic practices, as the Society of the Sacred Mission – an Anglican order where the members live in a community, remain celibate and take vows of poverty, chastity and obedience – had started a daily Mass in town which included some examples of ritualism. However, the tradition of St Saviour's Church – set up by Widdicombe – was evangelical, and that was certainly what the white Anglicans in town expected. Keable continued with a weekly service for them – matins, evensong or communion – but put all his energies into changing the services for the other worshippers. He introduced solemn evensong with incense, requiem Mass, children's Eucharist and daily Mass, and he made sure they celebrated all the saints' days, even the lesser saints. The main service on Sundays was a sung Mass at 9.30am with elaborate ceremonial. Canon Dove in his book *Anglican Pioneers in Lesotho*, explained:

> He introduced the Three Hours' Devotion on Good Friday, Devotions to the Blessed Sacrament, and processions of Corpus Christi, Palm Sunday and Our Lady. The ceremonies of the New Fire and the Paschal Candle at Easter began along with the Stations of the Cross, the rosary, the Aspergses and extreme Unction. There were Guilds of the Children of Mary and of the Blessed Sacrament.

He also got the Bishop in 1915 to bless a tabernacle, and he had a *baldacchino* – an ornate canopy often seen in Roman Catholic churches – erected over the altar. Archdeacon Balfour, who continued to live in Hlotse, did not approve and, once Keable had arrived, he hardly ever conducted a service, and indeed rarely set foot into the church again. One can imagine his reaction and that of the more elderly Europeans in Hlotse. If Keable had introduced all of these changes in an English parish, only ten years before, he could have faced prosecution under the Public Worship Regulation Act.

Keable had a missionary zeal to welcome as many people as possible to the church, and one result of his changes was that it began to fill with more and more black worshippers. This was not always the case. In another church in the diocese built by white people for their own use, all gifts received were on condition that no 'native' should ever set foot inside. In contrast, Keable welcomed everyone, although the majority of the congregation and helpers for his main services were black. Kathleen Molteno was persuaded to drop into one of the services and described it as being 'very high church' and noted that:

> boys and men took part in the ceremonial, some wearing red and some purple cassocks under their surplices and the whole time they seemed to be doing different things – carrying huge lighted candles, one swinging incense, another rang a bell at different stages and of course there was a lot of bowing and crossing and moving about.

Having dramatically changed the services and ceremonies, Keable moved on to reach out to the rest of the parish. Although Hlotse is in the north-west of Basutoland, Keable was also expected to care for parishioners over in the east as far away as Mokhotlong, more than sixty miles away, reached then only by horse on bridle paths. When he arrived in 1915, there was just one outstation in Mahhoas where services could be held. Gradually, Keable set up more and more outstations in Raphokas, Motsoanes, Senyokothos, Mokhachanes and Motsekis, as well as maintaining a series of house churches and congregations in the mountains on the way to and from Mokhotlong. He tried to visit the outstations as often as he could, riding out from his home and travelling for more than a week before returning home.

One problem Keable faced, as documented by Jackson Steward Lincoln, is that, at the time, many Basothos would only convert to Christianity if they had a dream telling them to convert. Keable told a story about a woman he was asked to visit living high up in the mountains. She had had a dream where her late husband told her to see a priest and be washed of her sins. A few days after, having done nothing about it, he appeared again in another dream – angry but silent. Keable reported:

> From that time she had eaten next to nothing, and had been in a kind of fit all day long, merely reiterating that I must be sent for. But the night before she had dreamed that a white priest came in, in a white vestment, and laying hands on her had healed her.

Arriving at her house:

> I heard her moaning, like that of an animal in pain, some distance from the hut, and she took no notice of my entrance. When I could see no sign of ordinary sickness, I knelt and prayed, and in my prayer commanded her to be at peace and laid my hand on her. Her moaning died down at once. They concluded soon after I had finished the prayer. She sat awhile not speaking, but then arose and gave me food. From that day she entered on her instruction and was baptized last year; and she bought with her a dozen or more from that village.

Perhaps the best measure of his success in Leribe was the increasing size of the congregations. He looked to welcome as many new people into the church as he could. Canon Dove reported that for the Easter service in 1910, a few years before Keable arrived, there were 160 communicants at the church in Hlotse, but that by Easter 1920 – Keable's final year there – that number had risen to 430. In addition, in 1920 there were fifty-one communicants at the service in Makhoas, twenty-three at Raphokas and 123 at Mokhotlong.

There is no doubt that Keable's success in the parish was helped by the hard work of his wife, whom he married soon after he arrived.

Keable had met Sybil Armitage in Bradford when he was a curate there. They both worked in the parish spreading the Gospel and helping the poor, and for a while they 'walked out' together. Hugh Cecil suggested she was impressed by his energy and missionary zeal. However, she wouldn't have been under any illusions about marrying Keable then since she knew that he was planning to become a missionary with the UMCA, which insisted on celibacy.

While in Zanzibar, Keable wrote regularly to her and they saw each other again when he returned to England in 1914. According to her niece, Doris Trewolla-Hulme, they became engaged at the outbreak of the war, and once he was settled in Basutoland at the beginning of 1915, he sent for her so they could marry.

Sybil Keable, as she became when they married, was four years older than Keable. A number of people have speculated as to why they married. RH Benson rather unkindly suggested Keable sought a wife as a means of evading the temptation of becoming a Roman Catholic priest. Hugh Cecil's impression was that:

Keable probably liked her looks and above all I think he thought she would make a 'suitable' wife for a missionary, as she was. But I don't think he was really physically attracted to her or else he found her too inhibited, as was the case then… It was other clergy who went on about her beauty! She was obviously a fine-looking woman and full of spirit and loveable but much too over-masterful for him and didn't like anyone to disagree with her.

Her niece, years later, said Hilda in *Simon Called Peter* was Sybil Keable. There is no real description of Hilda in the book, and it seems unlikely that she was as naïve as Hilda. The obvious similarity between her and Hilda was that both were betrayed by their partners. Perhaps their father's reaction to a marriage was also similar. In *Simon Called Peter*, Keable wrote that Hilda's father was:

> a person of distinction when at his club, [who] would have been seriously annoyed that his daughter should consider a marriage with a curate whose gifts had not yet made him an income.

Sybil Keable's father was a Bradford merchant not a London one, but this may also have been his reaction to Keable. A more obvious portrait of her is Edith in Keable's novel *Peradventure*, written in 1922, although Keable claimed she was a composite of various people. Composite perhaps, but there are many similarities between the fictional Edith and Sybil Keable, including the work they did in the parish and the decision to convert to Roman Catholicism.

I am really surprised that Keable did not use their wedding in Durban in May 1915 as the source for a few pages in one of his novels. Keable was an author who used all of his life experiences in his writings. His graduation ceremony at Cambridge gave him a few hundred words in *Peradventure*. As Dr Douglas wrote:

> Keable never wasted any material of emotional experience that would serve his end as a writer. Even during his strenuous early activities in Zanzibar he had gone around with pencil and notebook in hand, literally and metaphorically.

There are no descriptions of weddings in any of Keable's novels. In *The Mother of All Living*, Cecily does marry Hugh, probably in Durban, but there is no description. In his other novels, the main characters do not marry. Julie and Peter dither over the possibility for two books (*Recompense* and *Simon Called Peter*), Monty runs away from the possibility of marrying in *The Madness of Monty*, Richard Thurstan and Lady Ann Carew avoid marriage in *Lighten Our Darkness* and Paul Kestern in *Peradventure* is keen to live with Ursula, unmarried, for the rest of their lives. My guess is that, away from all their friends and family, the day was neither a joyous nor a memorable occasion.

Once married, Cecil suggested Sybil Keable slotted into her role with ease. He claimed she was:

admiringly equipped to be the wife of a parish priest: passionately religious, with a strong social conscience and robust health, her exuberance and her cheerful ripples of laughter were said to have a tonic effect, particularly on children.

Keable was out in the parish for long periods of time, often staying up on the berg – the mountain range that stretches across the area – for a few nights, visiting far-flung villages, and leaving his wife to take care of running the home and his office.

Having married Keable during the first year of the war, his wife could easily have been a widow nine months later.

*

In April 1916, Keable, his curate, Rev A Lawton, and two servants were on a tour of the outstations. At the end of a long day, they decided to call in on the officer in command at Mokhotlong police station. Jameson Smith was away on patrol and, with darkness setting in, they decided to spend the night in the compound, with Lawton and Keable using Smith's hut, which had a couple of beds. What they didn't realise was that a prisoner called Khomoapinya, who was thought to be insane, was also being held in the camp that night.

As there was no gaol, local policemen had been instructed to keep watch over him, but inexplicably the order to keep him in handcuffs and leg irons had been ignored, and Khomoapinya had been allowed access to beer, and was drunk. As Keable and his companions slept, the prisoner slipped his guards, collected a rifle and ammunition from the officers' mess, and walked into Smith's hut with the intention of killing him. Unaware that one of the sleeping bodies was Keable, he fired two shots, one of which smashed through Keable's thigh bone. Somehow, Lawton managed to push Khomoapinya out of the room, barricade the door and window and bandage Keable's wound to stop the bleeding. Lawton later told a friend that he spent the night guarding the door with the only weapon at hand – a stirrup iron at the end of his stirrup leather – expecting Khomoapinya to return at any moment, with Keable sitting up beside him in real pain.

At the time, Keable played down the seriousness of his injury but later used the event in his novel *Recompense*, where he graphically described the injury:

51

The bullet had entered his right leg above the knee, obviously ricocheted from the thighbone, shattering it completely, and passed out high up on the left side, driving a splinter of bone before it. It had caught him as he bent to pick up his boot, and a trifle higher would have gone through the stomach… despite the pain, the swelling, the completely shattered bone, haemorrhage had all but ceased, and it was obvious that the danger lay chiefly in unskilled treatment. The effect of the shock upon him, the chances of mortification, of fever, of tetanus, he could not and did not try to estimate.

The next morning, after much discussion, the decision was taken to take Keable down the mountain into South Africa, where the nearest medical care was available. A local chief organised sixty men on rotation, to help carry him down the very steep Sani Pass – then a rough path of about 5 miles that dropped more than 4,300 feet – and on to Himeville, a total journey of fifty-five miles. From Himeville, a hired car took him to hospital in Pietermaritzburg.

This incident was clearly mortifying for the British police force and made more embarrassing when Keable started to ask who would pay the sizeable bill of £115 – the equivalent of over £10,000 today – for car hire, doctor's bills and his stay in a private hospital.

Since the money was owed to South Africans, the issue became a major diplomatic incident and led to the Resident Commissioner in Basutoland, the Right Honourable Viscount Buxton, writing to Andrew Bonar Law, the then Secretary of State for the Colonies:

> I do not know whether the Administration can be legally held liable for the charge but I fear that a certain moral responsibility does exist in view of the fact that no provision is made for the care of lunatics.

Two months later, a letter came from Downing Street, signed by A Bonar Law, agreeing that:

> the expenditure incurred by Reverend R Keable as a result of the injuries received by him through an attack upon him by an insane native in Basutoland [could] as a special case be met out of Basutoland funds.

In October 1916, Keable was sent a cheque from the British authorities for the full amount that he was owed.

Reports of Keable's shooting came out slowly in several publications, although none made reference to the mistakes of the local police.

The quarterly newsletter in his parish reported:

It is with great regret that we heard that the Revd. R. Keable had been seriously wounded by a mad native at Mokhotlong, who got hold of a rifle and fired at him through the window of the Government hut and fractured the bone above his knee.

The Magdalene College magazine described the events in its April edition, saying Keable wrote to his wife to say: 'I have broken my leg, but it is nothing'.

Keable had a lucky escape. Though the operation to repair his leg was largely successful, it was left about an inch and a half shorter, so that he walked with a rolling limp for the rest of his life.

Chapter 5

Simon Called Peter – writer to novelist

As far as Keable was concerned, his reputation for himself as a writer had been established before *Simon Called Peter* was published in 1921. He had had some success with *City of Dawn* published in 1915, which described his experiences in Zanzibar. During the war, he had written devotional pieces for an Anglican newspaper in South Africa, the *Church Chronicle*, and these were eventually collected into several volumes – *The Loneliness of Christ, The Perpetual Sacrifice* and *This Same Jesus* – all published by Nisbet and Co. All three were well reviewed by the *Church Times*.

Before the war ended, Keable managed to persuade another publisher – Skeffington and Son – to produce a collection of stories under the title *The Drift of Pinions*, which appeared in 1918. This was his first attempt at fiction. It is a strange book, telling of spiritual experiences of different people around the world, each one with a touch of the mystical or supernatural. The *Church Times* review is gloriously dismissive of the *TLS* for the way it classifies the book. 'Some people apparently find it difficult to understand Mr Robert Keable's *The Drift of Pinions*. The *Times Literary Supplement* reviewed it under the heading of "Religion and Theology", which makes us wonder if the reviewer would class Mr Thomas Hardy's novels under the heading "Agriculture"'.

The reviewer was a partial fan of Keable:

He has great gifts for this [fictional] kind of work. He joins a vivid and picturesque style to great ingenuity in telling a story, though sometimes the introduction to the story is too long. Whether he has the gift of drawing and developing character is not yet evident, though there are signs, even in the limited scope here, that he may possess it.

Following the war, Keable wrote two more books: *Standing By: War-Time Reflections in France and Flanders* and *Pilgrim Papers from the Writings of Francis Thomas Wilfrid, Priest.* These were published in England in 1919 and 1920, respectively, receiving favourable comments although very low sales.

Standing By was an account of his time during the war. It remains an interesting read today with its hotchpotch of chapters on various topics. Trips to Versailles and Paris, Jumièges and Crecy; reflections on the work of army chaplains, WAACs and prostitutes; accounts of restaurants and army concerts; and, perhaps most moving, the experiences of the men under his charge, from working in the hangar unloading ships' cargo and celebrating Christmas to the hundreds of deaths when the SS *Mendi* sank in the English Channel. For some, the book is seen as a criticism of the Church of England and its ideas about the role of a chaplain. Father Bede Jarrett, an English Dominican friar, wrote:

I thought at the time and still think that it was the most admirable story of the war from the standpoint of religion, with its insistence on the two types of Christianity, Catholic and YMCA, that is, the priestly religion, authoritative and sacramental, and the religion of clubs, libraries, gramophones and cups of tea.

Largely ignored by critics in England – Keable blamed a 'damned bad publisher' – the book was well received in America, with a review in the *Philadelphia Ledger* calling it 'one of the great spiritual books of the war' which 'range[d] through a wide scope and deep, of interests and reactions brought and wrought by the war, mainly religious, it is true, but sometimes military, aesthetic or social'.

Pilgrim Papers was more personal still to Keable. He described the work as a collection of papers belonging to Francis Thomas Wilfrid, a retired priest, describing his thoughts and experiences as a missionary in Basutoland. However, Cecil noted:

The closeness of Wilfrid's views to his own, on many points, suggests the possibility that Keable may have written the 'letters' himself, as a means of conveying some unconventional opinions of his own, and that Wilfrid may have been a literary creation.

After much research, Tim Couzens – who visited Lesotho while researching Keable's life – noted in a letter to Cecil that 'there was no priest called Wilfrid' and 'too many co-incidences with Keable himself'. The book is filled with Keable's muddled thoughts. For Couzens, the book's merit lies in the 'mountain writing and mountain philosophy'. Couzens understood how the awesome desolate countryside moved Keable, and he believed it played a significant part in his thinking and development.

Though unappreciated in England, there was, again, more recognition in America, where it was published in May 1921. The *New York Tribune* described it as 'an important document in the literature of Christianity'.

*

Between 1918 and 1921, Keable had published three non-fiction books in England through different publishers but had earnt very little money from them. If he was to resign as a priest, it was very clear to him that to make his living as a writer it would have to be primarily as a novelist. And he also knew that he would need to appeal to a very different audience from those who had read and enjoyed his non-fiction work. Having written *Simon Called Peter*, he confessed to Sadler that he had written his second novel as a 'library' book, very much with his readership in mind. He told Sadler he thought it might be 'a jolly book for Xmas presents and girls' school prizes'.

He had already written *The Mother of All Living* before *Simon Called Peter* was published, and began work on his third, *Peradventure*, while teaching in Dunstable in 1921. Neither had any connection with *Simon Called Peter*. Both his English publisher, Sadler, and American publisher, Macrae, were eager to publish a sequel as soon as possible, but Keable was keen to get two more novels under his belt first.

The Mother of All Living is a romantic novel set in southern Africa. It includes a description of a week-long trek in Basutoland which ended in Mokhotlong, where Keable had been shot before the war. The novel begins with a young girl, Cecily, returning from six years of education in England, falling in love and marrying Hugh – a farm-owning, English-born public-school boy. Three years later, having had a child, she falls out of love with him and is attracted to Christopher, a novelist and traveller. Cecily's friend Pamela does not trust Christopher and agrees to go travelling with him to test his faithfulness to Cecily. Despite Pamela's attempts at seduction, Christopher stays loyal to Cecily. By the time they return, Cecily has decided to remain with Hugh, and Christopher invites Pamela to come travelling with him again.

One could read the novel as another story of sexual indiscretion, and some critics tried to, but, as a reviewer in the *Aberdeen Press and Journal* pointed out, there 'is nothing offensive in the novel' and 'at least the author has the merit of introducing no scandal or divorce into his pages but presents a piquant and original ending'.

Keable was very keen for *The Mother of All Living* not to be compared with *Simon Called Peter* and admitted in a letter to Michael Sadler that he had made sure he had not written anything 'sensationally wicked or violently pious'. Given the uproar that *Simon Called Peter* had caused in some quarters, he changed the plot so that Christopher only kisses Cecily, when in the first draft he slept with her.

As soon as *Simon Called Peter* was published, in May 1921, Keable started to badger Sadler to publish *The Mother of All Living*. Sadler held back publication while *Simon Called Peter* continued to sell well, but eventually published the novel in December 1921. Although not nearly as successful as *Simon Called Peter*, the 7s/6d edition had sold 17,000 copies by April 1923, earning Keable almost £900 on top of the £250 advance – three times his annual salary as a teacher.

Over in America, Macrae was also eager to get *The Mother of All Living* published. The reader LW, who had so hated *Simon Called Peter*, was full of praise:

This is a great book; one of the finest studies of human nature I have ever had the pleasure of journeying through, it rises to the heights, and gives you lofty and great ideals of womanhood and manhood.

Macrae instructed his printers to set up the novel and print the first edition. There was one problem. Keable's American literary agent, Paget, had already sold the novel to a rival publishing house, GP Putnam's Sons.

Macrae was furious, writing to Paget, 'As I understand it, we have the right from Mr Watt to the refusal of *The Mother of All Living*. There would be no reason for making contracts, if they were not intended to mean what they say'.

It is clear how the confusion arose. John Macrae and Paget had agreed a two-book deal for *Simon Called Peter*. Paget thought *Pilgrim Papers*, not *The Mother of All Living*, was the plus one. Keable, unaware of the risks Macrae had taken in publishing *Simon Called Peter*, upset with its delayed publication in America and knowing Putman's were offering considerably better terms for *The Mother of All Living*, asked Paget to stick with Putnam's.

As soon as Macrae found out, he took the first boat to England and summoned Keable to a meeting in London. Following 'a long personal talk', they reached an agreement. Keable would let Dutton publish *The Mother of All Living* if Putnam's had the next book, and first refusal on the two after.

When he heard the result of the negotiation, Major GH Putnam flippantly wrote to Macrae: 'You certainly fly across the ocean and back again very quickly', and then, perhaps unwisely, seemed to gloat about what he called a 'bothersome' matter. Macrae responded in real anger in a private letter:

> Naturally if you follow as Keable's publisher after *The Mother of All Living* we withdraw completely and forever from any publishing relations with that author, beyond the books we now control and publish... I admit your moral right to enter into any kind of arrangement you may see fit with authors and authors' agents, but there is a point involved in this arrangement which to me is quite obvious, namely, that [after] my acceptance of the book in hand, your people outbid my royalty proposal 5% and they allowed it to be placed in the contract a five-year leasing clause. I have with absolute sincerity refrained from bidding directly or indirectly against my fellow publishers' authors... I am being so bold as to make this letter almost brutally frank to you and all because of the many years of splendid cooperation which has existed and persisted between the houses of EP Dutton and Co and GP Putnam's Sons.

It seems clear, having read the private letters of Macrae, that he was very badly treated by Keable and his advisers. However, that is the nature of the publishing business, and for Keable, the situation was win–win. He ended up with a very generous advance for *The Mother of All Living* in America and a new publisher, offering a better deal, for his future novels.

When *The Mother of All Living* was eventually published in America, it received a pretty good press. In particular, Louise Maunsell Field wrote a very long review in the *New York Times*, noting:

> Mr Keable's talent for description is already well known, and the present novel is full of admirably drawn pictures not only of pass and mountains and valley, of village and isolated post, but of big, prosperous farms and such busy places as Durban.

She was particularly taken by Pamela, whom she described as:

> far and away the most interesting character in the book, this vivid, passionate, intelligent, widely read, ruthless and strong-willed but generous, fascinating and lovable Pamela, who dabbled in strange arts and ran strange risks, besides playing an ugly game from excellent motives. It is difficult to imagine any man or woman of intelligence bored in her company.

Pamela is considered by many as Keable's best-realised woman character. His introduction to her in the novel is pure Mills & Boon:

> Her best friends never called Pamela pretty, but equally her enemies (of which she had more than her share as life went on, especially among women) never called her plain... As for her eyes, one rarely saw them fully open. They looked at you provocatively, and you called them brown. But if you ever saw them really open, you knew them to be grey. Women said they were hard, but no man ever saw anything hard in them. If there was a hardness in them, it lay behind, and men were no longer reasonable creatures when they penetrated so far.

Keable was very open about the fact that he wanted *The Mother of All Living* to be seen as a popular romantic fiction. *Peradventure* was a very different novel altogether. His most personal one, it drew heavily on his time at Cambridge, including thinly disguised portraits of his wife (as Edith), his father (Mr Kestern), Frank Weston (the Bishop of Moçambique) and – with great affection – RH Benson (Father Vassal).

His own comment on the book, written to Sadler a few months before it was published, was: '*Peradventure* is useless. It is too true to life to be interesting until it becomes so untrue as to be fantastic'.

But perhaps surprisingly, when the book was published in England, in September 1922, it received good reviews. A typical one in the *Daily Mail* hailed Paul Kestern as 'one of the characters of the year' and suggested:

> Mr. Keable has lost none of his considerable power of depicting mental strife... The chapters dealing with Cambridge are delightful and Mr Keable catches the undergraduate spirit, the mixture of affection and sincerity... The book is a technical advance on anything Mr Keable has yet done, and I think he will yet write a great novel.

Robert Keable

Although *Simon Called Peter* was Keable's greatest commercial success for Dr Douglas – the author and biographer – *Peradventure* was his best-written book. He suggested 'Keable got beyond the propaganda of rebellion, to a depth of feeling which was as moving as anything in *Simon Called Peter*'.

The influence of RH Benson is apparent to Dr Douglas. Not only is one of his main characters, Father Vassell, an accurate portrayal of the Roman Catholic priest but:

> Keable's style is in many places somewhat like a serious parody of Benson's, rather than an expression of an independent personality.

Keable must have been concerned as to how AC Benson would view the portrait of his brother, but he received a nice letter from him:

> My brother and I have been reading Peradventure, it seems to me a book full of life and energy and I am not surprised at its success... The picture of my brother and Hare Street is admirable, both matter and manner – though isn't the stammering overdone?

In America, *Peradventure* was the first of Keable's novels to be published by Putnam's, which seems to have organised very little publicity. Few newspapers reviewed the book and those that did were not keen. The *Evening Star* in Washington called it a 'sincere and tedious story', while the *New York Times* was damning in its faint praise of his progress:

> Keable, having obtained a large (and undeserved) success with Simon Called Peter and a lesser though still visible popularity with The Mother of All Living has attempted to 'put over' a third success with Peradventure. His method is to mix theology and passion, but in the case of this latest there is too much religion and too little passion.

Once *Peradventure* was written, Keable started on another novel, examining eugenics and communism. However, both Sadler and Major Putnam were increasingly impatient for a sequel to *Simon Called Peter*. Keable had said, in response to the initial reaction to *Simon Called Peter*, that he intended to write a follow-up, but the truth was that he had really given the idea no thought. Having come out of the war a changed man, he had no desire to let the Peter and Julie story mirror his own life.

CHAPTER 6

KEABLE AND THE WAR

When the First World War began, the sense of duty Keable felt at that time weighed on his mind. He had tried unsuccessfully to join the regular army as a chaplain after war had been declared, and soon after the First Battle of the Marne in September 1914 – he, and others, realised how awful it was going to be. In a sermon in Pimlico the following month, before he left for Basutoland, he spoke of 'the terrible sorrow of the disease-stricken trench' and 'the sorrow of the women, wives, mothers, lovers, and of the children of Belgium, France, Russia, yes and of Germany', while at the same time insisting the war was 'just'. And he called out the:

> bitter shame that in this age countless hosts of men, themselves neither desiring not rightly understanding it, should be hurling death the one upon the other at the bidding of forces that are scarcely human at all. It is as if we were all in the grip of a heartless and awful machine.

As Keable was leaving England for Basutoland in January 1915, thousands of men his age were joining up, and heading to France. Conscription did not come into force until the following year, but Keable had been a member of the school cadet force at Whitgift, which had trained students to fight. Many of his contemporaries at school and university volunteered. More than 250 former Whitgift students died in the war, including his younger brother. Magdalene, one of the smallest Cambridge colleges, recorded the death of sixty-five graduates or undergraduates. Other, larger colleges such as Trinity (619), King's (202) and Jesus (158) had more deaths.

When Keable arrived in the Union of South Africa in January 1915, the country was under threat. He wasn't necessarily escaping the war. German forces from South-West Africa (now Namibia) had invaded the Northern Cape, and it wasn't until July that year that the Germans in the region finally surrendered.

As Keable took over his parish in Basutoland, there was a mass exodus of Europeans. Some 190 of the 366 young male Europeans – in the colony – joined one of the forces going to war. The South African Overseas Expeditionary Force was set up in July 1915 and started to send white men from across southern Africa to fight in German East Africa, where many of those with whom Keable had worked in Zanzibar were being held by the Germans. Soon after, white men from across southern Africa were heading to the Western Front. White men, not black men, as South Africa still feared, as it had feared during the South African War, that black men might consider 'themselves the white man's equal' if they fought together.

And meanwhile, Keable, not yet thirty, was working in his parish in Basutoland and reading in the papers every day of more men sacrificing their lives for their country. He could not help but feel guilty, but unless he resigned from the church and joined the regular army – and some priests did that – there was little he could do.

Keable tried to do his bit. He preached about the war and encouraged the wealthier members of his parish to contribute towards the financing of the war. After the war, he proudly pointed out that the Basotho 'raised the equivalent of £55,000 voluntarily for War funds'.

The situation changed for Keable when South Africa approved the formation of the SANLC, following secret talks between the British and South African governments. To tackle an acute labour shortage in France, the British offered to pay for black labourers to come to help with the war effort in auxiliary roles. Similar labour corps from Egypt, China and India were also set up. Initially, the SANLC recruited only in South Africa, but soon the catchment area was expanded to the British protectorates of Basutoland, Bechuanaland (now Botswana) and Swaziland (now Eswatini).

After local chiefs proved fairly unsuccessful in recruiting men to join the SANLC, local priests and magistrates were asked to help, and Keable began to encourage his parishioners to join. At the time, there were few jobs in Leribe, and many men ended up going to South Africa to work in the mines. So, a well-paid job in France must have seemed quite attractive. Norman Clothier, author of *Black Valour. The South African Native Labour Contingent, 1916–1918, and the Sinking of the Mendi,* explained why men joined up:

> For some it seems there was a genuine emotional response to the appeal to serve their king and country, just as that rhetoric motivated the white volunteers. Many of them would have preferred to fight, but though they were only called upon to work so as to relieve others from fighting, they still came forward. For the leaders, there was the additional desire to travel and learn, to see for themselves what European civilisation was like, and the hope that, when they had served their country well, the South African Government would show gratitude by improving the privileges and the status of black peoples. For the young and unsophisticated, the chance to go no doubt appealed mainly to their spirit of adventure and they saw it as a challenge to their manhood.

It was the better-educated men who were the keenest to join. Estimates by missionaries calculated that 25% of the total number of men who volunteered to go to France were from the educated elite. According to the chief chaplain, John Lennox, they were men who had left their schools, their businesses and their congregations. This was especially true of those who joined from Basutoland.

Keable was successful in persuading some of his parishioners to go to France. He wrote about visiting men's wives and their parents to reassure them that their sons would be safe to travel. He explained that the men were going to be well treated and well paid. The rate was £3 a month, which could all be sent home. This was almost double the one shilling a day that white South Africans received from their government when they signed up as privates in the army.

Keable may have assumed that the men would be treated better in Europe than they would be treated if they went to South Africa. Certainly, Stimela Jason Jingoes, who had been educated in a mission school in Basutoland and spoke about his war experiences, explained that: 'One of our preachers had told us that we would find no colour bar in England', although he added: 'but we did not believe him: how could there be a country where black men were treated the same as white men?'

In total, nearly 1,400 men from Basutoland joined the 21,000 men who served in the SANLC between 1916 and 1918. Of these, 367 men volunteered from the Leribe district, many of whom Keable knew. Keable wrote about two different groups of thirty from his church travelling to France, and also mentioned that nearly all the members of his church band joined up.

One man from Keable's parish who did join was Michael, who Keable described as a lithe and 'well knit' man with a tendency to spill porridge all over his face when he ate it. He was one of the first to join from Keable's church, leaving his pregnant wife, Agnesi, and joining twenty-five other Basothos at the Rosebank training camp in Cape Town. On 25th January 1917, Michael boarded the SS *Mendi* and set sail for France. There were 823 passengers on board the ship, mainly black members of the SANLC, along with some white officers. The labourers were confined to their very cramped quarters throughout the voyage. The ship called into Plymouth on 19th February before starting to make the Channel crossing. A thick fog formed in the Channel and from midnight the ship, supported by British destroyer HMS *Brisk*, crept slowly forward towards France. At 4.57am, as the *Mendi* was 20km off the southern tip of the Isle of Wight, a mail steamship, the SS *Darro*, twice the size of the *Mendi* and sailing at full speed, emerged from the dark and fog, emitting no warning signals, and drove into the side of the *Mendi*. It cut into the hold where Michael and the other men lay asleep.

There weren't many boats in the area to pick up the men. HMS *Brisk* got lost in the fog, although they did launch rowing boats which desperately searched the sea for survivors. The crew of the SS *Darro* were too concerned about the minor damage done to their boat to send help.

Keable imagined in *Standing By* how the men had tramped up on deck in their heavy boots and unlovely blue uniforms and lifebelts and were made to form up as if on parade. How the officer in charge had ordered the men to jump into the freezing water even though very few could swim. And how 'six hundred boys of the King's black people chilled for ever'.

In the end, Michael and 617 other men died that night in the English Channel. The news of their deaths was not announced in the South African Parliament until March. By that time, Keable and many of his parishioners had already been accepted into the contingent and had either started their training or were about to start. It fell on Keable, as the parish priest, to make his way to the small village of Maluti to tell Agnesi of the death of her husband. In *Standing By* he wrote:

That steady jump of those black boys ought to still the slander in
more white throats than it does, and at least for me I am not ashamed
to say that I honour the race that did it.

Keable wrote this in 1918, two years after the tragedy. The 'slander' came
from many of the men he met during his time with the SANLC, for he didn't
know, when he joined the contingent, how badly the men under his care were
going to be treated. And he certainly didn't know that the setting-up of the
labour corps was an experiment.

BP Willan wrote in his essay, *The South African Native Labour Contingent
1916–1918*:

Once the decision had been taken to send the SANLC to Europe,
a number of missionaries, Native Affairs Department officials and
others concerned with the native problem realized fairly quickly that
the scheme provided an ideal opportunity for testing – in what would,
it was hoped, be carefully controlled conditions – the practicability
and effects of the implementation of certain segregatory devices
of social control; the lessons and results of this experiment could
possibly be utilized in South Africa itself. It was perceived as a test,
in other words, of the efficacy of ideas that were coming increasingly
to bridge the gap between hitherto rather more distinct liberal and
segregationist positions.

Many who travelled with the SANLC were not as liberal in their views
as Keable. Among them was Captain LE Hertslet, a medical missionary who
served as a doctor with the SANLC, and who was one of the few to survive
the sinking of the *Mendi*. In 1911, he had written a short book, *The Native
Problem*, where he discussed many questions relating to the future of black
men in South Africa. He suggested that the nub of the problem was how to
preserve 'racial purity' and the 'virtues of a white society', surrounded as it
was by a 'sea' of 'native's ignorance, laziness, sensualism and superstition'. One
of his biggest concerns was 'What steps can be taken to stop the creation of
the half-caste?' He described a:

typical black dwelling [as] dark, dirty, insanitary, and often
overcrowded… The character of the dwelling is the result of ingrained

habits of laziness: the style of living caused by such a dwelling eventuates in future laziness.

And he added:

The idea is ingrained in the native's mind that work, for work's sake, is unnecessary and foolish, and only many years of teaching and example will remove the false conception.

Unbeknown to Keable, when he applied to become a chaplain with the SANLC, most of the white men recruited to look after the labour force shared Hertslet's views. The white officers were initially chosen on the grounds that they knew how to 'control and handle natives… and for their willingness to use physical force in dealing with them'. Many were unfit for active service but were chosen because they had a good knowledge of at least one local language and experience of working with black men. They tended to be retired civil servants or men who had worked in the mines.

Originally, there were no plans to send white chaplains with the labourers, but this was changed following a call from the editor of the *Christian Express* in South Africa, who asked for 'some experienced white missionaries in order to assist the officers of the SANLC in keeping the men from moral dangers and perils'.

Ten of the twelve white chaplains who joined the SANLC had lived for many years in South Africa, where the colour bar and race discrimination were an accepted way of life. They probably expected that the labourers would be treated very differently from other men working in France. The chief chaplain, Lennox, a Presbyterian working at Lovedale College, was head tutor and acting principal of the then large school. He had forceful views on dealing with black students and the importance of strong discipline.

Unlike most of the other chaplains, Keable had never lived or worked in South Africa. His experiences in Zanzibar, and to a certain extent in Basutoland, had been of a multicultural, multiracial society. Keable had been used to meeting and working with people of all races and creeds and believed the level of one's education was more important than the colour of one's skin. He wasn't naïve enough to believe the men he was recruiting were not going to face some racism, but he had not imagined they would be so badly treated.

He wrote in 1918:

it ought not to be necessary for a white missionary to defend his attitude towards his black people. Honestly, I love and admire them – not all of them, nor altogether, but neither do I love all white people, or admire wholly the white races. For myself I have friends among the black people who stand as high in my esteem, and whom I would trust absolutely.

Keable was as guilty of racism as any white person born at the end of the nineteenth century. Some of his books contain racist language and some characters are racial stereotypes – as is true of nearly all white writers writing before the Second World War. However, he may not have encountered such overt racism until he joined the SANLC.

It was towards the end of 1916, having recovered from the bullet wound to his leg, when Keable asked his bishop for permission to join the SANLC and travel to France with them. He went to see JH Sims, the Leribe Assistant Commissioner, who recalled:

He came into me one day and said that as many of his congregation were joining the Labour Corps he felt it was his duty to go to the War with them as Chaplain. I said I disagreed as he had worked up the mission to a good degree and a lot of people were now dependent on his Ministry and looked up to him for help, whereas there were plenty of priests, African and European, for Chaplain's duty which would be in a sense routine and only temporary until hostilities ceased. However, he insisted and eventually sailed overseas.

Keable was not an obvious choice to work for the SANLC, and the fact that he was a High Church Anglican could also have been a concern to the other chaplains in the contingent. Only three years before, he had been on Bishop Frank Weston's side in the Kikuyu incident, criticising efforts to push for ever closer union between Anglicans, Methodists and Presbyterians in Africa. Keable was going to be one of only eleven white chaplains to travel to France as members of the SANLC. He was joining one other Anglican, three Wesleyans, two Congregationalists, two Presbyterians, one Methodist and a member of the Dutch Reformed Church, all of whom were likely to have opposed Bishop Weston's charge of heresy.

To Keable's credit, he did write later:

I had no right to dismiss Presbyterians and Wesleyans, Congregationalists and Baptists, as I once did. Their religious systems do not attract me, and chiefly I wonder that they have wandered so far themselves from the tenets of their own founders, but what I have admitted perhaps only in theory, I now know to be a fact. There are true followers of Christ among them from whom I would learn and whose ministry is blessed.

Ultimately, there were two simple reasons why Keable was appointed to the SANLC. Firstly, he applied to join. Very few priests did. Secondly, with the unexpectedly large number of Basothos joining the force, a chaplain was needed who spoke their language. It is also clear that the Archbishop of Cape Town, who appointed him, didn't ask too many questions. If he had, he might have discovered what Keable's friends already knew. Intriguingly, an old friend wrote much later:

I once heard... that he had left the Mission and was serving in the Diocese of Basutoland, where it was said that he killed a white man who was ill-treating a Native. This, though probably an exaggerated tale, I can well believe, for he was always on the side of the 'under-dog', and he did not always have his temper under control... I heard he was serving as a chaplain in France. Here he got into further trouble as he was against military authority.

As we will see, it is one thing to be against military authority but quite another to be able to do anything about it.

Keable learnt he had been selected to join the SANLC in January 1917 and, after performing a number of baptisms in his parish over Easter, he officially joined the contingent on 24th April 1917 with the rank of captain. While his wife stayed on in the parish, Keable headed off to Rosebank camp in Cape Town, where the labourers received their rudimentary training.

Arriving at Rosebank, Keable immediately witnessed racism from some of the white officers. He later wrote that he met white officers who disliked 'educated natives' and particularly disliked 'natives in clerical dress'. The officers denied all privileges to the black chaplains and one officer said to Keable, 'Now we shall see what these blessed padres of yours will do when properly treated.'

Kept away from the labourers during their training, Keable tried to support the black chaplains who nominally came under his charge, but he was annoyed by their attitude. They disliked having to eat the same food as the labourers; for example, they were used to having sugar and milk on their porridge and jam and butter on their bread. Once on the ship, they complained they were made to sleep near the men and share a lavatory.

Keable was heavily criticised later for writing about this – not least because it was easy for some to work out which black chaplains he was talking about. He knew that the black chaplains had been promised the same rank as interpreters and shouldn't have been treated as they were. Of course, travelling as a captain, Keable had much more comfortable sleeping quarters for the three-and-a-half-week voyage, and better food.

When the SANLC first arrived in France, the British tried to break them up into small groups and share them out among different units. However, by the time Keable arrived, the South Africans were concerned about the increasing opportunities for black men to mix with white people and had managed to withdraw the men from the front to six northern French towns, where they were housed in large closed compounds.

Closed compounds had first been introduced in South Africa in the Kimberley diamond mines in 1885. They were self-contained structures with a mesh roof over the entire compound, and the workers moved between the compound and the mine through enclosed corridors. The compound gate was always closed and, once a worker entered the compound, he was isolated from the outside world and could not leave until his contract expired – or until he did.

Lieutenant Colonel Godley, second in command of the SANLC in France, commented in a confidential letter that:

the conditions of our men in France as regards freedom of movement are similar to those applying to prisoners-of-war, and the camps occupied by our men and the prisoners-of-war are identical in every respect.

The only difference being that the 'locality of those occupied by the prisoners is in the majority of cases more favourably situated'.

Members of the SANLC had to follow very strict rules. No labourers could leave their camp unless accompanied by an officer. They couldn't enter any establishment that served alcohol or enter or be entertained in any local houses. White officers were told:

> care should be taken to prevent unauthorised persons from entering the Camp and conversing with Natives and specially to prevent all familiarity between Europeans and Natives, as this is subversive to discipline and calculated to impair their efficiency as working units.

Their camps were kept far apart from others. In *Standing By*, Keable described travelling for a day to visit one camp, where eventually 'we climbed the hill to the notice-board on the tree which tells you that here is a camp of negro workers and you must not loiter'.

Keable was initially posted with the 17th Labour Group in Rouen, but before Christmas 1917 he was transferred to the 14th Labour Group's Headquarters in Le Havre. He described the area where the SANLC camp was situated:

> there must be more beauty in the flames of hell. For miles around there stretches a hideous wilderness of railway lines, dumps, docks, and waste places scattered with refuse, old scrap-iron, and filth. The camp, like many about, was once the swampy mud-flats of the Seine mouth. Cinders have been collected in vast quantities, tar and sand have been freely used, the most incredible ugly utilitarian huts of wood and iron erected, and so camps have been made. Any few bushes that once grew here have been long since rooted up. Except for sea-birds and for rats, there is no wild-life here. A hundred factory chimneys belch out smuts every day; railway engines add their quota of filth; our own lesser incinerators and fires shower their blacks upon us. The very sunlight is dirty. When it rains, one wades through leagues of mud, and not clean earthy mud, but civilised ghastly mud that hides filth. Every form of building is hideous and except where the buildings are those of the Government, practically all the houses are in more or less decay.

The location of the camp was close to Cinder City, a giant camp with a YMCA in the middle, set up for soldiers who had 'done their bit' but were not yet fit enough to go back to work. That, too, had been built on swampy marshland that had been buried under embers.

The set-up of the SANLC camp was very much at odds with the propaganda disseminated by the Committee for the Welfare of Africans in Europe, formed in London in 1916 under the chairmanship of the Earl of Selborne. It set as its first objective the erection in each camp of a large heated hut, where men could meet for recreation. In March 1917, after a fourteen-day trip round the camps, Sir Herbert Sloley, a former resident commissioner of Basutoland, claimed that the accommodation and facilities there were good and that most camps already had a hut set aside for recreation. Keable, however, wrote that his men had 'no canteen, no recreation room, no spare cubicle even, and the boys sleep and eat in great huts taking sixty or so'. When the supposedly independent Aborigines Protection Society in London visited the camps, it reported that they were run 'in the best traditions of paternalism' and was impressed by the way in which Africans were cared for.

The men worked in a giant hangar at the port, unloading ships. The hangar was an iron and steel shed half a mile long and 250 feet wide into which ships would roll, be unloaded and then roll out, all through the day and night. *Standing By* contains a vivid description of a visit Keable made to the hangar with the men, describing their work and the unloading of:

> the food of three million men, the food of their horses, the food of their guns – guns themselves, tanks, rolling stock, waggons, automobiles – all these are poured continually on these wharves.

The men worked incredibly hard and were considered stronger and faster than labourers working for other labour corps. They set the record for unloading sacks of grain – 170 tons per hour – which the deputy controller of labour described as 'an absolutely unique achievement and in spite of a great deal of experience of what can be done in handling sacks, we were ourselves utterly astonished by the results'.

This, then, was the job of his company. Unloading and loading, day and night, for many hours; and when not working, locked away in a cramped, dirty camp awaiting the next shift.

Keable's job as chaplain, along with other colleagues – George Herbert Eva, a Wesleyan Methodist and Henry Charles Newell, a Congregationalist – was to cater spiritually for 2,000 men in four camps. The labourers worked twelve-hour shifts, longer than men in other labour corps, so were exhausted. On their day off, there was no time to attend religious services, as they were expected to clean the camp. Keable made sure he saw his own parishioners as often as he could, offering them confession and religious services when they were free. About a quarter of the labourers in the SANLC were practising Christians, and Keable was expected to cater for men of other denominations as well as his own. That meant he had to quickly learn how to deliver appropriate services for Presbyterians, Congregationalists, Baptists, French Protestants, Zionists, members of the Salvation Army, Wesleyan Methodists, Dutch Reformists and Seventh-Day Adventists.

The only group he was not allowed to provide services for were the seventy Roman Catholics, as their Church had very strict rules, and a priest from a Protestant church certainly could not offer confession or communion. With no Roman Catholic chaplains working for the SANLC, Keable felt sorry for this group and wrote to both the assistant principal chaplain and the ACG assistant chaplain-general, complaining that Catholics in his camp had no access to the sacraments. Only when he threatened to provide rosaries himself did they finally take action, sending a Catholic priest to say Mass. Not that Keable was impressed with the priest they sent. As he explained:

> We had a big camp and a cramped camp, and we send out gangs by day and by night. Where his reverence expected to say Mass, how he expected to gather a congregation from boys sleeping, or eating, or arriving or falling in or falling out or lounging around, or digesting either supper or dinner or breakfast, as the case might be, especially as he had no Sesuto, had no assistant and was even without a bell...
> I cannot tell.

The other white officers did little to support the labourers. It was left to Keable and the other chaplains to set up and run informal schools, at night for the majority or by day for those working the night shift. However, the men were so exhausted that few attended.

The chaplains were also in charge of handing out the flow of comforts and warm clothing – such as woollen mufflers – sent by the Committee for the Welfare of Africans in Europe, as well as organising recreational activities. Keable described the main topics for discussion at chaplains' conferences as:

> whether it would be better to purchase magic-lanterns than cinematographs; bands; marquees; organs; gramophones; night

schools; [and] our financial relationship with the society that provides us with material.

Timothy Winegard – in *Indigenous Peoples of the British Dominions and the First World War* – suggests that concerts were put on 'to portray the SANLC as happy and well-maintained'. Keable helped to organise one, which featured a group singing ragtime to a banjo accompaniment; a choir performing a chorus from an oratorio; a corporal reciting Abraham Lincoln's dedication at the Gettysburg Cemetery; a few singing a mission hymn; a Zulu war dance in costume; and finally, of course, a rousing rendition of *God Save the King*.

Keable spent only one Christmas in France and wanted to make it memorable for the men from his parish. He decided to organise a special midnight Mass, but this was impossible, as the authorities planned to vaccinate the men on 23rd December, give them twenty-four hours off and then send them out on a twelve-hour shift starting at 6.30pm on Christmas Eve. The Sergeant Major told Keable he could only have the sergeants' mess – the one suitable room in the camp for the private service – early that morning. So, Keable held his Christmas service at 7.00am on Christmas Eve with eighteen men singing Christmas Mass. Before the service, the men had waited outside in the snow, taking it in turns to come in and out to make their confession. Later that evening, they headed out for their twelve-hour shift.

On Christmas Day, all work in the hangar stopped at midday and the SANLC labourers had a free afternoon. Keable joined his men for a proper turkey lunch with plum pudding and mince pies and was still there at 2.30pm, when a group of drunken British soldiers came down to the camp. They called across the barbed wire to the labourers, suggesting they come outside and enjoy themselves like everyone else. The situation quickly became ugly, with everyone arguing about why white and black men were being treated differently, and why the labourers – alone – were subject to the closed compound system. The officers managed to get all the labourers back into their huts and then handed over to Keable to lead evensong in one of the big huts.

That evening, Keable did, however, manage to get special dispensation to take three dozen of the men from his parish out of the camp and over to the Catholic church in town. After the French priest had finished his service, Keable was given permission to gather his men around the crib and they all said the rosary, watched by many of the French congregation and a few attending English soldiers. The tradition in Basutoland was to visit the cribs in local churches. Keable was very critical of the display in that church, with the baby Jesus disproportionately big, and Joseph, Mary and the oxen looking like they had come out of a child's Noah's ark.

*

Despite the welcome break of Christmas, Keable became more and more demoralised by the treatment of the men. He couldn't fail to notice how upset the labourers were by their treatment. Albert Grundlingh – in *War and Society* – revealed secret reports that indicated many of the workers had not been prepared to tolerate the treatment handed out to them by bullying supervisors, and that they had retaliated. He suggested that instances where workers 'resisted authority' or 'offered violence to superior officers' were almost daily.

What Keable did report on, after the war, was the overt racism of the white officers in the SANLC. In *Slave, Serf, Citizen – And the Way Back*, he recounts how an SANLC officer 'in an applauding [officer's] mess', declared that Basutoland was the 'plague spot of South Africa' and that 'the Basuto are growing too well educated and too numerous and ought to be "thinned out"'.

A problem for Keable was that the white chaplains were seen by many of the labourers as part of the problem. Holding the rank of captain, the chaplains were expected to make sure the labourers followed the rules, and the chaplains were often put in charge of a camp when other officers were off duty. There were incidents where labourers suffered racism at the hands of the white chaplains.

One of the worst incidents involving a chaplain occurred in 1917 just after Keable arrived in France. Charlie – a young labourer whose surname is not recorded – left the compound one morning to do his laundry at a nearby stream, having just worked the night shift. He was ordered by an officer to bring water into the compound instead, and do his washing there, but he refused and was arrested. His friends went to the chaplain, Captain Barritt, a Wesleyan minster who was in charge of the camp at the time, to ask why Charlie had been detained, but Barritt refused to tell them. The situation quickly got out of control as the men started to demand Charlie's release. Clothier's and Grundlingh's versions of the story differ slightly – Grundlingh described the men using a pickaxe to try and break down the fence of the compound – but both agreed that white officers and NCOs ended up shooting at the men, resulting in the death of Charlie and at least three others.

Barritt returned to South Africa soon after the incident, having served in the SANLC for only a few months.

Stimela Jason Jingoes – the only labourer in the SANLC who travelled to France to write a first-hand account of his experiences – also had a run-in with a chaplain, who he said came from Fort Hare (which could have only been the chief chaplain, Lennox). Jingoes claimed the chaplain had him arrested for speaking so strongly, after he complained his officers treated him worse than the dogs and that he had found weevils in his food. He was suspended from work and court-martialled, where if found guilty he could have been shot. At his court martial, Jingoes reiterated his complaint to the presiding captain, who immediately went into the kitchen, where he found weevils in both the porridge and the uncooked mealie-meal. The Captain asked why the chaplain hadn't believed Jingoes's allegations, to which he replied that he didn't believe black labourers would tell the truth.

Because of this incident, Jingoes reported that he began to hate all white ministers, although his friends later persuaded him that they weren't all bad.

One company of labourers refused to accept the poor standard of rations and insisted they were given the same food as the white troops. The fact that there were two major outbreaks of scurvy among the labourers of the SANLC – an illness almost unrecorded among soldiers in France – suggests they did not receive their food rations. The official reason given for scurvy in the corps was that the meat and vegetables had been cooked for too long, destroying anti-scorbutic vitamins.

Despite the poor food, there were fewer medical problems than expected, and the two hospitals that catered exclusively for the men of the SANLC were never more than half full. The sick rate was the highest among the men Keable knew, the Basotho, which was attributed to the fact that more of the men from Basutoland were from the elite groups unused to manual labour. In all, 463 men were reported to have died from illness out of the 21,000 who travelled to France.

The two hospitals were hidden away, one near Dieppe with 500 beds and a second near Boulogne with 200. Keable described visiting one of them:

One rides to it up the beautiful little river-valley, with the great woods on the left and the high ridge crowned by the ancient castle on the right… It is, of course, trim, clean, and neat, and from the pole in the midst of the careful little garden droops the Union Jack and the Red Cross.

How many died in France from Keable's parish is not recorded, but he wrote of visiting one in hospital:

I see one who greets me eagerly, very glad that I should have visited him. I go and stand over the bed, and I read the signs, the wasted flesh, the hectic cough, the tell-tale chart… He is sure he must be better, and at any rate the year is up in a couple of months, by which time he will see Africa again… The doctor knows and I know, but we two only, that that will not be… The boy could not stand the voyage.

One man who died, who Keable knew, was Private Mopedi, number 21,987 of the SANLC. Keable officiated at his funeral, with a group of Yorkshire soldiers carrying his coffin and acting as the firing party.

One can imagine how Keable must have felt about the treatment of his parishioners, having persuaded them to come to France in the first place. He was a patriot and believed the war was being fought for a just cause, so he probably didn't regret asking them to lend a hand. But, when he saw their treatment, he must have felt some responsibility and guilt. And how did he feel when he read the letters dropped by German planes on the SANLC camps? The pamphlets read: 'In this war I hate black people the most. I do not know what they want in this European war. Where I find them, I will smash them'.

Keable was not able to do anything very practical to improve conditions for the men under his charge, or spend as long with them as he would have liked. He admitted in *Standing By* that he wasn't allowed to smoke with the labourers or to share the lives of his men as other military chaplains could. He was only allowed to learn the lesson of the army.

The lesson is one's own relative unimportance… The Army teaches that life is a great machine in which each of us matters remarkably little… 'Do your own job and don't worry about the next man's'.

He added sarcastically that you can do what you like, as long as you don't break some regulation; observe what you like, although using a camera was banned; and record what you like, provided you pay attention to the censor. The rules and regulations under which the labourers lived and worked had been agreed by the South African government, and nearly all the South African officers Keable served with supported this treatment of the men. The chief chaplain, Lennox, who set the tone for the other chaplains to follow, clearly supported the experiment. He was awarded an OBE after the war, the only SANLC officer to get such an honour.

I do not know how vocal Keable was in his complaints about the treatment of the men, but it is instructive how vehemently the chief medical officer, Captain Lewis Hertslet, the author of the racist pamphlet *The Native Problem*, denigrated and ridiculed Keable in the South African press.

In January 1918, Keable wrote an article for a little-known publication, *The East and the West: A Quarterly Review for the Study of Missionary Problems*, about the training of Africans for the priesthood. He felt this had become more about trying to turn Africans into Europeans, or even English, rather than preparing them to go out among their people. 'True education consists in drawing out, not in perpetually moulding to a given form', and he wanted the Church in Africa to build on African traditions and culture. He observed that the African chaplains in the SANLC wouldn't eat the same food, share the same lavatories, or stand for medical inspection alongside other Africans, and he suggested they 'had come to despise their own people and to consider that they are no longer "bone of their bone"'. At the same time, he made it clear that the chaplains faced racist abuse from white officers. Though Keable did not name the four chaplains to whom he was referring, it would not have been difficult to identify them. In total only fourteen African chaplains travelled to France during the war.

It was unsurprising that Keable's old bishop in Zanzibar, Frank Weston, wrote to *The East and the West Quarterly* to complain about Keable's article, suggesting Keable was expecting from African priests a standard of life which as an Englishman he had never proposed for himself. Weston accused Keable of libelling the four priests and suggested the article would never have been published if it had been about white priests. It was also not surprising that the Archbishop of Cape Town, who selected the African chaplains, should also write a gentle rebuke:

no doubt that Mr. Keable acted from the highest motives, [but it was a pity] he thought it right to publish to the whole world… certain criticisms of three or four South African Native Priests with whom he had been in contact for a few weeks.

Hertslet, however, took his criticisms to another level, writing a long article in a leading Natal newspaper in which he accused Keable of being 'inconsistent and stupid'. In the article, Hertslet claimed he had made it his 'business to get to know the chaplains (white and native) and came into touch with nearly all of them at some time or another'. So, he knew Keable, either personally or by reputation. He asked if Keable 'were a Chaplain to white troops (which heaven forfend) would he be consistent and live with the Tommies or with Officers?' And he wrote:

> Mr Keable has a long way to go, he is inexperienced and unwise, he has gone out of his way to malign his ministerial brethren, he has through his stupidity done considerable damage to the cause of his own Church, and incidentally condemned himself.

Hertslet did not address or make any reference to Keable's claim that the black chaplains had suffered racist abuse. However, in another article credited to 'Native' – who was almost certainly FZS Peregrino – the writer disputed Keable's account of any cases of racism and detailed the excellent conditions and treatment of the men. He wrote, 'It does not, therefore, appear to us that the officers disliked educated Natives as much as Mr. Keable would have us believe'.

The personal nature of Hertslet's attack on Keable suggests he was trying to do more than just correct the record. Hertslet was, by then, the chief apologist for the SANLC experiment. In November 1917, he had written to a South African paper claiming: 'The disadvantages, involving contamination, to which he (the black labourer) has been exposed have been small', and he championed the success of the experiment.

BP Willan explained:

> For obvious political reasons… it was important that the difficulties involved in effectively running the SANLC 'along South African lines' did not become known inside South Africa. Information which did find its way into the South African press (African and European) about the organization and behaviour of SANLC units in France

was almost uniformly favourable – the outcome of several layers of censorship and the need to encourage further recruitment. Many of the accounts that were published came from European officers attached to the SANLC, and in these the degree of ideological vested interest in presenting the experiment as a success was often clearly apparent.

In South Africa, it was important that men like Keable were either kept quiet or discredited. Keable decided his best hope of highlighting the treatment of the men was to write a book. While on leave in England in February 1918, the book he had written about the SANLC was accepted for publication by a respected Christian publisher, the Society for the Promotion of Christian Knowledge (SPCK). However, the director confirmed in 1959:

> Mr Keable's manuscript of The First Black Ten Thousand came to us… When it had been set up in proof, the censorship refused permission for publication, without giving any official reason. We destroyed all proofs in our possession and distributed the type, because the book would have been unsaleable if we had waited until after the war.

The manuscript is lost. What is certain is that it was censured because it contained unfavourable comments about the treatment of black labourers. The law at the time – *The Defence of the Realm Act* – allowed books to be censured if they were: 'likely to cause disaffection or alarm among any of His Majesty's forces or among the civilian population'.

A few years later, Keable stated in *Nonsenseorship* – a collection of essays on censorship – that *The First Black Ten Thousand* had been 'censored out of existence' because he 'had given slight hints of the truth about the racial situation in South Africa'. The *Church Times* suggested years later that the book was censored because it 'described with unusual power the native, and particularly the Christian native, behind the lines in France'.

Two other books which spoke uncritically about the SANLC were published during the war. Both Sir Harry Johnston's *The Black Man's Part in the War*, which briefly mentions the SANLC, and FZS Peregrino's *His Majesty's Black Labourers: a Treatise on the Camp Life of the SANLC* were propaganda plugs aimed at extolling the virtues of the experiment, and excellent work, of the SANLC.

Keable, unable to spend much time with his men, and easily bored, took any opportunity to get out and see things. He made sure he travelled around as much as he could, and in *Standing By* he describes visiting Amiens, Crecy, Paris and Versailles, as well as the ruins at Jumièges, often 'plodding wearily along on a heavy Government bicycle, [while] the Colonel roars by in a motor-car...'

By the time Keable arrived in France, there were no SANLC companies near the front lines, so he rarely faced any danger from the enemy. The closest he came was when he and three others had stopped in a small village for lunch and a lorry was blown up outside the restaurant where they were eating. Keable's chauffeur, cleaning the car's windscreen at the time, was badly cut by broken glass but far worse was the lorry driver, who, according to Keable, 'from his waist downwards... [was] mangled untellably'. A doctor on the scene realised he could do nothing for the driver and handed his care over to the nearest priest – Keable – who saw him die moments later.

Wanting to help closer to the front line, Keable volunteered to work in an advanced dressing station for a few days. That experience clearly left a profound impression on him. For the first time as a priest, he felt completely unwanted. He had expected the injured and dying to seek comfort from him and was surprised when they turned away as he approached. It was almost ten years before he confessed how ineffectual he had been.

Imagine an enormous French barn, retaining a roof by a kind of miracle, and lit fitfully by half a dozen lanterns. It was shaken every few minutes by the sound of exploding shells. It was crammed to its limits by I do not know how many men, lying on straw and even on the bare earth, groaning in every degree of pain, if not mercifully unconscious. Stretcher bearers poured continually in, to the increasing despair of the doctor-officer in charge. And there stood I in the midst of them, the only padre, who should have been a consolation and a strength to those men in their hour of need, and who was not idle because I was useful now and again for jobs which have nothing to do with my profession. I could shift a bundle of straw or light a 'fag', if I had been a trained nurse I should have been more useful. I think in all that night of horror I was only once asked by any one of the wounded to supply the consolations of religion, and that was a black Catholic soldier from Senegambia.

Keable was shocked by how many men did not know or did not want Christ in their lives. Many of Keable's obituaries suggested the war had been the knock-out blow to his faith. Maybe it was the horrors of the war that challenged his faith. Maybe it was a realisation that as a priest he was unable to support his men. Or maybe he was turned away from his faith by temptation.

With the exception of that short trip up to the advanced dressing station, Keable was based behind the front line throughout his time in France, first in Rouen and then in Le Havre.

Le Havre was set up as the main base camp in France for the British Expeditionary Force once the war had begun. Although briefly evacuated in August 1914, it was quickly re-established for military purposes. By the end of 1917, the town housed the base camps and depots for, among others, the Royal Garrison Artillery, the Royal Horse Artillery, the Army Service Corps, the Army Ordnance Corps, the Army Veterinary Corps, at least six infantry British regiments, at least five Australian divisions, the Canadian Forces and the Canadian Lumber Corps. There were two general field hospitals, a number of stationary ones and a veterinary hospital. There was a school of cookery, field butchery, army printing and stationery service and a degreasing plant. There were eleven rest camps within marching distance. All this and Le Havre was one of the main ports through which troops arrived in France and returned to England.

Filled with so many service men and women, many resting up, Le Havre became a party town. For many single men, this meant eating, drinking and having sex. In response to a review of *Simon Called Peter*, Keable admitted life behind the lines was largely 'a devil's trinity of drink, damns and debauchery', suggesting it may not have been 'hell itself, but at least it was the antechamber'. He also mentioned the 'houses of lust' which were 'kept for the troops, where men lined up for immorality at a few francs a time'.

In *Sex and the Trenches, from The First World War Story*, Dr Clare Makepeace wrote that the British forces were allowed to visit brothels – legally – throughout the war. She claimed that 171,000 British troops visited the brothels of just one street in Le Havre, during just one year of the war. Long queues outside the brothels were common. A letter from a Private Richards recorded that, when he visited a 'red lamp' in Bethune, he found a queue of 300 men waiting patiently outside. Makepeace quotes an unnamed MP who insisted to officers that the continuance of regular sex in brothels was 'neither impossible not harmful'.

Whether Keable succumbed, we do not know. He wrote in *Standing By* that when he met the girls in the street, 'cheerful, human, gay', he involuntarily smiled back at them. And that they made him feel 'hotly indignant, rather tender, and very pitiful'.

Unlike the men he was responsible for, Keable was allowed to go into town and enjoy himself. He had nothing in common with the white officers in the SANLC but there were plenty of other men and women with whom he could socialise. Keable liked to drink, and he liked good food. He was clever and funny and good company. Cecil wrote he was 'an all-round good sport – his hands full of kindly occupations... a smoker, not adverse to a glass of whisky and soda'.

So, he began to socialise. JH Sims, the local administrator in Leribe, wrote many years later:

I heard more of him later through our officers overseas who said after a time a change came over him and he began going out with the lads on leave excursions and became, one might say, very worldly.

Sims could only have heard about this from SANLC officers reporting back to a senior official in Basutoland. Were they trying to discredit him? When he was finally released from the SANLC, his official war record testified, very succinctly, that he was of 'good' character, 'sober' and of 'good' efficiency. Was this untrue?

If Keable's attitude and behaviour did change while he was out in France, it is likely that a chance meeting with a nineteen-year-old lorry driver was one of the causes.

CHAPTER 7

SIMON CALLED PETER'S FORERUNNER – THE CHILD

Simon Called Peter was not Keable's first story to explore the idea of a priest choosing between a woman and God. Keable was writing throughout his time in France and in December 1917, he published a short story, *The Child*, in the *Treasury* magazine.

Although only six pages long, *The Child* gives us an insight into his thinking at the time. As in *Simon Called Peter*, the main character is a priest who falls in love with a young woman. They have the same first names – Edith and Paul – as the two main characters in his semi-autobiographical novel *Peradventure*, published in 1923. In the first part, we meet Rev Paul Weston and Edith Valency working together in Sheffield, on a religious magazine, during the First World War. Paul is 'strangely moved' by Edith, who is 'a tall handsome powerful girl'. Paul plucks up courage to write to ask if he may 'drop a bit of... stiffness' and call her Edith. If so, she should wear a red rose in her buttonhole the next day. She wears the rose, and they are soon walking out together.

In the second part, Paul breaks the news that he has decided to join up – although not as a priest but as a soldier. Although upset, Edith understands his decision and, before he goes, they share a long and silent kiss.

The third part begins with Paul and a Canadian soldier in a trench with a German soldier who is on the point of surrender. The Canadian charges forward with his bayonet and kills the man. Paul protests, only to be told: 'Why not? I'm not going to send another prisoner to eat grub in Blighty while the swine starve our chaps in the hells of prison.' Almost at once a bomb explodes in the trench, injuring Paul and we assume killing the Canadian. Paul ends up in hospital and writes to Edith to tell her he loves her but doesn't want to see her again, as he 'doesn't want the world he used to know'.

In the final part, Edith, allowed to travel to see her fiancé, tracks down Paul in Paris, where he is convalescing. He insists they separate but she persuades him to go into a nearby church where they sit together and view, behind the altar, a statue of the Virgin Mary holding her infant son. The sight moves Paul so much he agrees to marry Edith.

Although *The Child* has a similar theme to *Simon Called Peter* – a priest falling in love during the war – in some ways, it is a much darker story. The war crime is all the more shocking today because it is so simply told. And the reason Paul gives for joining up as a soldier is not surprising, in light of Keable's experience:

> England doesn't really want chaplains. It wants men who can be lively and bright to cheer up the Tommies, but it doesn't want chaplains – or only a few to do the necessary decent things, like burying the dead. We've got to make her want us as chaplains, if you see what I mean. She's got to take us as soldiers and find something in us that will make her want what a chaplain can bring, and turn spontaneously to us to bring it.

The choice of the church they visit – Notre Dames des Victoires – is significant. It is a Roman Catholic church with a close connection to many famous French Catholics, as well as foreign mission seminarians and priests, and where John Henry Newman gave thanks for his conversion. It is also one of the main churches along the pilgrimage route to Santiago de Compostela in Spain. The dramatic statue of the Madonna and Child, both crowned, is still in place behind the altar today. Paul and Edith were being welcomed into the Catholic church together. At the end of *Simon Called Peter*, Keable also used the device of a revelation that changes the course of a protagonist's life during a visit to a Catholic church.

One significant difference between the short story and the later novel is the character of the young woman. In *The Child*, she is a devout Christian, perhaps based on Sybil Keable. In *Simon Called Peter*, she was portrayed – according to Keable – as pagan, and it's likely she was based on Jolie Buck, whom Keable had met in France.

Chapter 8

Keable's secret affair

In America, particularly, the character in *Simon Called Peter* who attracted the most attention was Julie. The *Boston Transcript* wrote:

> How few authors could have seen or depicted Julie! She is wayward, intoxicating and tender. She is gay and observing, friendly and loyal, and in the end she is strong, strong beyond most. Most of all she is lovable.

The *Evening Ledger* went further:

> Beautiful, piquant, irresistibly human, but with a pervasive sense of the divine... Julie sacrifices virginity for the sake of greater love and then for the sake of greater love forgoes love itself. She outlaws herself from the moral code, casting aside the conventions for which she cares little, to make Peter happier.

Many newspapers claimed to be scandalised by the relationship between Peter and Julie in *Simon Called Peter*. How could a man of the cloth forsake his fiancée and have an affair with a nurse? Little did they know that the truth was even more scandalous.

Keable met Jolie Buck in Le Havre in 1917. *Simon Called Peter* is clearly based on Keable and Buck's relationship during the war, although Keable did try to disguise the fact. At the beginning of the novel, when Peter goes to France, he is engaged to be married, whereas Keable was already married. Peter is a young curate in London, while Keable was a parish priest in Basutoland. Peter is appointed chaplain to regular soldiers; Keable was chaplain to labourers in the SANLC. Julie was a South African nurse in her mid-twenties, while Buck was a nineteen-year-old English lorry driver. Changing her name from Jolie to Julie seems less than subtle, although he always called her Betty.

Keable never admitted publicly that Julie was based on Buck. It wasn't until November 1923, three years after Constable agreed to publish the novel, that Keable privately admitted to Sadler his relationship with her. That was almost six years after Buck and Keable had first met, and a year after the two had run away together to live as husband and wife. Keable wrote:

By the way, I trust you don't feel in any way hurt that I did not tell you earlier of [Buck]. I can't talk of these things easily. Also it wasn't only my secret, but I meant to do so when I got back to town and nearly did so in your office. Only it is hardly the place. And I am very glad you know. I hope that we have a friendship that is really going to mean something.

When he wrote *Simon Called Peter*, Keable wanted to keep his affair with Buck secret from his wife, his family, his clergy friends back in England, the SANLC officers, anyone back in Basutoland and the labourers he cared for. Buck was less concerned about the reaction of those she knew in France but needed her affair with a married priest to be kept secret from any of her mother's friends and anyone who supported her family financially.

Buck's brother William Buck, her friends Rita and Jack Elliott, and Sybil's niece Trewolla-Hulme all confirmed the novel 'was largely autobiography' and that Keable and Buck met in France during the war.

Grace Eileen Joly Beresford Buck – known to her friends as Jolie – was born in India in January 1899. She was named Grace after her aunt; Eileen, because it was a name her parents liked, but also the name of an old flame of her father; Joly after her godfather, Monsieur Joly; and Beresford was her mother's family name.

Her father, William Buck, the fourth of ten children, was also born in India but went to Cheltenham School, in England, before following his father, Major General Lewis Buck, into the army. He joined the Durham

Light Infantry in 1882, serving in Gibraltar and Malta before seeing action during a tour of Egypt. He was involved in the Battle of Ginnis, the last time British soldiers fought in red coats, for which he was awarded a medal and the Khedive's Star. He was stationed in India from 1887 and, in 1898, aged thirty-six, he married Eleanor Beresford, the daughter of Charles Beresford, the manager of the Delhi and London Bank.

Jolie Buck (top) with her sister, Kathleen, brother William and mother

In 1901, while Buck's father followed his regiment to South Africa to take part in the final months of the Second Boer War, Buck travelled to England with her mother and younger sister, Kathleen Buck. Two years later, the now-promoted Captain Buck was appointed deputy assistant adjutant general to Lord Kitchener. Buck's parents, along with their new baby, William, returned to India, leaving Kathleen and Jolie Buck in Bath with their Aunt May and elderly grandfather – Major General Lewis Buck. It was six years before Buck saw again her parents and William Buck, as well as another brother, Reginald Buck, who was born in 1905.

The growing independence movement in India at this time meant soldiers and their families were at risk of attack, and children were often sent home to

England for their own safety. There were other strong family reasons why the Bucks decided to leave their two young daughters behind.

In 1857, Buck's great-grandfather, his wife and five daughters were stationed in Delhi as Indian soldiers involved in the Indian Rebellion reached the city. Sarah, aged nineteen, and Rebecca, aged seventeen, were the first members of the family to die, hacked to death in the palace, where they had been taken to hide by a family friend. Later the same day, Buck's great-grandfather led his wife and their three youngest girls onto the roof of one of the Delhi Bank outbuildings. Wielding a sword, and his wife a spear, they tried to defend the stairs up to the roof. His wife killed two mutineers and the staircase became blocked with dead bodies. However, Indian soldiers managed to scale the walls and all five members of the family were killed. Agnes, aged six, Emily, eight, and Charlotte, ten, had their throats cut with broken glass. Their bodies were laid out on the steps of the bank for all to see. A ring Jolie Buck's great-grandmother had been wearing – a supposed gift from a maharajah – was retrieved later from her hand and kept within the family. The Beresford family still talk of the cursed ring, but there is no evidence that Buck ever wore it.

Even when Buck's parents and brothers returned to England in 1909, she and her sister continued to live in Bath, while the rest of the family settled in London. Her father had been invalided out of the army and he travelled abroad seeking a cure during the two years before he died. Her mother, Eleanor Buck, opened a dress shop on Bond Street where her clients were mainly her distinguished friends from India. Meanwhile, Jolie and Kathleen Buck continued their education at Hermitage House School in Bath before moving to board at the Royal School for Daughters of Officers of the Army, also in the city. The school was privately funded, and subscribers were eligible to vote on which girls could receive admission and at what rate their fees should be reduced. Jolie and Kathleen Buck were awarded the biggest bursaries of their intake in 1911, reducing their fees to £15 a year, compared to other families, who paid between £30 and £80.

After her husband died, Eleanor Buck, still only thirty-six, had four growing children and a pension of only £72 per annum. According to William Buck, their grandfather had 'champagne tastes' and left no inheritance. In dire straits, Eleanor Buck turned to Lady Waterford, who contacted the Officers' Families Fund on her behalf, which provided money and second-hand clothes for the children.

In November 1912, Buck left her boarding school in Bath, aged just thirteen, although her sister, Kathleen Buck, stayed on until she was nearly seventeen. It may be that the school was only prepared to offer one bursary and that Kathleen Buck won the vote. Whatever the reason, it affected the sisters' relationship. Kathleen Buck later wrote that, at home, her sister tried to get her into trouble by doing something wrong and blaming her. She also complained that her sister was always trying to steal her boyfriends, though there is no evidence that this is true.

So, while her sister stayed on in Bath, Buck joined her mother and brothers in London. They moved into a semi-detached house in Wembley Park, where they were joined by Miss Cunynghame, who Buck's mother had met at a séance and who lived with them for many years.

By 1916, the situation at home had deteriorated, as her brother explained:

[Buck] began to be difficult. She was 17 and refused to accept the rather dreary family life. There was a war on, and she wanted independence. She had been in a convent for some time, and eventually her Mother, who was at work all day, gave her an ultimatum that she must toe the line or get out. She gat, and went to live with Aunt Grace, whose godchild she was.

William's description of his sister 'gatting' was probably less dramatic than it sounds. Grace Godfrey lived not far away in Powis Square, Bayswater. Still, it gave her more freedom and an opportunity to get a job. Having learnt to drive, she volunteered as a driver for the army and ended up chauffeuring VIPs around London, based at the grand Hotel Cecil, on the Strand. Her sister, Kathleen Buck, who had left school in March 1917, began a job as a 'tracer' for the Air Ministry in London. The two met up a few times before Buck got a job in France working as a driver for the Canadian Forestry Corps. There is a photograph of her in her uniform, dated 1917, showing two badges on her coat, each with two trees and a crown, the emblem of the 238th Canadian Forestry Battalion.

The Forestry Corps was primarily made up of large numbers of Canadian lumberjacks who came over to the UK from 1916 onwards to cut down trees for the war effort, mainly to produce wooden supports for the trenches. The 238th Battalion was formed in Canada in 1916, with just over 1,000 men sailing to England in September. The battalion was then absorbed into the Canadian Forestry, renamed the 14th Company and sent to France.

Jolie Buck in the Canadian Forestry Corps

By November 1917, there were fifty-eight companies supplying lumber to the British and French troops. The main supply depot, where technical equipment was warehoused, was in Le Havre. Buck and the other lorry drivers were based there, ready to drive supplies to the various camps around France.

Her brother William Buck wrote that, early in the war, Buck 'got mixed up with a lot of strange medical types, none of whom seemed to be out of the right drawer'. Hugh Cecil suggests that her 'radiant sex-appeal made her an anxiety to her well-connected family' and that, as 'a spirited, pleasure-loving girl', she rebelled, although 'probably only to the extent of kissing and saucy conversation'. He went on to say:

> [Buck], though resilient, as she had to be, was neither hard nor morally weak. Despite her youth, she survived the punishing ordeal of the Western Front, seeing sights as horrible as had anyone who was there. Like other girls, she had to fend off the frequent attention of young officers whose demands were underscored by the threat of their imminent death. Not that she always rebuffed them. She was flirtatious and tender-hearted. She rebelled against the rules of conventional social behaviour and was naively excited by the effect she had on men.

Keable and Buck may have first befriended each other as fellow Brits, he surrounded by a sea of South Africans, and she by Canadians. In *Standing By*, Keable relates a meeting between him and a driver which could well have been based on their first meeting:

we are waiting for the Colonel in some deserted orderly room by the fire at night; I take out a cigarette case and as a matter of course offer it to her. As a matter of course she takes it. She crosses her legs, and the short skirts just suffice to cover her knees, and we chat of England and the world. She shall certainly go out to the colonies after the war, she says, blowing out the smoke. Yes, very likely motor-driving, except that there are two friends of hers on the land, who are thinking of a Canadian farm, and of course one would have a Ford and she might fit in there. I suggest we might have a walk one afternoon. Certainly she agrees, unperturbed; we can meet well out of town... The colonel comes in and we stand chatting a few minutes more. 'Well, if you are ready, Miss Smith,' he says... She cranks up; she knows her car, she says, and I should only muddle it.

Cecil speculates on why they were attracted to each other. He suggested for Keable:

[Buck's] significance was not simply that she stirred him romantically as no other woman had ever done, but she symbolised a new womanhood which beckoned to him to free himself from the past.

Cecil believed she needed 'someone who could take her in hand and treat her seriously', and that she saw in Keable 'a man of great earnestness, unusual talents and little obvious glamour' who 'combined experience with a kind of innocence, which made him relish new enjoyments of all sorts'. Father Dowling, a Roman Catholic padre, who knew Buck during the war, said she often spoke of Keable's thoughtfulness, patience and unfailing humour.

Though there was a twelve-year gap between the two, they were similar in many ways. Even after the war, Keable's friends still described him as boyish. He was a huge enthusiast for adventures. He loved to explore, go on bike rides and hike. And he was also very sociable. He loved to eat and drink and smoke. Buck's adventurous spirit was clear. She had left home and worked her way out to France, driving lorries for a band of Canadian lumberjacks.

Keable was the better educated, but she was keen to learn, and she enjoyed seeing the sights, such as the ruined abbey at Jumièges, and learning the history.

Rather peculiarly, *Simon Called Peter* is dedicated to Julie, with the lines:

She never lived, maybe, but it is truer to say that she never dies. Nor shall she ever die. One may believe in God, though He is hard to find, and in Women, though such as Julie are far to seek.

Dedicating the book to a character in the novel surely suggests the character is based on a real person. The relationship between Peter and Julie in *Simon Called Peter* seems to have drawn heavily on Keable's relationship with Buck: Julie's young confidence, her teasing and her childish sense of fun, and the jealousy Peter feels whenever anyone else chats or flirts with Julie.

Early in the book, Julie starts to call Peter 'Solomon', teasing him for being so wise. Interestingly, Buck also had a pet name for Keable – Bill – and he always called her Betty, perhaps after William Shakespeare and Queen Elizabeth.

The nicknames completely confused Sadler, who wrote to Keable in 1924 to ask: 'by the way, is her name Betty or Julie or both, and if so which ought one to use?' Keable suggested Jolie.

In the photograph of Buck from this time, dressed in her Canadian uniform, she appears much older than eighteen, staring seriously into the middle distance, perhaps trying not to laugh.

The words and phrases Keable used to describe Julie in *Simon Called Peter* could equally apply to Buck. Julie is described as spontaneous, fresh, lacking conventionality, daring, iconoclastic, free, mysterious, passionate and dominant. She, Julie, believed that love was 'an animal passion for the purpose of populating the earth', and 'she couldn't be respectable' as she 'talks about corsets in public' and 'doesn't wear them herself, except in the evening, for the sake of other things'. One can imagine, just as Peter fell in love with Julie, Keable also fell in love with Buck.

Julie, in the novel, is often seen puffing at a cigarette, smoking 'cigarette after cigarette furiously, only, however, getting through about half of each'. Even in the hotel as 'the fire glowed red', Julie was 'stretched out in a big chair, smoking a cigarette'. Before the First World War, smoking was seen as an almost exclusively male pastime and a decidedly unfeminine practice. Women who smoked in public were considered by many to be either masculine or to have a liberal attitude to drink and sex. But the war changed this perception. While before the war women were never shown smoking in cigarette adverts, during the war there were adverts suggesting that men and women might wish to smoke together! And more and more women started to smoke. One study by Rosemary Elizabeth Elliot suggested that the war saw:

> the beginning of changes in gender roles coupled with negotiation over the spaces in which these changes took place, which provided the climate in which the suggestion that women might also legitimately share a cigarette could be made.

The numerous references to Julie smoking in *Simon Called Peter* are likely to be more of a reflection of Buck's habit than a subtle attempt to pass commentary on her, or Julie's, morals.

We will perhaps never know how close Keable and Buck were during the war. In the letter Keable wrote to his, and Buck's, son in the days after she died, he claimed he had agreed to separate from his wife before he met his son's mother. However, unless Keable agreed to separate from his wife before he left Basutoland in 1917 (and took four and a half years to do so), Keable cannot be telling his son the truth. Maybe he wanted to protect his son from the extent of his adultery, or maybe when he said he hadn't met her before he decided to separate from his wife, he meant he hadn't slept with her.

Although Buck and Keable never wrote about their time together in France, it seems likely that the love story in *Simon Called Peter* mirrors theirs, with conversations, outings and a passionate weekend in a London hotel. Certainly, the book was banned from Sybil Keable's household, and years after, when her niece was caught reading *Simon Called Peter*, aged fourteen, all Keable's books were removed from the house and destroyed.

At the end of the war, Keable had to return to South Africa. He could not terminate his contract with the SANLC until he returned there, and, perhaps more importantly, he owed a debt to the men from his parish whom he had persuaded to go to France. He may have felt the least he could do was to accompany them home and make sure they were safely settled back into their old lives.

We don't know whether the couple broke up, seemingly for good, at the end of the war, or whether they arranged to meet again in England. The only clue comes in the letter from Father Dowling. He wrote to Keable, after Buck died, to say how much she loved Keable but, slightly cryptically, he wrote: 'She never had a chance until you gave it her and she was so proud and fond of you and so immersed in all your activities, that all the old sorrow and resentment had vanished'.

Was 'the old sorrow and resentment' about Keable breaking up with Buck when he returned to Basutoland?

*

Keable left France on 12th August 1918, returning to Africa by ship with a group of men who had finished their one-year contracts. Although the war had not finished, the South African government had decided to withdraw all the men from France. The last main group left in September, leaving only a few stragglers behind – sick men in hospital and a few working in the depot in Plymouth.

We now know that the South African government was concerned that the experiment had begun to fail. In a confidential letter, Lieutenant Colonel Godley of the SANLC wrote, in late 1917:

> the temper of a large proportion of the men is distinctly nasty...
> [there is a] constant undercurrent of feeling amongst the Natives that
> they of all the King's soldiers are singled out for differential treatment.

He went on to argue that the South African government should give serious consideration to abandoning the closed compound system. Instead, the government decided to abandon the experiment altogether, disband the contingent and ship the remaining members home.

As far as the British military authorities were concerned, the labourers had done a very good job. The official War Office account commented on the 'splendid reputation for good work under the hardest conditions conceivable' and Field Marshal Sir Douglas Haig, the Commander-in-Chief of the British Armies in France, expressed his 'warm appreciation of the good work done by them for the British Army during their stay in France'.

Willan suggested the main reason for the end of the project was that the

95

SANLC had become an embarrassment to the South African government, with the authorities perturbed by bad publicity, and rumours, reaching home. There was also an important political dimension to the decision, as Afrikaner Nationalists – who had opposed the setting-up of the SANLC in the first place – had become increasingly vocal in their calls for the SANLC to be disbanded. An indication of the dissatisfaction of the labourers was the fact that very few agreed to renew their one-year contracts.

There were rumours back in South Africa that attempts to segregate the contingent from contact with civilians had failed. Jingoes remembered how some French ladies had served Africans with tea before one of the white officers – and then offered the officer a cup used by an African. The officer said:

> When you people get back to South Africa, don't start thinking that you are whites, just because this place has spoiled you. You are black, and will stay black.

In fact, Jingoes, who left France in April 1918, said he had enjoyed his stay there, as it was his first experience of living in a society without a colour bar. He also claimed that, when the time came to leave, some of them had hidden in the houses of French friends. Most, he said, were caught by the military police, but some never went back to South Africa. Although there are no official records of anyone absconding, it could be true.

The South African authorities were terrified that if white women in France befriended members of the SANLC, then problems could 'spread' to South Africa. The law in South Africa at that time, looked at today, is really shocking. The 1903 Immorality Ordinance of Transvaal, which was still in force, stated that any 'white woman who voluntarily permits any native [defined as any person who manifestly belonged to any of the native or coloured races of Africa, Asia, America or St Helena] to have unlawful carnal connection with her is liable to imprisonment with hard labour for five years'. (The sentences in the provinces of the Cape of Good Hope and Natal were two years' hard labour.) If the relationship was consensual, the man would get six years in prison and twenty-four strokes of the whip. If it wasn't consensual, he would get a death sentence.

There were no such laws in Basutoland, although the authorities considered introducing new rules in the 1920s. Another British protectorate

– Swaziland – had adopted the same law as Transvaal and in seventeen years had just one case where, as the resident commissioner wrote, 'a degenerate white woman and her native paramour' were prosecuted and punished. Sexism and the patriarchy prevailed, and the rules about white men sleeping with black women were very different. However, the rumours that were later circulated that Keable may have been 'free with native women' while in Basutoland would have scandalised his parishioners.

Another problem in France arose when the men were unable to return home once their one-year contract was up. William Thomas Brownlee, a captain in the 1st Battalion, wrote, 'The men are all becoming very impatient and want to go now, now, now'. The men had been told that their contracts included the time it took to travel home. Those whose contracts had expired before they got onto the ship home not surprisingly were very reluctant to carry on working.

Keable's situation was different, as he was contracted to remain with the SANLC until six months after the end of the war. But the South African authorities didn't want any of the chaplains to stay around for long. Of the other eleven white chaplains who signed up with the SANLC from October 1916 onwards, three were released before the end of 1917, one more in February 1918, two transferred to the Royal Army Chaplains' Department and the other five were released between August and November 1918, round the same time as Keable.

Chapter 9

Simon Called Peter – the sequel

In the two years following the publication of *Simon Called Peter*, Keable received many fan letters, some asking him what had happened to Peter and Julie after the war, others inventing their own elaborate theories. Sadler was also eager for Keable to write a sequel, warning that he had to write it soon while his readers remembered the original story. Constable were still prepared to publish whatever novel Keable wrote, but the English market was still small, and, despite *Simon Called Peter* selling so well, it only offered him a £250 advance for the sequel. (Following its success, Constable paid a £750 advance for the subsequent novel, *Numerous Treasure*.)

Major Putnam, the managing director of Putnam's in America, was keener still for a follow-up. He had signed up Keable on the back of the success of *Simon Called Peter* and had agreed a generous contract for his first book with them, which would have been Keable's racy romantic novel *The Mother of All Living* if Dutton had not reclaimed it, and instead became the worthy *Peradventure*, with 'too much religion and too little passion'. The advance for *Peradventure* was £500. The royalties began at 10% for the first 3,000 copies, and then rose incrementally until they reached 20% for all copies sold over 15,000. The contract gave Putnam's first call on Keable's next two novels but included a clause which would see lower royalties paid if *Peradventure* failed to sell many copies. Keable had broken away from the loyal and appreciative publisher John Macrae at Dutton and he knew that if he didn't deliver a successful book for Putnam's soon, he could be out of contract.

Keable had no real enthusiasm for writing a sequel. He had other things he wanted to write, including a theatrical script for *Simon Called Peter*. But he promised Sadler as he left for Tahiti at the end of 1922 that he would write the book. A few months before, while writing *Peradventure*, he had written to tell Sadler that he had a huge plot for his next book – eugenics, birth control and communism. Not wishing to waste what he saw as good material, he decided to incorporate it into the sequel. He set the first half of the book in southern Africa, which gave him the opportunity to write about the beautiful, barren landscape of Basutoland. His attack in Mokhotlong, when he had been shot, was the basis for a central plot point in the first half of the story.

The sequel begins shortly after where *Simon Called Peter* left off. Having given up his affair with Julie, Peter Graham has decided to leave the priesthood, and the first chapter sees him in France as a private in the South African army. When the war ends, Peter then travels to South Africa to take a job as a trader in a remote area, while Julie returns to her old job in a hospital, not far from her former lover. Peter seems to have given up both the Church and Julie. Then, while asleep in a remote hut, he is shot by a madman. Using his experience, Keable described his hero 'waiting for death'. Peter is found by a doctor and Julie, who helps nurse him back to full fitness, but, despite sleeping with each other again, they agree to go their separate ways, Peter to Spain and Julie to England.

Sadler loved this first half of the book, writing to Keable in June 1923:

I doubt if it would be possible to fulfil more satisfactorily the expectations of the SIMON people than the first half... Right up to the time when Julie and Peter decide to go their ways together to Spain and there part, I felt that you had done the impossible and had written a sequel that was even better than the book that prompted it.

He was not, however, so impressed by the second half, which begins with Julie finding work in England at a maternity hospital that is experimenting in eugenics. Most of the second half concentrates on Julie's time there, with discussions on communism and the ethics of eugenics. Peter returns to England to see her and to say his final goodbyes. He has converted to Catholicism and decided to become a Carthusian monk. Julie decides to have a baby with the unhappily married doctor and champion of eugenics,

Maurice Sampson. Then, realising they love each other, Maurice and Julie agree to leave England for a 'far haven' – Corsica.

As Sadler wrote, 'The last part is not really a novel at all, but a eugenic tract'.

For many months, the book's title was *The Far Haven* as the manuscript passed between Keable, his literary agent, Watt, and Sadler. However, eventually they settled on the title *Recompense* to reflect the fact that Peter and Julie got the rewards they deserved, for the life they had led. As seen with *Simon Called Peter*, Keable liked to use biblical references and he based the title on a line from Hosea 9:7, which begins, 'The days of visitation are come, the days of recompense are come; Israel shall know it'. He considered calling it *The Days of Recompense* but preferred the single word.

No one was particularly happy with the manuscript, and Sadler was desperate for Keable to rewrite the second half. But, with Sadler based in London and Keable ensconced in Tahiti, there was no opportunity for a frank, face-to-face conversation. Letters were sent back and forth, crossing over each other and causing much confusion. Eventually, Sadler wrote: 'If you... say "Take it or Leave it" we shall of course take it'.

In response, Keable wrote in August 1923, 'I am sorry but I think there are only two things to be done – scrap it or publish it'. He knew it wasn't a very good book but was eager to move on to new projects rather than to engage in endless rewrites.

Recompense was finally published in February 1924 in England, and a month later in the US. Somewhat to the surprise of author and publishers, it received fairly favourable press. Sadler told Keable, 'Both the *Observer* and the *Morning Post* were good, and a number of minor papers have useful things.'

The *Times Literary Supplement* wrote:

Mr Keable still smarts from some of the censures passed on the old one (Simon Called Peter), but he has met his critics in the best possible way by lifting his second volume to an unmistakably higher level of thought and style.

The Scotsman was ruder, suggesting:

It is a pity that Mr Keable should take himself so seriously. The first part of the book, dealing with South African life, is admirable in

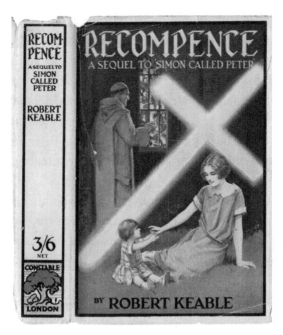

Recompense *book cover*

many ways, but when he changes the story to this country the story becomes a medley of absurdities.

Ultimately, with the subtitle *Sequel to Simon Called Peter*, the novel sold itself. Within a month of publication, it had already sold 24,000 copies, earning Keable over £1,600 – the equivalent of over £100,000 today. It proved to be Keable's second-bestselling novel in England, selling a few thousand more copies than *The Mother of All Living* but only just over half the number *Simon Called Peter* sold.

Although the novel was never nearly as popular in America as *Simon Called Peter*, it must have sold well, as Keable was paid a £1,500 advance for his next novel, *Numerous Treasure*. As *Recompense* launched, Putnam's was working hard to sell the rights to the book to Hollywood. It held back on a large advertising campaign, knowing that a movie tie-in was much more likely to generate good sales. He also wasn't that concerned about the views of the critics.

The *Washington Evening Star* reviewer, who guessed Keable's heart wasn't in the book, wrote:

Mr Keable had had no notion of writing a sequel to that much discussed romance. Nor did he wish later to do this. But people were shocked by the earlier story. That is some were shocked... And there was so much to-do over the matter that Mr. Keable devotes his talent for story telling to the business of giving the young priest a character.

Keable must have been pleased to complete the Peter and Julie story. In his introduction to the novel, he admitted he had written:

Not necessarily what I or [the many friends whom I made with my first venture] would wish, but what appears to me, in some form or another, given the natures of Peter and Julie, inevitably and substantially would be.

In May 1925, long after the book had been published, he could honestly tell the papers that the sequel was in no sense autobiographical, saying to a reporter: 'I never had the good fortune to meet a woman as attractive as the one in my novel.'

CHAPTER 10

KEABLE RETURNS HOME

JH Sims, the Leribe Assistant Commissioner, wrote: 'when [Keable] came from the ship before going back up country and I noticed a difference from the zealous priest I had known'.

It is not surprising that the man Sims saw arrive back in South Africa from France, in September 1918, was very different from the man who had left little more than a year earlier. Keable had a lot on his mind. His experiences in France weighed heavily on him.

He was angry about the way his men had been treated in France and his inability to do anything about it. He also worried that the war, which his men had supported and seen as their opportunity to show what they could do, would change nothing for the situation of black men in Africa, that things would revert back to how they had been, or worse. He was also concerned that the Union of South Africa might soon try to use their support of the British to seize Basutoland.

Having had an affair in France, Keable was also disillusioned with his marriage. He knew his wife was a good person, and he didn't want to hurt her, but he had come to realise that he didn't really love her. However, he was unsure what he could do about it.

His faith in the Anglican Church had also been shaken. He felt it had failed to offer support and preach the right message during the war. The terrible conflict had not brought about a revival of religion; rather, it had illuminated how ignorant and uninterested soldiers were in spiritual matters.

He was concerned that, if priests returned to preaching the same old message, to the same old cliques, then the Church in the west could die. He also had serious reservations about the future of the Church in Africa, having been optimistic about it in his early days as a missionary. He knew there were many who wanted to hear the story of Christ and to follow his philosophy, and he saw the potential for some great African priests. But he did not believe Europeans would deliver, fearing they would continue to run the Church as if Hlotse was Henley-on-Thames, and Leribe was Leicestershire.

Finally, and perhaps most unsettling of all, Keable was despondent about his own faith. The more he thought about it, the more he realised he couldn't justify remaining in the Church of England.

Keable returned to Basutoland with some of the men who had volunteered at the same time as him. He was formerly discharged from the SANLC on 4th October 1918, and carried out a first baptism back in Hlotse two weeks later, less than a month before the war finally ended. Sadly, however, Keable was quickly carrying out far more funerals than baptisms.

Perhaps ironically, the return of the SANLC labourers to South Africa has been blamed for the spread of the deadliest pandemic ever to arrive in southern Africa – Spanish flu. Recent research has revealed that, although a mild wave had spread from Durban in September 1918, the more virulent second wave was introduced into the country by the arrival of two SANLC troopships, the *Jaroslav* and the *Veronej*, which had left France a month after Keable's ship. These ships passed through Freetown, Sierra Leone – one of the hotspots for the virus – on their way to South Africa. Days after Keable and the men with him had been demobilised and had left Cape Town, the two ships arrived, with cases already appearing on board. All the men were briefly held in quarantine but were soon released and allowed to travel home by train, in the process spreading the virus. Some of the men were heading home to Basutoland.

The Spanish flu epidemic was widespread in Basutoland during October and November. There was no official system of registration of deaths at that time, but an official estimate suggested that at least 75% of the population were affected and 15,000 died.

Keable wrote tributes in the parish magazine for two stalwarts of his community who had died from the disease. Of Reverend Richard Giddy Makhobotloane, who had been a sub-deacon in Leribe for seventeen years, and who Keable had often stayed with on his station, he wrote: 'while many

Henry Keable

can preach and teach it is the few who can live Christ from day to day and year to year'. He added:

> Few English people realise what it means to a native to tear himself up by the roots in middle life and go to a college to study for the higher orders of the ministry. The leaving of home and cattle, the transport of goods and family, the commencement of an unfamiliar life is to them a great undertaking.

Keable also wrote about Edmund Mphuting: a 'keen young fellow' and 'a trained carpenter', who took up teaching when some of the schoolteachers had left with the SANLC to go to France.

Soon after he had arrived back in Basutoland, Keable heard that his younger brother had also died of Spanish flu, contracted in Malta. Family friends always suggested that Henry had lived in the shadow of his brilliant brother, and he had taken a very different course. After Whitgift, he trained to become an architect and, when the war began, he joined the Royal Navy. By 1918, he was working on a seaplane carrier, the *Manxman*, based in Malta.

The influenza epidemic took hold on the island in the summer of 1918 and Henry died just two months before the war ended. His commanding officer wrote to Henry's parents of their son's keenness, the affection felt for him by his brother officers and his 'straight as a die' character. Keable was not particularly close to his brother, but he heard, and later saw, the impact Henry's death had on his parents. His mother was distraught, and his father was told by a doctor they had to move from Croydon to a new parish, hoping that a new start might help her to overcome her profound grief.

It is unclear whether Keable mentioned his doubts about his marriage to his wife, but life seems to have carried on as before. When he returned, they had been married for less than three and a half years and, with his stay in hospital after the Mokhotlong shooting, and time away with the SANLC, they had lived together for less than half of that time. Sybil Keable had her own friends and had created a job for herself in the parish. Among the people in the town, she had a reputation as a cheerful, friendly and very nice Yorkshire woman.

For almost a year, Keable and his wife carried on living together as if nothing had changed. Cecil suggests:

She was not, unfortunately, an easy person to live with, least of all for [Keable]. Unlike him she was very certain of herself, and tended to be over-liberal with her advice, taking offence if this was ignored. Even those, including [Keable], who were the most fond of her, found her domineering. Emotionally, he and she were out of tune. Sentiment and poetry were a large part of his make-up, while she was down to earth.

Sybil Keable's niece offered an insight into the tempestuous nature of the relationship between the couple, remembering a conversation between two servants about Aunt Sybil and her notorious 'Uncle Bob'.

'Why did he leave her?'

'It was the war.'

'And the war was called Sybil, I suppose.'

Although her family were fond of her and her lively, positive personality, they also recounted tales that suggested she could be overbearing. Sybil Keable was heard to say to her brother: 'Harold, don't cross your legs, you'll crease your trousers,' and to her niece, 'Doris, you never did have decent taste

Sybil Keable in 1932

in clothes.' When her niece replied that she was forty, Sybil Keable responded, 'If I don't tell you, who will?'

Keable certainly annoyed his wife. He was not a good timekeeper and on at least one occasion completely forgot a dinner party that he and his wife were giving. Sybil Keable's niece reported years later that 'he had a particular gift of giving his whole attention to a person and making them feel unusually intelligent'.

The Rectory in Hlotse was pleasant, with a large garden and two pets: a collie – called Nuts – and a baboon. The baboon, which had been rescued when young, was chained to a large pear tree. May O'Shea, in *Bloomie Memoirs of the Twenties*, recounts that her family borrowed the rectory for a few months when the Keables were away, and she had to help look after the animals. She was devoted to the dog but terrified of the baboon, who actually bit her sister Mary.

The Keables would often throw dinner parties and have visitors to stay. To these guests, there did not seem to be problems with their marriage. Kathleen Molteno briefly described a party at Mrs Keable's which was very lively, with games and plenty of jokes and laughter. She recorded that Mr Keable could be very amusing.

Keable threw himself back into the life of the church with renewed vigour. In the parish, he had always had to deal with two distinct sets of parishioners: the predominantly Protestant, evangelical Europeans, and the Catholic, High Church, almost exclusively black population. His success and popularity lay with the latter group. He continued to recruit new members. On Boxing Day 1918, he baptised twenty-three children and adults; the following April, another forty-eight (in two different services); sixteen more that Christmas; and, on 4th April 1920, another nineteen. Most of these were adults, one described as 'an old man' and others in their twenties, thirties and forties.

There were rumours later that it was at this time that Keable began to worry some of the residents of Hlotse. Couzens, when researching Keable's time in Leribe, found reports about his behaviour towards women and suggested Keable had acquired a wolfish reputation. He found some gossip about Keable, but it is difficult to know to what extent stories were exaggerated or even invented years later. Canon Dove, who lived in Hlotse from 1952 to 1971, jotted down comments while researching his book *Anglican Pioneers in Lesotho*, although he did not include them in his book. He had been told that a Mrs Robertson, who used to play cards at Keable's rectory (without her husband) after the war, had felt uncomfortable when Keable escorted her home. Dove wrote: 'Mrs Robertson was afraid and suspicious of him (sex)'. He also quoted a local priest, Rev Falkner, who never met Keable, who suggested that Keable 'had a very passionate nature', 'that his wife was unresponsive' and that he was 'free with native women'. The gossip continued for many years. In a 1990 letter, Ken Wilson, a former acting officer in charge of Mokhotlong subdistrict, gave a brief account of Keable's life, claiming:

> In 1917 he went overseas as an army Padre: on his return his 'high Church faith' seems to have vanished. The tale goes that he organized a Xmas nativity play among the native parishioners at Leribe and is said to have seduced the girl who was acting the Virgin Mary. He was duly defrocked from the church; became a Catholic, was sacked for trouble with a choir mistress...

He concluded:

That there is much truth in this tale there is no doubt but, over the years it had probably grown to 'make a good story'.

They would have grown when Keable's novel *Simon Called Peter* became famous, and once the truth about his relationships in Tahiti a few years later became known.

It is difficult to know how influential Keable was in the black community in Leribe. He believed that the African Church needed to follow a different route to the Church in the west, and argued in an article:

> We have a teacher at hand, for the Bantu are social democrats. The scope of their natural socialism is very wide. As western Christianity has always tended towards individualism so African Christianity should naturally tend towards socialism.

One well-known figure who was surely influenced by Keable was the charismatic national leader, Keable Mote. Keable Mote, nicknamed the 'Lion of the North', was a significant early activist in the long fight against apartheid. He was born in Leribe in 1898 and was educated at Pietersburg in the Transvaal, possibly becoming a priest. He 'was a fiery speaker' who was very active in the 1920s and 1930s touring South Africa, campaigning to improve wages and, in successful campaigns in Bloemfontein and Port Elizabeth, to allow local people to brew their own beer. He was a member of the ICU in the mid-1920s, rising up to become provincial secretary in the Orange Free State and on the executive board of the All-African Convention (ACC) in 1937.

It seems very likely that Keable Mote took his name from Keable when he was baptised. Indeed, there is a reference to Keable Mote being WR Keable Mote, which could suggest he was baptised Wilfred Robert Keable Mote. It was not uncommon for babies to be christened with the name of the priest, but the fact that he must have been a teenager when baptised suggests it was his idea. He must have been impressed by his parish priest and it is possible that Keable's passion for reform in Africa influenced his views.

The most political article Keable wrote about Africa was published in the *New Blackfriars* magazine, in December 1920, called 'Slave, Serf, Citizen – and the Way Back'. He waited until he had left Basutoland before looking to get it published. The main section of the long article explained his fury at what he saw as the broken promises the British government had made to the people of the former German colony in East Africa, an area he knew well from his time in Zanzibar. In particular, he was disgusted by the decision to exploit the local people by reintroducing forced labour. He quoted the new regulations which meant 'every healthy native under fifty and not in regular employment, must do eighty-four days' labour for the government in the year'. He pointed out how unjust this was. Most of the men deemed unemployed were small-time farmers, or itinerant workers, supporting their families. For a start, it took some men two weeks to reach their labour camp, which of course wasn't deducted from the eighty-four days. But, more importantly, it meant taking many men away from their homes often around harvest, a key time of the year. It also provided cheap labour for the government's plantations. He was horrified that Lord Milner, the Colonial Secretary, condoned women, and children, being 'encouraged' to work on white plantations. Overall, he called the legislation 'ethically immoral and indefensible' and 'politically contrary to the spirit of the pledge of the Peace Treaty'.

He also discussed the fear that Basutoland might be absorbed into the Union of South Africa.

He contrasted Basutoland, the only 'territory left in South Africa in which the native is honestly, on the whole, his own master', with South Africa, where 'black men faced real discrimination earning less money for doing the same work as white men and put in prison if they went on strike'. He described watching men in East Griqualand in South Africa sheep-shearing from sunrise to sunset earning 15s a month, while a single blanket at the local store, made out of the same wool, would cost them 30s.

In this same article, he also highlighted the outrageous behaviour of the Legislative Council of Rhodesia (now Zimbabwe), who had used a couple of 'wars' in the 1890s to take the land from 800,000 indigenous people and given it to a few thousand 'invading foreigners'.

The article allowed Keable to say things he wouldn't have felt safe saying in southern Africa, but of course it made no difference. Unlike his article criticising the training of black chaplains, this one was not picked up by the South African press. However, an employee of the British South Africa Company took offence over his comments about the legislative council in Rhodesia and wrote to the magazine to defend her company, claiming that, far from being downtrodden, the 'natives' were flourishing. She gave as an example the fact that 'at the funeral of the late Sir Starr Jameson in the Matopos, a Matabele chieftain arrived in his own motor-car'.

Keable valued his work as a priest and missionary in Africa. He later wrote to Sadler to say that the reason he had been a good missionary was because he was an ardent propagandist. He strongly believed that religion made an African 'less subservient, less slavish in his estimation of himself, less satisfied with having small prospects and no racial future'. That, he argued, was why many Europeans were against missionaries.

Throughout 1919, Keable would often go up into the berg alone. It was then that he took the three-week holiday to write *Simon Called Peter*. Riding in the mountains gave him plenty of time to think about religion and his marriage and, in an effort to pull some of his thoughts together, he wrote *Pilgrim Papers*, which he dedicated 'To Sybil, a resolute pilgrim'. In the book, it is the passages where he discusses love and adultery that seem the most personal. He wrote:

It seems to me that more often than not the love of any two persons means bliss to them, but agony to others. If it is so, then this Love is a strange, ravening thing, and maybe our forefathers did wisely to seek to tie it down by conventions and proprieties and shibboleths. But what in the world did they do with their hearts, do you suppose? I think those Victorian folk must have cramped their children's hearts from the start, like the Chinese women their babies' feet, that they should have succeeded in arriving at such apparent placidity.

He goes on in the next chapter, *To the Ten Commandments*, to discuss the seventh commandment, thou shalt not commit adultery:

Take the seventh. Here are a man and a woman trapped by Nature into a marriage by the false lights of what was passion, but which they once thought was love. And then love and a third enter in. If love is, indeed, the supreme achievement, life for the two is a barren, wasted thing, and for the third it will never be achieved, if they keep all the Commandments.

In the next chapter, *Of God or Allah*, he moves on to marriage and complains that banning divorce could blight two lives. It is possible that Keable – too afraid to openly discuss separation with his wife – tried to use the book to persuade his wife of the immorality of staying with someone you didn't love.

Pilgrim Papers includes some essays extolling the merits of Catholicism and the problems with Protestantism. Later, in a letter to his old university friend, Grimble, he admitted that, ever since he had been at Cambridge, he had thought 'the only historical and reasonable and possible form of Christianity' was Catholicism. And he confirmed that in 1919 he 'brought seven years' struggle to an end by feeling definitely that the only possible claimant to Catholicism was Roman'.

Keable had never been afraid to advertise his Catholic views. At the UMCA, and later in Basutoland, he was as high an Anglo-Catholic as you can get. In October 1917 in a letter in the *Church Times*, where he defended the views of Rev PT Forsythe – who had recently written *The Justification of God* – he asked: 'Do you think it will ever be possible to persuade Protestants that Catholics are not altogether lunatics?'

In *Standing By*, he devoted a chapter to Rome – championing the fact that Roman Catholics would never accept different services for black and white people (as was the practice in South Africa and in the services for the SANLC) and that the Church of England played fast and loose with the truth. Ultimately, in that book, he did defend the Church of England, but the seeds of doubt were there for all to see.

Sybil Keable took her Christian faith extremely seriously and began to think about becoming a Roman Catholic, hoping that her husband might do the same. A friend of Keable's father, Dr Linnell, told Dr Douglas that Keable had entered into a pact with his wife that they should become Roman Catholics, but that Keable 'ratted at the last minute' and would not join Rome.

Keable waited a year before he started to discuss the possibility of leaving his job. He must have thought a year was the appropriate amount of time for him to spend helping and supporting the men, and the families of the men, he had persuaded to travel to France. Apart from his wife, no one in the parish knew that Keable was having doubts about his religion.

Keable eventually resigned as the priest on the grounds that he wanted to become a Roman Catholic. This of course made life a lot simpler for him. It was easier to explain to his parishioners, who could then accept he was going to continue to be a Christian and would not have to worry about what Keable had preached to them. And easier to explain to the bishop.

One imagines in those days, if you told your bishop you were giving up the priesthood because you had committed adultery, or loved another woman instead of your wife, then you would have been sent away to a retreat for a month of prayer, and reflection, and contemplation, and daily cold showers, and then, after a month, told to get back to work and pull yourself together. But tell the bishop that you were thinking of becoming a Roman Catholic and you would have been out of the door as a hopeless case before you could say anything else. Keable had heard how his friend RH Benson had been treated by the Church of England when he became a Roman Catholic, so knew how quickly the Church would try to wash their hands of someone (although admittedly RH Benson's father had been the Archbishop of Canterbury).

Telling the bishop he was going to become a Roman Catholic allowed Keable to leave the parish with his head held high. He did believe that Roman Catholicism was wonderful, and beautiful, the best form of religion, and the only possible home for him. But he later admitted he had too many doubts about the Church's teaching on transubstantiation, divorce and adultery to realistically join.

I do not know whether the couple discussed the state of their marriage, but Sybil Keable made it very clear that she did not believe in divorce. She also did not want to be around when her husband finally announced he was going to leave the Church, so they agreed he would say nothing until she went back to England at the end of 1919. He would then hand in his notice, pack up their house and head home. In the meantime, she would spend some time with her family and friends in Bradford and then look for a house for them to live in, for when he arrived back in England.

Keable began his novel *Lighten Our Darkness*, written in 1925, with a priest leaving the Church. Richard Thurstan is a Catholic priest (educated at Oxford), who having been a priest for ten years now works in a remote parish in South Africa. Keable recorded Richard's excuse for giving up the priesthood:

I can no longer honestly and sincerely stand at the altar or sit in the confessional because I cannot continue to profess that the Catholic Church is the infallible Body of Christ.

So, in the novel, doubts about transubstantiation provide the excuse for leaving the Roman Catholic Church. Perhaps Keable used the opposite argument for wishing to leave the Church of England. In *Lighten Our Darkness*, the Bishop begs the priest to remain, reminding him of how many people he has brought into the Church. Keable must have faced a similar conversation.

In the end, he was relieved to give up his vocation and move away from the parish. In *Lighten Our Darkness*, the protagonist gives away most of his possessions; his horse, Swiftsure, to Philip; his desk to Stephen; his *prie-dieu*, crucifix and statue of Our Lady to Paul. Nathaniel gets his old suit and flannel trousers, all his books go to the sister's library, and Abraham gets his sheep rug. His tobacco jar, made in the shape of a skull, goes to Nathaniel and the schoolmaster, Moruti, gets his typewriter. The names may well have been changed but one can believe the gifts are real. Presumably, he told his wife to choose what she wanted sent home, and the rest would be given away.

Once Keable finally left Hlotse, he decided to take his time travelling back to England. He had written to Bede Jarrett, a Catholic friend, to ask for letters of introduction to some Dominicans in Spain, explaining he had taken off his clerical dress and resigned his mission and was perhaps thinking of converting to Catholicism.

The last record of Keable in Basutoland was at a christening he did on 28th April 1920, so presumably he left St Saviour's Church for the last time soon after that.

Although Keable was mocked after he died by a few white members of the community – one letter doing the rounds suggested 'he had bought an island in the South Pacific where he had a harem of hula hula girls and died, reportedly of over indulgence' – his reputation among the black members remained high. When news of his death came through, a requiem Mass was held at Hlotse for the repose of his soul. Even in the 1950s, Canon Dove recorded that he was still well remembered by many people, and everyone spoke of him as a devoted priest and strong personality, having an able mind.

St Saviour's Church is still there today, little more than a large hut with a long corrugated roof. Couzens and Cecil visited it and made a small cross out of two pieces of wood they found within the church, which they later presented to Keable's son Tony.

Chapter 11

Simon Called Peter on Broadway

Following the success in America of the novel *Simon Called Peter*, there were producers keen to turn it into a stage production. When Keable first heard that there was interest, he decided he would have a go at writing the script, and a press release at the end of 1922 suggested he planned to go abroad to write it. In the meantime, William A Brady, who thought a play featuring a priest, prostitutes and a pretty young nurse was an excellent suggestion, decided to try and acquire the rights.

Brady was the leading theatrical producer across America, having already produced more than 150 plays on Broadway. He admitted that he had begun his career following the old-time tradition of piracy and plagiarism, and he was twice taken to the Supreme Court accused of stealing ideas from other plays – losing both times. He had to compete with other producers for the rights to *Simon Called Peter*, but the local press in America confirmed he had bid more than others and went on to say: 'when Brady is after a thing it is a known fact that he generally gets it. He secured the rights'.

Brady did not give Keable the chance to deliver his script and instead turned first to Jules Eckert Goodman, and later to Edward Knoblock, to do the job.

For Brady, there were risks involved, especially if the play focused on the more salacious elements of the story. With the book having been banned in Boston, he knew the press were likely to speculate on how rude and risqué his production was going to be. It quickly became apparent that Brady intended to sail as close to the wind as he could.

The play began touring in early 1924 with the plan to gradually sharpen up the script and cast ready for Broadway. It opened at the President Theatre in Washington, where, due to popular demand, it ran for three weeks. It was soon obvious how Brady aimed to appeal to audiences. As the first review explained: 'Every effort was made to visualize the bedroom scenes as closely as possible without necessitating action on the part of the local police'. The play was far too long, with eight acts, and the reviewer suggested there was a lot of mopping-up to be done before it opened on Broadway.

As the play toured, theatres did all they could to try to generate an audience. One advert described a play with 'love, strife and life' and boasted: '2 million read it. 2 million will see it'.

By the time it reached Chicago, in May 1924, it was a tighter play. However, the young *Daily Worker* reviewer, Alfred Frankenstein (just seventeen at the time but later a prestigious critic with a long career), was furious with the changes from the novel:

> After seeing *Simon Called Peter*… one has a strong itching desire to go after Jules Eckert Goodman and Edward Knoblock, the dramatic butchers who ruined Robert Keable's novel to make the play, with a large bottle of some effective but torturesome poison in either hand. For Keable's story and what might have been a good play are both spoiled by one of the most asinine happy endings ever put on a stage.

His disgust concerned the final act, which had the priest, Peter, preaching from the pulpit and announcing that he was going to leave the priesthood because he had sinned according to the laws of the Church. Frankenstein recorded that Peter was interrupted by Julie running through the theatre crying: 'Peetah, Peetah, forgive me.'

After initial interest, audience numbers fell off during the Chicago run and the cast took a pay cut for the last week, having been promised by Brady that they would all be going on tour with the play over the summer. Instead, after the last night in Chicago, Brady cancelled the tour and asked Jules Eckert Goodman and Edward Knoblock to go away and work on the script. The cast, furious with Brady for the perceived deception, took him to arbitration with the support of Equity, successfully forcing him to make up the final week's pay cut.

In November, with a new cast, a revised version of the play reached

Indianapolis, Indiana, for a week-long run. The publicity suggested that this new production was really shocking. It was claimed in the *Indianapolis Times* that *Simon Called Peter* was 'the only play which created a sensation on the road without the usual New York endorsement', and that:

> It is the first big play, it is said, that the war has brought. It will provoke much discussion. It will stir no little resentment, but few who condemn it for its utter frankness or who take issue with its big problems will question that it is a play of real distinction… we find the Church of England minister searching for God and for his own soul in strange places and with strange companions of both sexes.

The week before the opening, at the Murat Theatre, the local mayor, Mayor Shanks, declared that he had heard the play was 'a little rough' and threatened to stop the show if it failed to pass his censors. He appointed the police chief, the president of the board of safety and another board member as his censors. The *Indianapolis Times* reported:

> The Mayor attempted to get in touch with Nelson Trowbridge, Murat manager, to warn him any indecency would be stopped. More than a dozen attaches at the city hall volunteered to act as censors. Selection by the Mayor was difficult.

On the opening night, every seat and most of the standing room was taken, with the chief of police and members of the board of safety sitting sternly in the box they were given by the theatre. The editor of the local paper, Felix F Bruner, who also attended, reported that the 'audience sat on the edges of their seats expectantly' and the theatre manager was 'hopefully awaiting arrest'.

Bruner was disappointed. He wrote that the audience saw 'less than can be seen at most musical shows', and he went on to bemoan the fact that 'it would require a stretch of the imagination to call [the play] dirty in comparison to many other modern plays', and concluded, 'Don't go to *Simon Called Peter* looking for a shock – unless you are easily shocked'.

The play finally opened on Broadway at the Klaw Theatre, on 45th Street, on 10th November 1924, starring Leonard Willey and Catherine Willard. It was Willard's second Broadway appearance; her third was as Jordan Baker in

The Great Gatsby, also produced by William Brady, which opened a year after *Simon Called Peter* closed.

As with the book, the Society for the Suppression of Vice took an interest. The relevant law at the time, the 1872 Comstock law, banned all things 'obscene, lewd, or lascivious'. John Summer was running a crusade to remove any suggestion of sex, obscenity, blasphemy and other inappropriate activities from the stage. Brady, as the play's producer, was contacted before the play's opening night by the Society, and asked to show them the script, so they could see if there was any blasphemy or smut. He refused.

The day after *Simon Called Peter* opened, the Society's lawyers applied for a court injunction to halt the performances. They argued that the play promoted immorality by depicting a clergyman soliciting sexual favours from a prostitute and having sexual relations with a young woman. They complained about the scene in which the prostitute, Louise, unbuttoned her blouse in an attempt to entice the priest. The court refused the injunction but the city authorities agreed to launch an investigation into whether the play was immoral.

Some newspapers started to complain about the play, though it is not clear they had seen it. One in Seattle reported:

> Broadway is verminious with such salacity this season, masquerading under the holy names of art, salvation, messages to Garcia and what-not. These dirty shows keep children out of the theatre. For every Peter Pan there are a dozen Simon Called Peters. Their nudity and their obscene language render even decent-minded and beauty-loving adults with severe cases of mal-de-theatre.

The publicity, of course, encouraged more people to buy tickets, and the newspapers continued to do their best to try to suggest the play was racy. One explained that most of the second act was devoted to Louise's attempts to seduce the chaplain:

> When the minister-hero won't reach down for the key, the temptress tears her waist to convince his companions that he had lost his foothold on virtue's slippery path. And then, after it's all over, the audience goes home and tells friends that nothing happened when the waist ripped but maybe it might another night.

Brady did everything he could to generate publicity for the play. He cast a former beauty queen in the part of the prostitute, Louise. Lota Sanders, born Lota Cheek, much to the disbelief of an *Evening Journal* reporter who had to check, had become an actress two years before after winning a contest to find Boston's most beautiful girl. She had gained further fame when she was named in court as the new wife of a bigamist – FL Seimmons – whose real wife was suing him for divorce. Brady promoted the fact that, halfway through the Broadway run, Lota got married, for the fourth time, to another actor in the cast, Harry Tyrrell-Davis, an English actor who played Lieutenant Bobby Jenks.

Brady also started to talk about a possible movie and, just after the Broadway run began, he encouraged the *New York Times* to report that preparations were under way to film *Simon Called Peter* at the Fort Lee studio in New Jersey, with 'elaborate sets' in the process of being erected. Although Brady had produced films at that studio during the war, he didn't produce another movie after 1919, and this film was never made.

In a well-publicised attempt to win over the clergy, who strongly objected to the play, Brady put on a special matinee performance just for them and their families, and hosted a panel discussion afterwards on the Church and theatre in general, and *Simon Called Peter* in particular. The *New York Times* reported the event with some glee, quoting a Dr Straton, who suggested that theatres put on 'the most salacious, absurd and even indecent productions' and that the moral life of actors and actresses was deplorably low.

Perhaps fortunately, the investigation into the suitability of the play was not completed by the New York authorities before it closed, having run for a respectable eighty-eight performances.

Keable, more by luck than judgement, was in New York during the run and went to see the play. According to *Time* magazine, 'he had little comment'. In fact, he had plenty to say privately, and wrote to Sadler:

Simon Called Peter is the most incredible and awful production that ever anyone dreamed of. Thank God I have a certain sense of humour. It is so totally unlike the book that no human being, however foolish, could see my hand in it. There are perhaps half a dozen lines that I wrote and there may be a third of an incident.

He was not the only one who did not enjoy it. Judah Waten, a drama critic, expressed his reaction in verse:

The dowagers wept in the stalls,
And I really can't see,
Why the man next to me
Repeatedly said it was balls.

Unlike many other plays, *Simon Called Peter* did not tour again after it closed on Broadway. Brady had managed to squeeze every ounce of publicity out of it and decided to rest on his laurels.

The experience did not prevent Keable selling on the rights of his book *Numerous Treasure* to Brady. As he wrote to Sadler:

Old Brady is fearfully keen to get hold of the book for stage and film. I think he might as well because I am perfectly certain no one would stage and film it as I should like to see it done.

Chapter 12

Keable – no longer a priest

Keable arrived back in England in September 1920. He had spent the summer on what he called a 'jaunt'. As he explained to Grimble:

> I went to the Canaries, got on a cargo steamer, knocked about the islands, crossed to Minorca, wandered up the coast (Mogador, Agadir, Rabat, Casa Blanca, Tangiers) then crossed to Algeciras and walked home most of the way through Spain.

In Spain, Keable stayed with Dominicans. He later described in his novel *Recompense*, memories of different towns and cities:

> I went to Ronda... the gorge by moonlight... a great drop cut sheer between the two halves of the town that itself is a fortress standing up clean out of the Vega, encircled by mountains... And then Grenada. The Alhambra is wonderful... but the Generalife – that is the dream of Grenada... then Seville. You have to disentangle Seville. It's a flourishing city. I found a view from across the river... Then I went on to Cordoba. Imperial Rome is still there... Then, oh, well Madrid. Pizarro's sword held me there... And then Toledo. The Cathedral. Of course it's just the Catholic Church in miniature: austere, ornate; poor, rich; imperial, republican; old, young; dead, alive; a dream of beauty, and a Person at whose feet one falls as though dead.

Back in England, Keable went first to his parents' in Pavenham, where his father had taken on the role of parish priest in October 1919, aged sixty-seven. Since he had chosen to leave the Church voluntarily, Keable legally remained a minister of the Church of England. That annoyed him and he asked that people stop calling him 'rev', although later he said he didn't mind if he was introduced as an 'ex-Anglican minister'. Although his parents must have been shocked and upset by his decision to leave the priesthood, he remained close to them for the rest of his life, writing regular letters when he was abroad and taking them on holiday when he could afford it.

Eventually, Keable joined up with his wife, who had managed to borrow a cottage in West Wratting, near Cambridge. For six months he wrote, managing to finish *The Mother of All Living* and to get two articles published in *Blackfriars* magazine, including 'The Sword of Pizzaro' – about the exhibit in the armoury in the Royal Palace in Madrid. His long-term plan was to become a full-time writer, but in the short term, having given up his, and his wife's, only serious source of income, he ran out of money. His non-fiction books and articles earned him very little money. Eventually, he admitted to Sadler that he was 'gloriously financially embarrassed owing to the fact that my wife is a perfect lunatic for paying bills'. So, on his return to England, he had to find a job and turned to teaching, first for a term at Dulwich College in south London, and then from September 1921 at Dunstable Grammar School.

What is surprising – considering how rude Keable was in his private letters about the 'utterly damnable Dunstable' – is how active he was in the school. The first school magazine of the year was already full of praise:

> We extend a hearty welcome to Mr Keable MA, as English and History master. Mr Keable has a vast experience both in teaching and travelling, and his little anecdotes of Africa and elsewhere, sprinkled liberally over his classwork, make his subjects some of the most fascinating on the school timetable.

Although he only taught at the school for a year, he managed to give two lectures to students – one about climbing Mount Kilimanjaro, and the other about travels in Moorish Spain – and took part as a main speaker in three debates – on an arms limitation treaty, on spiritualism and on communism. He also helped run the school magazine, leading the student editor to write at the end of the year:

To pay a just tribute to the advice, help and consideration that he has given during the three terms he has been here is impossible. Behind practically all the improvements in the magazine is the mind of a man whose equal we shall probably not see for a long time to come, and certainly the keenness, enthusiasm and skill seen in Verse and Prose section is entirely due to him.

He clearly made a lasting impression on his students, as a few years later a former pupil contributed to his obituary in *The Sun*:

[Keable] was always tolerant and reverent, never a bitter scoffer. He was the most inspiring teacher I have ever known. In history it was he who for the first time gave us the idea that the whole world had a story behind it, apart from the ten-sixty-six, the Elizabethan Rovers and the Reform Bill of 1830. He had a broad and comprehensive mind and he taught us in terms of the flux of civilisations, the rise and fall of empires, the sweep of migrations, rather than of dates and royal poisoning. He opened us to a new vista of peoples and of cultures, by means of his enthralling lectures and his fascinating maps and charts and even when he was obliged to teach the small details of rebellions and civil wars he could make them interesting to a degree that we had never believed possible. As an English teacher too he was beyond praise, acting as an astonishing stimulus to the school's reading and encouraging original creative work, which had been practically non-existent till then.

... Being a man of charming personality and a splendid companion, he was extremely popular out of school. At the cricket match even on big match days he would have a small shoal of boys squatting around him forgetting cricket in the magic of his travel stories of Madagascar, Spain, France, Italy, Africa, and he would discuss literature without end and always illuminatingly.

... it should be said that he never attempted to preach, or even to mention, his ideas to us at school. He was the inspiring teacher and the charming companion.

In boarding schools, there are some teachers who prefer the camaraderie of the staffroom and spend their free with other teachers; and some teachers who prefer the company of students, spending free time helping them with their work and running extra-curriculum activities. Keable fell into the latter camp and made little effort to get on with the other teachers.

Writing to his friend Grimble, he explained he was getting on all right at the school because he loved history, but that the situation was a bit farcical. He confessed that the kids adored him because he saw school as a 'standing joke'.

Keable seems to have had less success with other teachers. Dr Douglas contacted Dunstable Grammar School in 1960 for information on Keable and was told:

> There are two members of staff who still remember Keable. They recall him as an irreligious person, somewhat cynical in outlook and inclined to be lax in morals. (The view seems to have been widely held that Simon Called Peter was largely autobiographical.) He was of violent temper – one informant remembers him as hurling a tennis-racket at a colleague in public during some heated argument. During his year at Dunstable, he was accompanied by his wife, who seems to have been a delightful woman of considerable charm and talent.

Although Keable was desperate to escape teaching at the end of the year, as always, he used the experience in a later novel – *The Madness of Monty*. Dunstable Grammar was relocated to south London and was renamed Wearstone College. The low assistant masters' salaries, the obsession with school uniform, and the desire to be a proper public school remained. Monty, the eponymous hero, was a history teacher who wanted to explore the major period changes in history and to give his students 'a sense of time and sequence and comparative chronology'. He suggested English history should be about the revolts against autocracy and aristocracy and not 'tripe' like the Field of the Cloth of Gold. Monty's boss, Mr Caltrop, the senior history teacher, complained to the headmaster that Monty: 'has practically set aside his text books. He actually discourages their use among the boys and relies on his own teaching… [which] will be disastrous.' He went on to say: 'I do not hold with all these new-fangled ideas. Unless I am very much mistaken, there will be a disastrous record in the Locals.' An obsession with exams clearly existed even then.

The average salary for teachers in 1922 was £271, and new teachers at

Dulwich, one of the wealthiest schools in the country, started on around £300. At Dunstable Grammar Keable had signed a one-year contract and, with a first-class honours degree and 'life experience', he would have been paid £350, at most. Enough for him and his wife to live on, as long as they stayed together.

His letters to Sadler in 1921 and 1922 reveal the dawning realisation that he might eventually earn enough money from writing so that he could give up teaching, and then that he was about to become rich. In September 1921, he wrote to a friend saying he hoped to earn about £400 from his books in the following year. After he received an interim payment from his publisher in March 1922, he thought he might earn a little bit more than that. Once Putman's started talking about a £500 advance for each new novel, he could see he had seriously underestimated his future earnings. By the end of 1922, he had earned, from royalties and book advances, at least eight times his annual teacher salary.

The situation at home was not easy. After *Simon Called Peter* began to sell, he wrote to his old university friend, Grimble, about the possibility of going abroad:

> It is absolutely between you and me but I'm not very happily married. Never mind why. I've no kids too. She might come with me; she might come after me; she might be rather glad to see me go for a bit. I expect I'm a beast to be with, especially now. You see she's R.C., conventional, English and awfully good to me, but we're cut out of different moulds. While I was a parson it was possible; now we tend to go apart at a little speed. She hates my books – but then, why wouldn't you? Besides, what can one do?

After Keable decided to leave the priesthood, he seems to have met a number of women, though it is unclear how far these relationships progressed. One was writer Peter York's grandmother, Lizzie Whittington. Following a book review of *The Red Earl* by Selina Hastings – a biography that references Keable – Peter York, born Peter Wallis, added in a postscript:

> Keable, a pretty gruesome writer himself, was the love of my grandmother's life. I'm named Peter after his 1920s hot book *Simon Called Peter*.

Lizzie Whittington was an accomplished musician training in France before the First World War and had travelled widely after the war with her husband, spending time in South Africa. It was a loveless marriage, and she told her daughter that Keable was the love of her life and suggested she name her son Peter after the hero of *Simon Called Peter*. It is possible that Whittington met Keable in South Africa in 1919 and that they spent some time together during the few months after his wife had returned home.

Martha Smith, an editor who worked with Sadler at Constable, became a good friend of Keable, and the two used to meet when he came up to London. In 1921, he wrote:

> Monday I will be in town and I am going to one of my rabbit holes for Monday night as Tuesday is full up with arrangements. Will you dine with me there, Monday night? There, will be a private sitting room and we will have a quiet and simple dinner in it... I hope you will come... We can chat in front of a fire at our ease and I promise to behave.

Later, when she agreed to meet him, he wrote:

> You don't know how pleased I am. Without reason, it seems to me a kind of adventure. Let's make it so. Let's meet and go anywhere on the spur of the moment – not to any of the ordinary places I mean... I propose: 6.00pm Brasserie of the Criterion in Jermyn St. Don't dress. Then after a cocktail, we will walk into Soho and dine somewhere foreign leaving it to chance and fate. What do you say?

Keable wrote to Dean, his old friend from Whitgift School, in May 1922: 'I have a box to your show on Sat night May 6: if you are in the theatre do pop in. I shall have a most charming girl with me'. It is unclear who he was referring to, but it seems unlikely to have been his wife.

At some point during 1921, Keable met up with Jolie Buck again. Possibly in June when he was living and teaching in Dulwich and she was working as a dance teacher at Filigrees, Baker Street.

They often frequented Gwen Otter's salon at No. 1 Ralston Street. Sadler may have introduced Keable to Gwen's salon, since another of his authors, Katherine Mansfield, was also a frequent visitor. Both Buck and Keable mention Gwen in letters: Buck telling Sadler that a travelling companion – Mrs Bohun Lynch – was like her; Keable telling a friend he entertained the novelist Alec Waugh in Tahiti and gave him a good time 'for Gwen's sake'.

Gwen Otter was an eccentric figure who liked to play host to the young bohemians in London in the manner of other wealthy women, such as Lady Ottoline Morrell, Ada Leverson and Violet Hunt. She claimed to be descended from the native American woman Pocahontas, dressed only in purple or black, sported baggy trousers and a dramatic turban, and often carried her parrot on her shoulder.

In his first autobiography, Alec Waugh described her sitting room – decorated by Marcel Boulestin, the famous chef and interior designer – with its dark blue ceiling, silver walls and alabaster lamps. There was a pen-and-ink drawing of the occultist Aleister Crowley by Augustus John on one wall and ink drawings by Aubrey Beardsley on the other walls. Waugh claimed that, since she was very deaf and could never remember anyone's name, she preferred being a hostess to being a guest. If anyone wanted an invitation to her salon, you only had to invite her to yours and she would insist you came to hers instead. As she had a particularly good cook, an invitation to lunch or dinner was very desirable. Otter invited a cosmopolitan crowd to her salon: Waugh reported meeting novelists Rebecca West, Berta Ruck and William Gerhardie, art historians James Laver and John Rothenstein, actors Marda Vanne and Ernest Thesiger, and Aleister Crowley.

Equally eccentric was Gwen's brother Frank, who sometimes co-hosted their parties. He had been one of the characters of Edwardian London and, despite an addiction to alcohol and gambling, he was still going strong during the Second World War, by which time his genial face was the colour of a ripe Victoria plum. Thanks to his excessive drinking, Frank would have occasional episodes and Gwen would ship him out of town to stay with Rita and Jack Elliott, the son and daughter-in-law of her good friend Wuffy Elliott. Gwen introduced Keable and Buck to the Elliotts, and they quickly became friends. The Elliotts lived in the then sleepy Chilterns village of Stokenchurch, where Jack was the local general practitioner, and Keable and Buck sometimes stayed with them.

By the beginning of 1922, Keable had started to consider leaving his wife. Later, he wrote to his son: 'My legal wife is an R.C. and would not divorce me, nor could I, English law as it was then at any rate, divorce her'.

Divorce in 1922 was both rare, with less than 2,500 divorces that year in the UK, and difficult to obtain. It was particularly hard for women, who not only had to prove their husband was an adulterer but also that there were aggravating factors such as cruelty, rape or incest. For a man, the best hope of divorce was to prove his wife's adultery, although he would also have to prove he had not colluded in or condoned the adultery. By now, Sybil Keable had become a devout Roman Catholic, attending church every Sunday, without Keable, and often going on retreat to a nearby convent. She was not going to commit adultery, nor did she want a divorce.

By now Keable had very strong views on marriage. In an interview with a New Zealand journalist in 1922, he explained what he believed:

> The old view that the marriage is a church sacrament ordained by Almighty God has gone by the board. We know perfectly well it is a contract entered into between two individuals for their mutual advantage. Like every other contract it ought to be dissoluable at the will of both parties. My ideal of the relations of man and woman is this; if they are attracted to each other they swing together, and quite frankly tell their friends 'We are in love with each other and are going to live together.' If the relationship is spoiled then they should part. The State should register all such contracts, if only to ensure that wrong use would not be made of such a slack law. If married people do not love each other, yet continue to live together, it is gross immorality.

Later, Keable developed these ideas in his book *The Great Galilean*:

> The mistake which the Church has made... is that it has taken for granted that every marriage which it solemnizes is a true marriage. No two human beings who have ever been unquestionably in love, who have known the depths and wonder that are possible in the union of two souls, can doubt that those whom God has thus joined together cannot be put asunder. But to say that every two human beings who approach a magistrate or who stand before a priest and take a traditional and often impossible vow dictated to them are thereby indissolubly joined together by God is to say something at which the world of free men and women will one day ring with Homeric laughter. It is simply the commonest of common knowledge, not only

that men and women approach the magistrate or priest again and again, for mixed or unworthy motives, but that it is characteristic of us poor humans that when under the influence of sex or when in the heyday of youth we most often do not know our own minds.

Keable went on to defend 'swinging together', or 'free love', although he made it very clear that, while 'free love is precisely the only sort of love worth having, and, indeed, the only kind of love that can exist', it did not mean 'promiscuous lust' and indeed the two things were 'absolutely contradictory'.

Keable's view on free love should be seen in the context of the time. In the UK in the late nineteenth century, free love movements, such as the 'Fellowship of the New Life', initially advocated that all sexual matters, such as marriage, birth control and adultery, should be private matters and separated from the state. Adultery, or at least sex outside marriage, became the focus for many writers such as Bertram Russell, HG Wells and Bernard Shaw. Keable would have had plenty of opportunity to hone his views on free love, not least during his visits to Gwen Otter's salon. James Laver discussed the risqué conversations at Sunday lunch when some of Gwen's guests – like the well-known gynecologist Norman Hare – happily discussed sex.

In England, the views Keable expressed on marriage and free love could be seen as part of the ongoing debate which led to minor reform of the divorce laws in 1923. He was part of a small minority who sought much more extensive reform.

By February 1922, Keable started to make plans for what he would do after his year of teaching. Without mentioning Jolie, he wrote to Sadler:

Since I saw you I have squared the domestic side of it. I should take my wife to pay a round of visits in South Africa which she is keen to make and go on myself to Australia and the Pacific.

For the Easter school holidays, Keable went travelling in Germany. He told Sadler that he was going with an old clergy friend. Back at school and with news that his book was selling well, his plans started to shape up and he admitted to Sadler in June:

since I anticipate being away over a year and considerable wanderings during that year, I have to leave my financial affairs settled behind me.

Keable was not entirely straight with Sadler, as he had still not told him about Buck, or that his long-term plan was to live abroad. He was looking to escape an unhappy marriage and a judgemental society. And, like many, he also wanted to re-evaluate his life, after so many his age had died fighting in the war or from Spanish flu. There was much he disliked about England that he wanted to escape.

For a start, there was the weather. The summer of 1920 had not been a good one, with unseasonably cold spells, and it had been a long, hard winter, with very heavy snowfall across the country for many days in December. That winter was the first full one he had spent in England for ten years. His health wasn't brilliant, and some doctors thought he would be better off somewhere warmer. He had the occasional bouts of malaria, which he had first caught in Zanzibar, and a kidney infection which reared up every now and then, giving him excruciating pain.

The British economy was also in a bad way. The optimistic bounce that occurred at the end of the war had fallen away and, as in America and the rest of Europe, the country was in a deep recession. GDP fell by over 20% between August 1920 and May 1921 – not that different from the Covid recession of 2020 – and unemployment was high, rising to 17% of the working population. With deflation and falling wages, there was civil unrest. More working days were lost through strikes in 1921 than any other year – apart from 1926 – in British history. Working as a teacher, Keable had managed to avoid the worst impacts of the economic crisis, but his plans to become a full-time writer, with fluctuating earnings, meant he could be affected in the future, especially with rising income tax. Not that he ever complained in any of his letters about taxation – which was 30% on income in 1921. Even though he had champagne tastes, he saw himself as a socialist. A few years later, he talked about communist Russia in *The Great Galilean* and conceded that, although he did not support the political upheaval, he did appreciate the thinking behind their economic policies. He argued that, in the west, 'we have got wealth into a wrong perspective'.

Worst still for Keable was the political situation. He had absolutely no faith in the political leaders of the west who, despite all their talk of rights and freedoms, he believed had 'no longer any standard as to the one or the other'. He was dispirited by what he saw as the failed opportunity of the Treaty of Versailles and also by reports of the awful behaviour of the Black and Tans in Ireland. He was angry about the treatment of Africans by all the colonial powers, and he was also angry about what was happening in Europe. On his visit to Germany in the Easter holidays, he heard accounts of the appalling Austrian famine. He detailed his disgust in his novel *The Madness of Monty*, giving one of the characters, Enid Fillimore, this powerful speech:

England, France, America – all the Allies – are officially starving a million women and children to death in Austria. But the words convey nothing. If you had seen naked children crawling on the floor of decent houses last winter, their little bodies swollen horribly, their little voices almost too weak to speak, while the mother, without underclothing or what you or I call boots, was prepared to sell her body for the waste crusts of a hotel that was making a small fortune out of tourists and a splendid display of all races and variety of prostitutes – yes, and not getting the crusts because the management could sell them to somebody else with a little something more left to pawn – if you could have seen that, you might understand. And not a few cases. Street after street. And not Austria only.

At the same time as there was the awful famine in Austria, Russians were also suffering, and Keable donated money to the relief fund. When, the following year, Keable decided to buy some land in Tahiti, he told Sadler it was because:

Any damned thing may happen to the madmen who run Europe and America and the bottom may tumble out of anything, but a valley [in Tahiti] will remain.

Keable and Buck had decided to go and live in Tahiti together. For Buck, the more important factor was to escape any publicity. In truth, any comments about an adulterous relationship couldn't really cause more harm to Keable, or his family, since any damage to his reputation had already been done with the publication of *Simon Called Peter*. But, for Buck's family, a public scandal could have had dire consequences.

Although well connected and from a good family, Buck's mother was really struggling for money, and she was supported through a scheme that aided deserving gentlewomen. Buck's two brothers, William and Reginald, had needed generous foundational scholarships in order to be educated at

Wellington College – awarded only to the sons of deceased members of the military. Buck knew how horrified her mother's friends and family would be if they found out she had broken up the marriage of a good woman, let alone had an adulterous affair with the notorious author of *Simon Called Peter*. The fear was that such a family scandal could cost Reginald Buck his place at Wellington College; could make it very hard for William Buck – who was about to leave school – to find a respectable job; and could also make it more difficult for Kathleen Buck in her search to find a husband. As William Buck loyally (but when it came to Sybil Keable, not totally accurately) recorded:

> suddenly out of the blue Jolie ran off with Keable, who had given up the church. He, unfortunately, had a wife already, about whom I know little, beyond the fact that she was in a mental home, and in consequence of her religion divorce was not possible. The whole business was an awful shock to us, divorce in those days was unheard of.

For Buck and Keable, French Polynesia, as somewhere to hide from the glare of publicity, was perfect, with the added attraction of escaping the English-speaking world.

Although leaving his wife to be with Buck was Keable's main concern, he also really wanted to marry her. Buck was by now twenty-three. At that time, twenty-one was the median age for getting married – as many older as younger – and, following the war, there were almost six women to every five men in her age group. Her brother William Buck suggested his sister Kathleen, then aged twenty-two, had been terrified 'she would be left on the shelf', and so had married a tall, handsome cavalry man who was a 'complete rotter' – Captain Reverley. (They separated soon after their marriage.) Buck, being so unconventional, was probably less concerned about marriage, although she had waited a few years for Keable, and admitted that she turned down several marriage proposals. She later wrote:

> I can't think how grateful I am to my small amount of common sense that I did not marry the first man that proposed to me, but waited for the right one to come along, and I am afraid I should never settle down and be a respectable and dull and dutiful wife.

As it was impossible for them to marry, Keable and Buck decided they would live together as man and wife, and that, as soon as they left England, Buck would change her name to Keable. She didn't need to change her name by deed poll, as there was, and is, no law against anyone choosing to change one's name, unless one is impersonating someone else.

In July 1922, as they prepared their escape, Jack Elliott's mother, Wuffy Elliott, who lived in Burghfield near Reading, suggested Buck should leave London and move in with her. Buck stayed for a few months, later admitting how 'bored to death' she was by the young women round Burghfield, with their futile conversation and their 'utter inability to see farther than their noses'.

Keable and his estranged wife drew up a separation agreement; a letter confirms he had it with him in Tahiti when he died. AC Benson mentioned something of the arrangement in his diaries when the Bishop of Kampala, Gresford Jones, came to preach at Magdalene College, Cambridge:

> We had a long talk about Keable who was his curate... He put his troubles down to sex suppression. But now he tells me he has separated from his wife, a nice and handsome woman, and given her an inadequate allowance.

The allowance was £400 a year, more than Keable earned as a teacher but perhaps ungenerous when seen against his later royalties.

So, in September 1922, Keable and his wife said goodbye to their respective families and set sail for South Africa. They travelled on the SS *Bendigo*, a new one-class P&O ship which had been launched at the beginning of the year. Sybil Keable left the ship at Cape Town and Keable stayed on. The following year, he wrote to Sadler to say:

> My wife is remaining in South Africa and is teaching the Roman Catholic religion to little white children. She is far happier with out than with me.

Two weeks after Keable sailed, Buck, giving Wuffy Elliott's address in Burghfield as her last address in the UK, and calling herself Miss EJ Buck, set off for Australia on the SS *Omar* via Naples, Port Said, Suez, Colombo, Freemantle and Adelaide, finally reaching Melbourne five and a half weeks later. Keable had also stopped off in Perth but finally disembarked in

Jolie Buck on her way to Australia in 1922

Melbourne on 27th October 1922, by which time Buck had caught up with him. A couple of days later, she wrote to Rita:

> I am only 2 days off Sydney now. I saw [Keable] for a moment in Melbourne but only because my boat came in earlier than expected. Curious voyage – two proposals, one from a sweet boy from Haileybury 2 years my junior. I told him everything – he hero worshipped [Keable] – and still would marry me!

And she signed the letter – 'Jolie Keable'.

CHAPTER 13

SIMON CALLED PETER IN AUSTRALIA

By November 1922, *Simon Called Peter* had been on sale in Australia for over a year. Constable had the rights to the novel for both the UK and its colonies, including Australia. So, they began to import it into Australia as soon as it was first published in the UK.

News that Keable was planning to visit Australia was first reported in the press there in May 1922, by which time Keable was well known across the country. A journalist calling herself 'Maggie Wylie' (the name of the heroine in JM Barrie's play *What Every Woman Knows*) suggested he was due in June and complained that, although *Simon Called Peter* had caused a tremendous sensation everywhere, it was 'impossible to get it just now in Sydney'.

The Australian market, considerably smaller than the English or, indeed, American markets, was not helped by having a much more scattered population. The total population of Australia in 1921 was still only a little over five million, compared to over forty-five million for the UK and over a hundred million living in the US.

Initially, Constable did not promote *Simon Called Peter* in Australia and newspapers were not sent review copies. However, word of mouth proved to be very successful. The *Sydney Daily Telegraph* explained:

When the book *Simon Called Peter* came out a few months ago, all the dear afternoon tea people said, 'Shocking!' And when they were told what a thoroughly wicked book it was, they immediately ran and bought it.

Among the few newspapers that did review it, the critical reaction was mixed. The *Sydney Sunday Times* suggested it was 'the best novel of the war and the most honestly human love story of recent years'. A few months later, they called it 'the finest and most human of the war stories written behind the lines', while admitting that 'some of the skimmers have found in it nothing but a design to shock the thoughtless crowd'. Another article, in *Table Talk* magazine, acknowledged that certain critics had called it 'a thoroughly wicked book'.

A *Perth Western Worker* journalist later wrote that, when the book first appeared, it 'made Wowserism shriek at the top of its screechy voice'. Wowserism was a denigratory label applied to a Protestant social reform campaign in Melbourne, led by WH Judkins, who embraced the Wowser label as 'We Only Want Social Evils Remedied'.

In Australia, new novels were then seen as expensive – six shillings, which today would be the equivalent of $25A – and there were other options for those who could not afford to buy. Book clubs, such as the Sydney Book Club set up in the 1890s by Angus and Robertson, were very popular. For an annual subscription, readers could borrow books from a list of popular fiction and other titles. *Simon Called Peter* first appeared on the Melbourne book club list in August 1921. It was also stocked in libraries and in reading rooms that were run by literary institutes or local bookshops.

Though at that time Australia had one of the strictest censors in the world – with the Commonwealth Customs Department often banning books even though they were considered suitable reading in Europe and America – *Simon Called Peter* managed to slip through the net and did not face any legal attempt to prevent it from being imported into the country.

However, in February 1922, the committee of a Sydney literary institute voted to remove it from their shelves, even though some of the committee hadn't even read it. The *Grenfell Record and Lachlan District Advertiser* reported Messrs Howarth and Metcalf as having dissented from the vote, with the institute selling their only copy to Mr Howarth after the meeting.

Many reading rooms attached to bookshops also refused to loan out *Simon Called Peter*, although they allowed those who wanted to read it to buy a copy. This, *Table Talk* reported, was 'good business for the bookshops'. Ten years later, one newspaper reported that a Sydney bookseller had forbidden his sales assistants from reading *Simon Called Peter*. Keable had made that shop his headquarters when he visited Sydney and, unaware of the prohibition, left autographed copies of his novel for the young women on the manager's table, with a note asking him to hand out the books on his behalf.

Still, not all lending libraries were so puritanical, and the Sydney School of Arts reported in July 1922 that, although *If Winter Comes* was their best-read novel, *Simon Called Peter* came a close second. And there was a rather sad plea in a local newspaper from another reading library asking for *Simon Called Peter* to be returned, as it had 'run off'.

Without promotion, many readers in Australia had no idea who Keable was, and, almost a year after the book was published, the *Sydney Daily Telegraph* stated that:

> Mr. Keable, whose identity has so far been somewhat of a mystery, has been accused by ignorant critics of being a silly youth, with a desire to sound wordly and wicked.

Once Constable knew that Keable was planning to visit Australia at the end of 1922, they tried to put this right, and put more effort into promoting his second novel, *The Mother of All Living*, making sure they included more extensive biographical details. Newspaper reports began to appear detailing his pedigree. The *Sydney Morning Herald* ran through his career from a scholar at Cambridge to resigning from the Church, which it claimed was because he could no longer 'confess the orthodox creeds'. He had written devotional books and travel volumes, it continued, while waiting for the inspiration to write his first novel.

Newspaper articles appearing just before Keable's arrival in Australia went from being headed 'Naughty Novelist' to 'Popular Novelist' and by the time he arrived in the country, 'Noted Novelist' and even 'Famous Novelist'.

When Keable arrived in Australia, the media still retained a strong provincial link with the UK and America. As David Carter has shown in his article 'The Conditions of Fame, Literary Celebrity in Australia between the Wars', the Australian media did not like to attach celebrity status to Australian authors but were happy to do so for British or American ones. As an English author, Keable was seen as a fully-fledged celebrity. His books were popular in Australia and the fact that he was prepared to make the long journey to visit was much appreciated.

When Jolie Keable (as she now called herself) briefly saw Keable in Melbourne in November 1922, she wrote that her new 'husband' had looked tired and was hating both the country and the bully reporters. Outwardly, however, he seems to have cheerfully embraced the media circus, spending his time on a round of visits, interviews and photos.

The press interest was partly generated through Constable's efforts. Sadler commented: '[I'm] very glad… to learn our advance booming of your arrival has such an absurd and embarrassing effect'.

His arrival in Australia made the front page in Adelaide's main newspaper, the *Register*, a city he didn't even visit. It reported he was in Melbourne for a short visit and, although initially intending to stay longer, he needed to get to Tahiti to complete a dramatised version of *Simon Called Peter*. In a wide-ranging article, it also discussed plans for 'two' sequels to *Simon Called Peter*; the success of his latest book, *The Mother of All Living*; the soon-to-arrive new novel, *Peradventure*; his movements after the war; the voyage to Australia meeting new immigrants; his recommendations of up-and-coming young British novelists (Rose Macaulay, DH Lawrence and Michael Sadler); and the difficulty of distinguishing fiction from fact.

Thanks to Constable's 'booming', Keable was engulfed by the press. He was taken around town to be interviewed and photographed. The *Melbourne Herald* took him to their Herald-on-the-Yarra festival, and a *Sun* reporter followed him on a visit to the law courts. Keable was amused by the subsequent headline:

Keable's blank day – No divorce cases – Dull day in the Courts.

The *Sydney Sun* quoted at length Keable's views on Australian women under the headline: 'Keable's Misfortune – Hasn't seen enough of our girls – They know how to frock'.

Keable was alleged to have said: 'The Sydney girl struck me as showing extraordinary good taste in her frocking, being smartly dressed with a true sense of color.' He was further quoted as saying English girls had 'less freedom of choice… in their clothes', while Spanish girls 'pay great attention to their feet, ankles and hair', and French girls had a 'chic… sense of dress'. He also praised Australian mothers for being 'clean in mind and body' and

KEABLE'S MISFORTUNE

Hasn't Seen Enough of Our Girls

"THEY KNOW HOW TO FROCK"

(Specially written for "The Sun" by Robert Keable, author
of "Simon Called Peter.")

Mr. Robert Keable

THE Sydney girls are wonderful. One regret that I take away with me is that I have been prevented from seeing more of them. During the week I have been in Sydney I have been constantly in the company of men; I have been interviewed by man reporter after man reporter, and welcomed at men's club after men's club. I wish that it had been possible for me to see more of the wonderful women of Australia, who made their name in France just as your Anzacs made their name at Gallipoli.

The Sydney girl struck me as showing extraordinary good taste in her frocking, being smartly dressed with a real sense of color. The average Sydney girl knows how to frock immensely better than the average English girl, each according to her class. The Australian girl has a much greater freedom of choice regarding dress than her English sister. The Sydney girl appears to have something of the chic which is distinctive of the French girls' sense of dress, who know so well how to wear their clothes.

Sydney Sun, *10th November 1922*

female Australian office workers for 'their alertness, their capabilities, and their charm'. Though he commended the 'absence of prudery' exhibited by Australian women on the beach, he found the rule that men and women have to lie face down when sunbathing on Bondi Beach to be 'ridiculously absurd'. The article is probably explained by Keable's admission to Sadler that: 'in Melbourne one blighter got me at 11.45pm and I did not recognise a word of what I had said next day'.

The *Sydney Sun* wrote three articles on Keable, each over 500 words long. Commenting on *Simon Called Peter*, Keable was quoted as saying:

> In the book I made Julie a South African nurse... That may be because
> I spent twelve years in Africa, but though Julie is not a photograph,
> the girl who suggested her was actually an Australian nurse.

This was a strange comment, given that Keable spent only six years in Africa and that Keable's family were convinced that Julie was based on his

139

new 'wife'. It was possible Keable was trying to protect her, since she was with him in the city at the time.

He had been asked to give a series of lectures but ultimately gave just two, both in Sydney. At the first, a lunchtime talk to the Ad Men's Institute, he spoke on 'The Author, the Press and Public'. The *Melbourne Sun* found it 'a creditable little lunch hour speech' and was most intrigued by his style of speaking and his very self-depreciating tone. Keable arrived 'looking fearfully surprised and apologising for the luck he had had' and after the speech he strolled away 'looking more surprised than ever – surprised at everything and everybody, including even himself'.

The speech itself covered a wide range of topics. He predicted that the decline of European empires would lead to a new world order, with a mighty empire based in the Pacific and centred on Sydney. The main point picked up by journalists, however, was his suggestion that novelists were beginning to replace priests and teachers as the leaders to whom the public were turning. One journalist used the speech to write a poem, which included the lines:

Take a tricky Juliet – christen her Julie,
Make her figure ravishing, drenched with patchouli:
Put a rosebud in her hair – nothing else you'll see,
Boldly put the bluff up, call it artistry,
Cultivate the pose of nude, make it naughtily,
Hint salacious goings-on, say it lustily,
Life is but a desert that missed the lechery
Incidental to the naughty, saucy novel S called P.

And concluded:

Make it reek *unbridled passion*, get yourself a dizzy fame
As purveyor of the 'soul mate' stunt, declaring it a shame
That anyone should criticise, or ever dare defame
The classy high-brow novel under Robert Keable's name.

The details in the poem – centred on Julie's time in the hotel with Peter – suggest the writer was confident that *Simon Called Peter* had been read by many of the newspaper's readers.

Keable's second speech, a public lecture at the Protestant Hall in Sydney, was far more controversial and received huge coverage across Australian media. The talk, 'Modern Marriage', was advertised in the *Sydney Daily Telegraph* as 'the only address to be given in Australia by the famous author of *Simon Called Peter*' and by the *Sydney Sun* as 'an address on the existing relationship between the sexes by an outspoken authority, whose recent utterances have caused much comment'.

In the talk, Keable rehashed many of his views on marriage laws, which he believed should be based on a couple's physical and spiritual needs rather than the teachings of the Church. He felt marriage laws were immoral if they meant two people who no longer loved each other had to stay married. He gave as an example a then current story in Australia, of a woman who had to remain married to a convict and lunatic for the rest of her natural life. He stressed that any new marriage laws must still involve some sort of contract and, when relevant, ensure that men took responsibility for their children.

Controversially, he criticised the Ten Commandments and was mocked by one report for saying they were not worth the paper they were written on, since they had been written on 'tables [sic] of stone'.

In general, Keable's views were fairly reported, although one paper did say Keable wasn't 'the sort of novelist to inspire confidence when you get on

Sydney Daily Telegraph, *4th November 1922*

the moral tack'. The *Sydney Sunday Times*, which also interviewed Keable, published a 1,600-word article on his talk, subtitled: 'Famous novelist gives special exposition of tenet that not Church authority but human love is true basis of union'.

Much of what Keable argued seems uncontroversial today, but some of the furious reaction in Australia showed how preposterous many thought his ideas were. The *Sydney Daily Telegraph* published a long article by Rev M Maddern, a priest from Willoughby, in response to what it called Keable's 'recently delivered… remarkable lecture in Sydney attacking the institution of marriage'.

Maddern complained the publicity around Keable's speech would not help the cause of morality. He called Keable's philosophy of marriage destructive and what he called trial marriages 'repulsive to all ideas of decency' and 'a reminder of the promiscuity which obtains in many savage races'. He argued, not unreasonably, that couples needed to work on their marriage, that a modicum of friction was inevitable and, perhaps less reasonably, that couples who believed they were incompatible should get over it.

Maddern also highlighted Keable's criticism, reported in the *Sydney Sun*, of the rules on mixed sunbathing at Bondi Beach, where men and women were not allowed to 'sun' on their backs. He argued that by calling the authorities' restriction 'sentimentally squeamishness and prudish', Keable had revealed his 'unconventional thinking'. And it was that sort of thinking, by Keable and others, that Maddern believed could lead to the:

slipping of the cables of propriety, and of drifting out on the wild, wide sea of passion, into excesses that are condoned because they are unconventional.

There is no doubt Keable caused a stir during his time in Australia. His appearance belied his reputation as naughty, or unconventional. He still had the air of the country vicar about him and was described by one journalist as tall, courteous and impeccably attired. Still only in his mid-thirties, he was a carefully spoken, boyish man – happy to answer any questions a journalist would choose to ask him as long as he could have a cigarette in hand, a comfortable chair to sink into and a cup of tea or glass of whisky at his side.

Many suggested he loved to shock. His obituary in *The Times* suggested:

[Keable] was for ever outraging his natural kindliness and reticence for the sake of a queer angry ideal of social freedom, so that the 'public' Keable became a rather monotonous rebel against convention and prudery, and thence – by an automatic exaggeration which it is easy to understand – against all reserve and all sobriety.

Keable reported that 'it appears they love religious controversy in Australia' and everyone was keen to hear his views. He made quite an impression on the journalists he met. Hector Bolitho, a prolific New Zealand-born writer, was full of praise:

Most of the great writers I have met have been a great disappointment in the flesh. But Robert Keable with whom I browsed on Friday evening smashes my little theory about great men. He comes like a flood of sunshine from the literary lights of London… Success has not changed him or made him self-satisfied… his books are, in many ways, the most important among recent fiction… He has called a spade a spade… He realises the mean tragedy of the modern shirking of truth. He has taught us that the nude is cruel only when it is half-veiled.

Bolitho found Keable:

a great talker, a friendly, deliberate talker. He has the much-mentioned and seldom-found source of conversation – a sense of humour. He is deeply religious in the great wide sense. He is very much a boy, and has all the enthusiasms that lend colour to an interesting personality… I liked him for himself… He has forgotten how to sneer and be intolerant.

Keable seems to have formed a less favourable impression of Australia and never visited the country again. He wrote to Sadler:

Australia is a place to get out of good and lively. In W.A. you positively can only get dinner between 6.00-7.00. FACT. No one is allowed to serve later. Drinks off at 6.00pm unless you are staying in the hotel or have a rail ticket. They're all hearty with a kind of if-you-don't-like-it-you-can-bloody-lump-it kind of air. And one gets a little tired of the excellences of Aussy.

To keep their relationship secret, at least from the Australian press, Keable and Jolie Keable did not travel together to the South Pacific. After the couple had spent a few days in the Blue Mountains, Keable left Australia on 9th November 1922, and after a quick stopover in Wellington, New Zealand, set sail for Tahiti on the *Manuguani*. Jolie Keable followed, two weeks later.

Chapter 14

Keable in Tahiti

Keable claimed in a letter to Grimble in 1921 that he had always wanted to go to Tahiti, even dreaming about it while still at school:

I've read everything there was to read on the Pacific in the Varsity library... I long to get out there; I have a notion that it may even be better than Central Africa... you write of 'emerald lagoons and an ocean of petunia in cobalt'?

It was clearly on his mind when he wrote *Simon Called Peter* three years before arriving in the South Pacific. Julie, the heroine, says to her lover, Peter:

Peter... Wouldn't you love to live in the Fiji – no, not the Fiji, because I expect that's civilised these days, but on an almost desert island?... But I don't want it quite deserted, for I want you, and three or four huts of nice savages to cut up wood for the fire and that sort of thing. And I should wear a rose – no, a hibiscus – in my hair all day long, and nothing else at all. And you should wear – well, I don't know what you should wear, but something picturesque that covered you up a bit, because you're by no means so good-looking as I am, Peter.

Before air transport, it took many weeks for European and American visitors to reach Tahiti by sea. But throughout the eighteenth and early nineteenth centuries, travellers had still visited the island, thanks to its reputation as a kind of paradise, an image fanned by writers such as Pierre Loti, Herman Melville, Robert Louis Stevenson and Jack London.

Immediately after the First World War, the island had been badly hit by Spanish flu, but, by the beginning of the 1920s, travellers had begun to return. Somerset Maugham's novel *The Moon and the Sixpence*, published in 1919 and loosely based on the life of the French post-impressionist artist Paul Gauguin, would have provided a fresh impetus to tourists to visit, and Cook's Tours began to arrange trips for independent travellers. According to some, Tahiti in the early 1920s was still an idyllic island untouched by western civilisation. Popular photographs of the day by photographer Lucien Gauthier show semi-clothed men and women in rural scenes, suggesting a peaceful paradise; and Herbert Moesbury's woodcuts, published in many newspapers, depict Tahitians canoeing, collecting pearls and bathing in the forest stream. Even Frederick O'Brien's *Mystic Isles of the South Seas*, published in 1921, details tranquil life in the rural areas of the island, although it does also describe some of the raucous behaviour of Americans and Europeans in the clubs and hotels of Papeete, Tahiti's capital.

Some discussed how Tahiti had already changed. Hector MacQuarrie in *Tahiti Days*, published in 1920, wrote that the 'amiable care-free child-like' Polynesians were slowly dying out, and suggested the country was being 'swamped' by Chinese migrants. George Caldron, in *Tahiti*, published posthumously in 1921, complained that the English missionaries and the French government had ruined the country and that Europeans and Americans had introduced:

Coffee, manioc, vanilla, oxen, goats, mice, mosquitoes, fleas, bicycles, sewing machines, telephones, ice-works, concertinas, cotton frocks, corrugated iron, Christianity, Mormonism, Munyon's remedies, mouth-organs, milk-shakes, tuberculosis, syphilis, and other amenities, which have flourished exceedingly in that virgin soil, and caused a number of modifications in the life of the native, known collectively as Civilisation.

ST de Goes, a former consul-general for Sweden in Australia, argued that Tahiti didn't live up to its idyllic reputation. He complained that the 'natives' were indolent and unreliable, their hospitality a thing of the past, and the place 'overrun by Americans, especially cinema actors and saloon-keepers who with their noisy ways, made Tahiti rather undesirable'.

An August 1921 *New York Tribune* article described how Papeete was overrun by American 'hermits' summer and winter. 'Stacked four deep in the hotel rooms, swarming the provincial sidewalks and crowding the cows out of the pastures'. Reporter Torrey Ford explained that tourists could stay in a range of hotels, including one with a golf course. They could visit movie houses around town and play quoits or roque or dominoes or chess in the park, listening to the band. And there was the 'added bonus' of sightseeing bus tours 'taking in all points of interest on the island including the Paul Gauguin shack and the Pierre Loti monument'. Ford suggested that those who looked to settle on the island, to escape the trials and tribulations of modern civilisation, were either bank embezzlers, long-haired writers, poets, painters, disappointed politicians, broken-down crooks, wife deserters or alimony dodgers. An article in an Australian newspaper in March 1922 suggested visitors were either tourists seeking '*dolce far niente*' (a sweet time doing nothing) or writers searching for copy.

When the Keables arrived, the population of Tahiti was about 12,000 – 40% of whom lived in Papeete. Those who had newly settled on the island were mainly French or Chinese, and many of them preferred to live in the capital.

Whatever they were expecting, the Keables were not on their way to a desert island. Nor did they want to escape the comforts of modern civilisation – they were soon shipping any modern conveniences they couldn't find on the island from San Francisco.

As he sailed towards the port, Keable noted 'the corrugated iron of rectangular stores', 'the lines of villa residencies' and the 'spires of churches whose builder did not think of the holiness of beauty'.

It was not a town he ever particularly liked:

Poor little Papeete! They dub her, the writers and visitors, the Paris of the South. God forbid, but if you want a Paris in the South Seas go to Papeete and deserve what you get... Papeete is well lied about, and she has a veil which the lies prevent most visitors from lifting.

As soon as Keable arrived in Tahiti, he went in search of Gauguin. He knew he was unlikely to find any art works. Somerset Maugham, in 1916, had managed to buy one of the last pieces left on the island, a painted glass panel from an old door – *Polynesian nude with apple* – paying about $35 for it, selling it thirty-five years later for $117,000. However, Keable did want to find Gauguin's house, the location of which O'Brien had described in his book:

> In Punaauia, the next district to Fa'a, was a schoolhouse, and on it a sign: 2 + 2 = 4... Near the school-house, a dozen yeards from the salt water, was a native house with straw roof, a mere old shell, untenanted.

Claiming to follow O'Brien's description, and ignoring the sightseeing tour bus, Keable drove out to Punaauia, ten miles south-west of Papeete, along the main road that circles Tahiti Nui, the larger portion of the island. There, Keable found it, a dilapidated shack among the many coconut trees. Beyond the shack was a beach curving round a glass-topped lagoon, protected by a reef from the white crashing waves. Further still was the shadowy island of Moorea, stretched out on the horizon.

Keable had been tasked by Jolie with finding a house to rent and knew, after a few nights at the Tiare Hotel, that he could not bear to live in Papeete. So, he decided to rent Gauguin's house. It had only two habitable rooms, but

Gauguin's house in Tahiti in 1922

Keable rather optimistically claimed that 'the greater part of the house' still stood. It had been unoccupied for a while, so the owner was prepared to rent it out, along with two or three acres of land between the road and the beach. Keable later claimed the:

> obtaining of a house was attended with as much beastliness as it is in London, perhaps with more, for swindling in London in such matters is impersonal.

Keable admitted the house 'in itself, it is not beautiful', but a huge attraction was the magnificent view across the sea to Moorea. As Keable put it:

> On either side of the bay the hills fall back so that Gauguin looked left to the mouth of the Panaruu and right to pointed iron-wood trees or casuarinas. But before him the sun sets daily in that wonderful Pacific glory of delicate colour upon feathery cloud, in the summer right out to sea and in the winter over Moorea. Since the reef is broken just here also, not only had he the everlasting murmur of the ocean upon it, but to one side is an open ocean beach upon which the great breakers thunder in south-east trades.

Keable clearly saw Gauguin as a role model. He wrote reverentially about the man, pointing out that it was 'easy enough to blame a man for the desertion of his wife and family' but arguing that Gauguin's 'gesture' should be seen in the context of the millions who find themselves tied to a job that doesn't fulfil them. Keable suggested Gauguin was a man who 'bravely, rent tatters the careful web of social custom, and traditional duty, and went out naked'.

There were barely a dozen houses scattered along the two miles either side of their new home. However, if the Keables had thought this was their chance to live among 'three or four huts of nice savages' as Julie had wanted in *Simon Called Peter*, they were very much mistaken. The Keables were viewed with deep suspicion by their new neighbours, who made no attempt to be friendly – not even smiling at a greeting. Keable complained, very uncharitably, that none of his neighbours was physically beautiful and that they all wore 'extremely ugly dresses'.

Jolie Keable arrived in Papeete two weeks after Keable, and she may have been horrified when she first saw the state of the house. However, since they arrived in the rainy season and couldn't go out much, they had time to concentrate on doing it up. It didn't take long to get the house rebuilt and decorated as they wanted. The long, wide veranda facing towards the road, and the two bedrooms reached by doors either end, were in good condition. They had the bedrooms – wall and furniture – painted white, and Jolie Keable chose towels and bed linen in different colours; green for their room, love-in-the-mist blue for the spare room. Beyond the bedrooms they rebuilt the drawing room, leaving it open to the elements. It was here where they spent most of their time. Jolie Keable explained:

> East and west there are no walls except bamboo breast high so that one gets a glorious view east and west of the sea. The walls are painted grey and the floor is polished and I have the most fascinating carpets of brown and green Chinese matting with brown leaves stencilled on. There has been built into one corner a topping little cosy-corner, and I have masses of green cool-looking cushions everywhere. There are heaps of armchairs and two settees and a huge desk for [Keable]. I had the armchairs made of bamboo, the furniture is all the darkish colour of the floor. There is no electric light, only lamps with soft green shades. I have masses of lovely tropical green plants everywhere and a huge green parrot who struts about, and of course there are flowers everywhere, but in huge clumps.

The last room, completely rebuilt, was a dining room, also painted grey, with windows on three walls and a door leading out to the sea on the fourth. Jolie bought a polished dark brown table and matching chairs, along with a settee, for the room, and she also chose the white and green patterned china. As was the fashion in Tahiti, the kitchen was a separate outhouse. They also had a shower and, unusually for Tahiti, a bath, which they were given by an Englishman returning home.

In front of the house was the reef that protected the large lagoon from the Pacific waves, meaning they could fish, canoe and swim safely.

Keable could not have been happier. The last few years had been quite a challenge. His *Times* obituary suggested:

> Keable's story is a veritable fairy story of a swing from poverty to

Robert and Jolie Keable on beach in front of Gauguin's house, 1923

wealth, from fetters to freedom. It began in righteous anger; went on to... revolt against authority; to a life of penury and struggle; to the writing down in a book the story of anger and revolt – and then the book's triumphant sweep over two hemispheres carrying Keable with it through half the countries of the world and landing him in a paradise of flowers and sunshine in the South Seas.

Keable and Jolie ended up spending nine months in Gauguin's house. Jolie was in charge and employed their Chinese cook, a gardener, a girl to clean the house and another who came to wash their clothes in the freshwater stream nearby. Jolie calculated they could live on 1,500 francs a month, about £250 a year, to cover wages, rent, washing, food and drink.

Being close to Papeete had its advantages, as they could get daily deliveries of fresh food from the early-morning market, as well as ice. Every day, *le truck* – both a local bus and delivery service – travelled down the road from Papeete. On it would be anything they had ordered from either Papeete or even San Francisco. For Keable, the priority was the best whisky on offer – 'very drinkable at ten shillings the bottle' – and good, cheap French wines.

They ate well, their cook specialising in Tahitian-style curries. The meat was always good, as the French government insisted on inspecting the market every day to check it was fresh. Jolie went into raptures about the burru leaves, which, when wrapped around meat, would tenderise it within minutes. She described how local people cooked their meat and fish – when they could afford them – wrapped in the leaves and placed on red-hot wood with red-hot coconuts on top. The leaves, which never burnt, acted as casserole dishes. She also loved the raw fish mixed with slightly fermented coconut sauce, made from nothing but shredded coconut.

Though she enjoyed fashionable clothes, she confessed it was a joy not to wear stays or shoes or stockings, unless she went into Papeete. Because there were no fashionable dress shops in the capital, she made all her own dresses, buying crepe de Chine and Chinese silks, which were cheap compared to English prices. Determined to remain fashionable, she travelled to Papeete every month, on the day the San Francisco ship docked, to see what the American tourists were wearing, and then copied their outfits. She explained:

> The only objection to buying ordinary materials here, is the fact that you are quite liable to see a Tahitian maiden in the same frock as you next week. So, I am extravagant, I only buy the best materials which I know they cannot afford.

As soon as they arrived on the island, they ordered a car from San Francisco – a Dodge Model 30 – which became Jolie Keable's runaround.

Together, she and Keable spent a lot of time planting the garden. Jolie admitted she was easily bored by gardening but admitted:

> one thing makes it more enjoyable here than at home, if you plant a hibiscus cutting in three weeks to a month you have a flower, the same with other plants. Practically before the week is out you see the new flower beginning.

Jolie Keable's biggest concern, when she arrived on the island, was how the French authorities were going to react to her, but, as she told Wuffy Elliott in a letter:

> The passport officials found out that my passport was not in the same name as [Keable's] but they all knew that we would be married if we could and that it is not a passing phase, so they are all simply charming to us and treat us as an ordinary married couple, and there are no people more exclusive than the French.

The French maintained a very clear social hierarchy on the island, based on those who did not fraternise with local people and, to begin with, Jolie stuck to it. The only 'respectable' women of Jolie's age were the daughters, or young married wives, of French officials, and she eagerly accepted invitations to visit them. The food, she reported back, was wonderful, although she was horrified by their twee houses full of knick-knacks and cushions embroidered with phrases such as 'God is love' or 'Doves of peace' on them.

Quickly bored of stuffy French society, Jolie encouraged Keable to start inviting the long-term English and American residents to lunch. Barely ten miles outside of Papeete, with a private beach, and soon their own boat, their house was the perfect location for gatherings. Within a few weeks of arriving, they had an open house once a week, for a disparate group of friends. Keable had always been generous, even when poor, but now, with his new-found wealth, he was, according to his *Times* obituary, 'eager to share with anyone the comforts and experiences that money had brought within his reach'.

Sundays were also particularly riotous, as Keable explained to Sadler:

Life is so utterly easy and haphazard... Every Sunday a feast arranges itself somewhere, not with Tahitians, they don't exist except in the incredible lies of O'Brien – but with the half-caste American citizens and Claude Rivière and the like. You should see me dancing the hula-hula after my nth rum-punch! Monday one gets over it.

Madame Claude Rivière was an eccentric woman who had worked for *La France* in New York and was in Tahiti to study the islanders on behalf of the French government. She showed Keable a Gauguin manuscript she had purchased called *The Modern Spirit and Catholicism*, which she and Keable spent some time preparing for publication. Later, Keable portrayed her in his novel *Numerous Treasure* as the adventurous painter and art critic Antoinette Verclos, as happy swimming near naked in a rock pool as debating the demise of Polynesian civilisation.

The rest of Keable's circle of friends were American or British. He and Jolie tended to befriend the more unconventional men who had come to the island to work or explore and, having fallen in love with the way of life, stayed on.

Frank Stimson, whose daughter still lives in Punaauia, was one. Later to become an eminent anthropologist, Keable described him as 'a fellow of real brain who has chucked the States to work as a clerk for bread and butter while he bathes in folk-lore and ethnology'. Stimson was a 'stout, irascible man – the "stormy petrel" of Polynesian anthropology'. Like many of the men who stayed on the island, Stimson had had a string of Tahitian girlfriends, before he eventually married a local woman.

RJ Fletcher was another friend, whom Keable described as 'an amusing cuss, a fellow with a cynical outlook, a brain, and a pleasant gift of speech, and he is handy too'. He wrote *Letters from the South Seas*, a gossipy book about Tahiti written under the pseudonym 'Asterisk' and published by Constable. Later, he agreed to oversee the building of a new house for them, and they travelled with him for a short while across France in early 1924. His niece was the writer Penelope Mortimer.

Two others, whom Keable mentioned in his first letter home from the island were Knapp – whom he called 'the greatest living authority on Tahitan [sic]' – and Nordhoff – 'a yank of the nicest sort who is in touch with American publishing and has left civilisation to settle here'.

Charles Nordhoff and his sometime writing partner James Norman Hall were perhaps the two most well-known Americans on the island at the time. Hall and Nordhoff had met after the war when they were asked to write a history of the Lafayette Flying Corps, of which they had both been members. Having completed the book, they were commissioned to write another and decided on a trip to the South Pacific. They had arrived in February 1920 and their subsequent book, *Faery Lands of the South Seas*, was published in 1921. They stayed on the island, Nordhoff for sixteen years, Hall for the rest of his life. Together, in the early 1930s, they wrote *The Bounty Trilogy*, based on the famous mutiny.

Hall and Nordhoff were keen to distance themselves from the tourists who visited the island, but happy to mix with those who came to stay. Like nearly all those who settled, they both married women native to the island. Charles Nordhoff married a nineteen-year-old half-Polynesian, half-Dutch girl called Tua Tearae Smidt, which ended in divorce some years later.

The same age as Keable, Hall was a remarkable man. At the outbreak of the First World War, he joined the 9th Royal Fusiliers pretending he was Canadian, since Americans were not permitted to serve in the British Army. He was a machine gunner at the Battle of Loos and given an honourable discharge when his nationality was discovered. Back in America, he wrote about his adventures in a successful book – *The Kitchener's Mob* – and then he returned to France to cover the formation of an American pursuit squadron. Instead of writing the article, he joined the squadron, learnt to fly and joined the Lafayette Escadrille along with other American volunteers. In June 1917, he had an encounter with seven German aeroplanes, was shot through his shoulder and lungs and fell 12,000 feet. Miraculously, he survived and within three months was flying again. When America entered the war, he joined the United States Air Service and was shot down again, this time behind enemy lines. He was captured and held as a prisoner of war.

The success of *Faery Lands of the South Seas* provided Hall with an income for a while, but he soon started to struggle. He was commissioned to write a book about Iceland, where he was when Keable and Jolie arrived on the island, but returned early, with writer's block, and never completed the book. He is first mentioned by Keable in a letter in June 1923 saying that they were about to go on a camping trip out in the wilds. Hall was unmarried when he first met Keable. According to his daughter, he was waiting for his half-Polynesian, half-English girlfriend, Sarah Winchester, to turn sixteen.

Other colourful characters on the island at the time included Sarah's father, Captain Jo Winchester, who had threatened to have Frederick O'Brien horsewhipped for the poorly anonymised portrait of him in his book. There was also the three Smiths – 'Whiskey' Smith, who drank; 'Seven Kilometre' Smith, because that was the distance of his house to Papeete; and 'Borneo' Smith. 'Borneo' Smith – Dr Harrison Willard Smith – was a retired professor from MIT, who, unusually among the British and American residents, lived alone in a little house doing his own housekeeping and cooking. He was a physicist turned botanist who set up the Botanical Gardens in the south of Tahiti Nui.

Once the house was refurbished, Keable was happy to settle down to write. He quickly got into the routine, getting up early, writing all morning and then going out for walks and a swim in the afternoon. Fairly soon, he heard that Brady already had a script for the theatrical production of *Simon Called Peter*, so he concentrated on trying to finish *Recompense* as quickly as possible.

His next project, once *Recompense* was completed, was to write a book about Tahiti. *Tahiti, Isle of Dreams* is an odd book, written as a money-making venture and serialised in magazines in both the UK and America – *Asia* magazine paid him $600. The book is a travelogue-cum-guide set to sell the dream of Tahiti, but Keable decided to tell it as he saw it, and he included

Jolie Keable and friends at Gauguin's house, 1923

some uncomplimentary details about life on the island. Ultimately, although it was published in England, his US publisher decided not to go ahead, protesting that 'the book would not have sufficient appeal for the American public to warrant Putnam's publishing it'.

Keable decided to structure the book round the famous literary and artistic figures who had visited Tahiti over the years. He went searching the island for traces of their visits, and for people still alive who had known them, taking with him a local photographer, William Crake.

Easiest to find were people who had known Paul Gauguin. Still living in a little native house across the stream from Gauguin's house was his *vahine*, who appeared in several of his paintings, including *Nevermore*. According to Keable, she had no desire to discuss Gauguin, but M Tessier, who Keable claimed had been Gauguin's best friend on the island, and whose estate adjoined theirs, was happy to talk about him over an eggnog or rum punch. M Tressier told Keable about his visits to the house Keable was now living in:

> He would come across in the morning to find the painter at his easel
> in his open-air studio under the pandanus-thatched roof, naked as

likely as not, bearded, smoking innumerable cigarettes, engrossed in painting and unapproachable... Gauguin would merely throw him a monosyllable and continue to paint while he sat down to watch... Or the artist would be making his strange carvings after the native manner, of incredible gods and austere nude humans and distorted twisted trees.

M Tessier also had happy memories of going with Gauguin to another Frenchman's house to eat '*omelette baveuse*', which he claimed the 'exiles' soul loved'.

The poet Rupert Brooke had lived in a house in Matiaea, on the southern side of Tahiti Nui, in 1914. Keable tracked it down and confirmed Brooke's description of it:

the most ideal place in the world to live and work. A wide verandah over a blue lagoon, a wooden pier with deep clear water for diving, and coloured fish that swim between your toes.

Brooke wrote a few poems here, including 'Retrospect' and 'The Great Lover'.

Keable managed to find a woman, Tetuanui, who remembered Pupure (Brooke's Tahitian name, meaning fair). She described how he would get horrendously sunburnt strolling around only in a *pareo* – the Tahitian sarong – and how he would write poetry in the morning and either bathe with the children or go upriver to spear fish in the afternoon. She explained he rarely went into town and claimed he 'never cared for the girls and drinking... as other white men did'. He had a girlfriend, Mamua, and she said he could swim even quicker than her.

Brooke had stayed at the Old Tiare Hotel in Papeete but, when Keable checked the register, he was amused to find that a part of the page had been torn out. Questioning Pare, the son of the hotel owner, Lovaina, he was told that a young American 'fan' of Rupert Brooke had torn out the 'Rupert' so that the entry just read: '___ Brooke, 26, Journalist, Cambridge, England, Jan 14'.

The writer Robert Louis Stevenson was already famous by the time he visited Tahiti in the late 1880s, having written *Treasure Island*, *Kidnapped* and *The Strange Case of Dr Jekyll and Mr Hyde*. Keable travelled to the village of Tautira to find where Stevenson and his wife had lived in 1888. He found the

Stevensons' home as lovely as Mrs Stevenson had described it. An elderly Tahitian who remembered Stevenson told him:

> We shall never see his like again in Tahiti. He is dead and we are dying. None of the Europeans are as he was, whose body, soul and spirit were white as the moon and pure as the stars.

He also visited the church which had been consecrated during Stevenson's stay in the village, but found it in a sorry state, windows broken and the door swinging from the hinges. Local people had constructed their huts against the wall of the church. (Today, it has been fully restored and stands tall, surrounded by a well-manicured lawn.)

Back at home, the Keables had to contend with a constant stream of tourists who came to see Gauguin's house and who had the added delight of finding the author of *Simon Called Peter* living there. He wrote to Sadler in June 1923:

> SCP looks as if it would make me an income for life, but it also looks as if it will prevent me ever being taken seriously in literature... Visitors here say S.C.P! Why certainly. You don't mean to say you wrote it!! I never can remember authors' names. Damn their eyes. I think I shall commit suicide outside the theatre in town... leaving a confession to say that I was Simon myself and Julie was the Russian Princess who managed to escape and is now living incognito.

Jolie Keable admitted Keable received 'hundreds of letters from adoring females and earnest young men' every time the monthly mail boat arrived in Papeete.

In *Tahiti, Isle of Dreams*, Keable was very critical of the tourists who came to the island:

> There comes to Tahiti a regular stream of nature-worshippers and beauty seekers (to give them the pleasantest names) who end up in hospital or prison or steerage on a cargo steamer or the cemetery and who make themselves a great nuisance in the process.

He went on to say:

If [the tourist] wants an amorous adventure he had much better go to Paris. If he wants primitive simplicity he had better go, as quickly as possible… to Central Africa. And if he wants every material necessity for nothing he had better shoot himself at once, for as far as I know such things are not obtained without labour save, on some accounts, on the Astral Plane.

And he continued:

The average young tourist who comes to Tahiti runs an even greater chance of contacting venereal disease than anywhere else in the world. The average lunatic in search of the simple life usually leaves in six months to rid himself of elephantiasis or something worse.

And he tried to dispel any myth that Tahiti was some sort of Garden of Eden:

There was a time in Tahiti when the fruits of the earth were held in common and when you could walk along and pick them. To-day we have land laws, and if you do that you break them and you will end up in prison. There was a time when the fisherman would gladly share his catch with you, but to-day he sends his superfluities to Papeete market where charity is as far to seek as in Covent Garden or Billingsgate. There was a time when damsels, sporting on the banks of the rivers, would call to you to join them and thereafter take you home and keep you for as long as you cared to stay. To-day… as for the damsels, who will sport with you on river banks, they must be obtained from Papeete, from another 'market', and it is you who will have to keep them.

Keable and Jolie had initially only intended to stay in Tahiti for a few months, but they eventually decided they wanted to make it their home. Reading their letters and looking at their photographs, one can see how happy they were, trekking into the centre of the island, swimming in the rivers, fishing and fish spotting near the reef, picnicking and taking canoe journeys. Keable described one day:

On Sunday afternoon… we were at our friend Mauu's place and

Jolie Keable being rowed around the lagoon, 1923

bathing sixteen of us, in one of the most heavenly pools you can possibly imagine… Clear limpid cool and sparkling water from the mountain; a pool under great rocks on one side and overhung by giant mape trees on the other; sunlight that is real sunlight dappling down on grass banks and stones, vistas of the swift river running to the sea, time no moment, life one long laughter. And such company! There was Louise, champion pearl diver from the Paumotus; her man an utter scream of a cinema boss, over here to make pictures of real native life and faking the thing that no longer exists as hard as he can; a Swedish artist, most charming and as poor as a church mouse; an American millionaire, literally, and his wife – bathing in thin chemise; three naked babies of five and six, swimming like little frogs; Mauu who is beyond description; his wife in love with me; two native men, such good chaps, and a few odd ugly quaint women of Mauu's house-hold. Back in the moon-light to crabs, prawns and rum-punch.

At the beginning of April 1923, Keable told Sadler he was 'thinking of buying a valley and settling here. It is a good investment for one thing'.

Jolie Keable at Mauu's party, 1923

According to the then British consul, Fred Devenish, Keable hired a schooner to sail round the island to find the perfect location for their new house. They eventually purchased a plot of land opposite their friend Charles Mauu's house. Keable described it to Sadler as 'the farthest corner of the island, next door to a Russian communist, a splendid person, and my Swede'. The view was spectacular, looking south at the rolling ocean waves coming from the horizon, and south-east towards the peaks of Tahiti Iti, the smaller part of the island.

They knew they had to go back to England to sort out their affairs and to give Keable a chance to sell his book on Tahiti. They spent their last couple of months planning for the new house. The site they chose was on the top of a small cliff, some fifteen feet high, with a view of the bay and 3,000-feet-high surrounding hills. They decided to use Walkers, a local shipbuilding firm, to build it, and imported many of the materials, including the roof tiles, from America. Their eccentric friend Fletcher was asked to oversee the project, including clearing the site of trees so that building could begin.

Keable was not in Tahiti when the house was being built, but Caroline Guild, who wrote about her experiences on Tahiti in *Rainbow in Tahiti*, built her house on the island in the same year. She described a whole new community arriving and setting up camp near her building site. Tradespeople set up little shops for her workers and soon there were a couple of small outdoor cafés and even a bar. The French authorities tried to punish her for running an unlicensed premises until she persuaded them the selling of alcohol to her workers was nothing to do with her.

Keable's new house needed water and Keable found a spring two kilometres away up in the hills and organised for water to be piped down to the house. Mauu – who owned much of the land through which the iron pipeline would need to be laid – agreed, as long as the water could be piped to his house as well. The house also needed electricity, so Fletcher was asked to buy a suitable generator and to arrange for it to be installed.

They even began to plan how to lay out the two or three acres of land they now had. Since they were hoping to be able to avoid going into Papeete, fifty kilometres away, they wanted to be as self-sufficient as possible. Seafood wasn't going to be a problem, as crabs, lobsters, oysters and fish were in the bay below. But they decided to plant enough trees to give themselves a supply of bananas, mangoes, limes and, of course, coconuts, while also leaving space to rear their own animals. Chickens and cows were the main priority, as they wanted fresh eggs and home-made butter.

In September 1923, as building work began, they were ready to leave the island. The plan was to spend some time before Christmas seeing family and friends back in England before spending a few months travelling in North Africa and southern Europe, which would allow them to shop for the house. The Spanish-style square that they planned needed some sort of sculpture to go with a fountain, and they wanted to buy paintings, wall hangings and furniture. After their mini grand tour, they would sail to America for a visit and some sort of promotional tour before making their way back to their new house in June or July 1924.

Before they left, Keable reported to Sadler that there had been:

bursts of parties in which everyone gets gloriously intoxicated and performs the miraculous. The last was the farewell to Tahiti of HL Wilson… and so at 3am on his last night I mixed him three cocktails of Gin and Vermouth and Eno's Fruit salt, being at the time under the delusion that he and I were very good fellows and with a new and divine cocktail. From such orgies I return to the peace of my country home, a sadder but alas never a wiser man.

In September 1923, Keable and Jolie left Papeete on the slow boat to Marseilles. The *El Kantara* took about twenty first-class passengers – mainly French, and a few more second-class – but it was the cargo that mattered to the crew. On the journey out to Tahiti, the cargo had included livestock, poultry, sheep and even oxen, but coming back, the hold was full of wool from Australia and exotic fruit from the South Seas. The joy of travelling on a cargo ship was that the formalities of some 1920s cruise ships – changing four times a day and only speaking to those of your class – was largely ignored. Keable and Jolie ate the same food as the crew, although not with them. They were served by a steward, who had an extravagant array of gold teeth.

Keable spent much of the journey planning out and writing sections of what was to be his next novel, *Numerous Treasure*. The novel is Keable's take on the opera *Madame Butterfly*'s story – which is based partly on Pierre Loti's *Madame Chrysanthème*. In Keable's novel, a young English graduate visits his old tutor, George Guiney, who now lives in Tahiti, and falls in love with a sixteen-year-old mixed-race girl named Numerous Treasure. Much of the novel is set in George's house, which is described in detail and plays a central part in the story. Keable's new house in Tahiti was clearly on his mind at that time.

The old twin-screw steamer took almost five weeks to complete the journey, travelling through the Panama Canal, passing by Madeira and through the Strait of Gibraltar before heading up the coast of Spain to their final destination, Marseilles, in France. From there, they moved on to Paris, to begin buying things for the house, and then on to the UK.

The couple spent only two months in England, mainly based at the then fashionable Hotel Belgravia in Grosvenor Gardens, before setting off again, just after Christmas, on their grand tour of southern Europe and northern Africa. From the French Riviera, they moved on to Algeria and Tunisia, stopping off in Malta on the way to Egypt and Syria, and sailed from Jerusalem to Greece before flying to London. By the time they arrived home in May 1924, Jolie Keable realised she was pregnant. A few months earlier, she had written to her friend Wuffy Elliott:

Talking of babies (this is for you alone) I must say I am extremely glad that Bill shares my views about them. I certainly do not want to

Jolie Keable in 1923

start having babies for at least 4 years. I don't really want them at all, in spite of the fact that every woman is supposed to long for them.

Although they were living as man and wife in Tahiti, they were not actually married, so their child was going to be illegitimate. With fewer than 5% of babies born out of wedlock at the time, illegitimacy was seen as a source of shame. In the early 1920s, nearly 3,000 unmarried mothers were forced to live in workhouses in England and Wales, while some were even consigned to mental hospitals under the 1913 Mental Deficiency Act.

Though Jolie's circumstances were very different from those of most unmarried mothers, her family, and Keable's parents, did not feel able to talk openly about her pregnancy for fear of a scandal.

As there was no modern hospital on Tahiti at the time, the couple decided to put off their planned return to the island until after the baby was born. This also meant delaying their visit to America. The plan had always been that, on his first visit to America, Keable would go on a lecture tour, promoting himself and his books. When he visited Australia, back in 1922, Jolie Keable had hidden in the background, but this time she would be able to travel with him as his wife. And now also with a new baby.

They rented a house down in Kent for the summer, after which they were invited to stay with the Elliotts, in Stokenchurch, where Jack Elliott, as a doctor, could keep an eye. The early stages of her pregnancy seem to have gone well, although Jolie Keable was afraid of giving birth – so worried, in fact, that she made Rita Elliott promise that, if anything went wrong, she would look after the child. Childbirth was still relatively risky in England in the early 1920s, where four in every thousand mothers died from complications, and one in every twenty-five babies died before the age of one.

Towards the end of her pregnancy, Jolie Keable was diagnosed with pre-eclampsia and was prescribed bed rest. A month before she was due, she was moved up to London to stay at 27 Welbeck, a nursing home in Marylebone, where three days later the baby was induced. Keable, who had a chance to wish her luck the day before, was kept well away from the hospital. During a painful labour, she was given chloroform, which was sometimes used at that time as pain relief. Shortly after her son, Tony, had been delivered, she died, aged only twenty-five.

Her death certificate listed the causes as influenza and toxaemia of pregnancy (pre-eclampsia). Her sister, Kathleen, later suggested that she died from a weak heart, but there is no evidence that this is the case. It could have been the chloroform that killed her. The American Medical Association had sought a ban as early as 1912, and in 1923 the *British Medical Journal* reported that a 'famous' London hospital had forty-two fatalities in eight weeks and regretted that 'week after week the chloroform holocaust goes on'.

After her death, Keable was summoned and spent a little time alone with her body. He cut off a couple of locks of her hair, putting one in an envelope for his newborn son, addressed: 'Your Mother's hair, which I cut as she lay dead'.

Jolie Keable's funeral was held four days later in Golders Green, attended by a small number of family and friends, including representatives from Keable's publishers. Her father had been cremated there thirteen years earlier and her family were keen for her ashes to be placed beside his. Records at the crematorium show that it was Kathleen Buck who organised the cremation and the purchase of a niche large enough to fit caskets for both Jolie Keable and her father in the Ernest George Columbarium. Keable confirmed in his will that he had paid for the niche, requesting that his ashes be deposited next to hers when he died. The initials J. E. B. K. (Jolie, Eileen, Beresford, Keable) were carved onto the metal casket along with the date 14 Nov 1924 and the simple Latin phrase '*In Pace*'.

Keable was distraught. They had been together, living as man and wife, for just two years, with their future all mapped out in Tahiti, in their new house. Only a few months before, they had written to ask Fletcher to add an extra room as a nursery. Rita Elliott later told their son, Tony, about:

> the supreme happiness the two shared together. She was young, modern and loving. He in her found an outlet that provided a happiness he never found in religion.

Rev Dowling, who knew Jolie during the war, wrote to Keable a few days after she died:

> It was only so recently that her spirit had come into the sunlight. She never had a chance until you gave it her and she was so proud and fond of you and so immersed in all your activities… One evening I took up some remark of hers and began big words about it, hoping to confuse her by noise if not by sense. The poor child looked at me for a moment and said 'Paddy you know all my thoughts are my husband's'. I was delighted, but said nothing. It proved her happy, and I could wish for nothing better. Hundreds of times she told me of your thoughtfulness and your 'patience' and your unfailing humour. She never repeated herself and she never tired of it. I like to think of those things just now. It's a wonderful thing when we have no cause to reproach ourselves in respond to those we love.

The stress of Jolie's death contributed to Keable's ill health. After collapsing at his father's house two weeks later, he wrote to Sadler:

> I've been ill – sudden heart attack that has led to revelations of an unpleasant sort. My blood pressure is 2½ times normal brought on by worry and excitement etc. and it has aggravated my kidney

trouble (sorry to worry you with butchers talk.) But there it is. If I go to Tahiti and be quiet I may live on happily (?) but if I don't I may sail off. This is confirmed by the Insurance Societies who won't accept my life at all. Cheerful isn't it? But with my [Jolie's] death it doesn't seem to matter. Still I can't bear the heart-failure feeling and this insomnia and I suppose for the child's sake also I might need to go slow.

Jack Elliott arranged tests and advised him that he needed peace and calm if he was to recover. After three weeks at his parents', he was feeling well enough to travel to America to fulfil his commitments there. Jack and Rita agreed to look after Keable's baby son, initially with the help of a full-time nurse paid for by Keable. There are no records of any formal arrangements that he made for his son, so it is difficult to know how much he saw this as a temporary solution, given his poor health and determination to return to Tahiti. Before he left, and six weeks after Jolie Keable had died, he wrote a long letter to the child, addressed: 'For my son, Robert Antony Keable, When he is 21'. In the letter, he explains why he couldn't marry his son's mother, who he called:

the most lovable, impulsive, child-hearted, devoted woman… I adore and love her a hundred times more than when we met and braved the world's indignation…

He then offers his son advice:

You must take charge of your soul. I think Truth, Beauty, Wisdom alone are worth following. Lie socially like a trooper, if you have to, but in your soul worship Truth.

Life is a great adventure. It's an odd business and I feared starting you off on a journey when I myself had so little knowledge of the goal. But I have come to see that any solution to our problems, if there be a solution, lies in living – experiencing, carrying on, not funking not shirking nature. Life is good Tony. I mean it even tho' I say it when I have had to face so many sorrows.

He continues:

You will be told how your dear mother died. No words of mine can tell you what it meant – and means – to me. But you cannot be told how much we loved each other. There have rarely been love stories such as ours. From the moment that we met we loved, and we staked all and gave up all, for love. Fortune smiled on us then and the two years I had with your mother were an earthly paradise. We travelled, I wrote, we loved and then, like a thunderbolt, the end came.

He explains:

I have left you my legacy. Wisdom – the best education I could provide; Beauty – foolish little memories of your mother, and her portrait: Truth – something, I hope of our nature for we did love truth. More I don't even want you to have from me. You must live your life. You must make your own way. If you can't – it is better you should hoe cabbages living by your own strength – than live in a palace on my money.

And he ends:

And, lastly, the day we die we can watch on those we love. Today those we love wait for us on the other side. I don't know as I write this. It has seemed to me that your mother is still alive and with me. But if it be, so we shall wait for you, Tony lad; come crowned.

    Yr loving Father, Robert Keable

Two days later, Keable set sail on the Royal Mail steam packet ship, RMSP *Orca*, from Southampton to New York. He wrote to Rita Elliott from the ship:

I did not realise quite what starting alone meant. I had a kind of re-action as bad as if Nov 14th was here again. She always loved ships and used childishly to prowl about with me learning the ropes. She would have loved this one – just right size and compact and so on. Oh Rita… I don't know which I feel the more: my loneliness or intense resentment against the fate that can shut her happiness so terribly and so swiftly.

Keable's fame preceded him and, once on board, he was asked by the ship's company for permission to photograph him for the company's annual report. Eager to avoid attracting further attention, and deeply mourning the loss of Jolie Keable, he stayed in his cabin for most of the voyage. His health still wasn't good, and he was nervous about the trip to America, remembering the frenzied reaction of the press when he first arrived in Australia.

It was a rough voyage. 'Boat is tossing delightfully', he wrote to Rita Elliott, 'but had affected my writing only not my lunch yet'. He underplayed the situation. The *Orca* was one of three ships delayed by storms, with the *New York Times* reporting that their captains declared that the hurricane on Thursday, 8th January, was about the worst day they had ever experienced in any part of the world.

RMSP *Orca* docked at Ellis Island on 13th January 1925. The contrast between the mood of the man who arrived that day in America and the one who had arrived in Australia two years before could hardly have been greater.

CHAPTER 15

SIMON CALLED PETER – THE SEQUEL IN HOLLYWOOD

In 1922, there had been discussions in Hollywood about turning *Simon Called Peter* into a film. At that time, Hollywood studios relied on tried and tested material, including novels, short stories and plays, for over half their output and particularly the big-budget productions.

In 1921, Edith Maude Hull's controversial novel *The Sheik* was made into a hugely successful film starring Rudolph Valentino, and studios were on the lookout for another shocking story.

However, following the infamous trials of Fatty Arbuckle for rape and murder, and stories of debauched Hollywood parties, the film industry's reputation was at an all-time low.

The *New York Herald* commented in March 1922:

Hollywood, the motion picture capital; a community of dissolute actors and actresses and others of the movie industry; the worst of them unspeakably vile, the best suspicionable; a colony of unregenerates and narcotic addicts; given to wild night parties commonly known as 'orgies'; heroes of the screen by day and vicious roysteres by night; a section of civilization gone rottenly to smash.

The studios decided to clean up their act by appointing Will H Hays, who went on to compile the 'Hays Code', advising directors to avoid 'lustful and excessive kissing' in their films. But, first, Hays drew up a list of books that should not be filmed. In 1924, he claimed that 160 books and plays had been kept off the screen, and it is very likely that *Simon Called Peter* was on it. This was not the time for a film about a priest visiting prostitutes and having an affair with a young nurse.

Having missed out on making a movie of *Simon Called Peter*, Hollywood studios were keen to film the sequel. Putnam's published *Recompense* at the end of March 1924 and signed a deal with Warner Brothers by the middle of May. Mr Grubb, Putnam's agent in London, explained the hurry in a letter:

You probably know that Will Hays is the Czar of the American picture world, he has what amounts to an index expurgatorius. His organisation places the names of certain books upon this index. It says in effect to its members 'This book is improper. Its utilization will be damaging to the industry. You shall not use it'. It was known to Warner and subsequently to ourselves, that *Recompense* was headed for this list. Once on this list it would have absolutely no possibility of sale in America – until a reversal had been arranged – which would be very difficult. However, after a book has been bought by a producer it is not put on the list. The ban could not be enforced then. Also it would stir up too much trouble. This being the situation Warner was anxious to rush this thing through. So were we.

Warner Brothers claimed that they beat their competitors to the film rights by sending an envoy into the mountains of North Africa to find Keable, who was away on his grand tour at the time, to get him to sign the memorandum of agreement. They knew that they would be able to sell the film on the back of the success of Keable's first novel and, indeed, all the publicity for *Recompense* described it as the 'sequel to *Simon Called Peter*'. The intention was always for the film to be a main feature and they paid Keable $15,000 for the rights, well over the then Hollywood film industry average of $5,000.

Warner Brothers, the only family-owned – and -operated – studio in Hollywood, was run by four brothers. They had begun as a nickelodeon business – running the earliest cinemas – before moving into distribution and then in 1918 started making films. In 1922, they built the West Coast Sunset Studio on ten acres of land and a year later could afford to upgrade it. The early 1920s was the heyday of Hollywood silent movies – talking films began in 1926 – and by the middle of the decade, over fifty million Americans a week were going to the cinema. Warner Brothers alone produced thirteen feature films in 1923 and seventeen in 1924, including the big hit *Beau Brummell*, starring John Barrymore and directed by Harry Beaumont. The success of that film meant that Beaumont had first pick of the next season of Warner Bros films, and chose to direct *Recompense*.

*

In July 1924, it was announced in the American press that Keable would visit America for the first time in the autumn to coincide with both the opening of *Simon Called Peter* on Broadway and the screen adaptation and production of his 'popular novel' Recompense. It also reported that he would give a series of lectures.

After the death of Jolie Keable, the trip was postponed. Warner Brothers issued a press release in December of that year which made no mention of a lecture tour. Instead, it confirmed Keable was visiting America at the invitation of the studio so he could confer on the *Recompense* script and that filming had been delayed until his arrival. After meeting with his publishers in New York, he would continue on to Hollywood to 'look over the entire picture industry' as their guest.

A week before Keable arrived, six weeks after Jolie Keable's death, Warner's announced in the American papers:

> Word has been received that Mrs. Robert Keable, wife of the author of *Recompense*, which is about to be produced, died in London recently.

Before Keable arrived in America, some local American papers, including Wisconsin's *Appleton Post-Crescent*, suggested his visit would launch a 'Keable year' with a play on Broadway, a film in pre-production and the imminent publication of his new novel, *Numerous Treasure*. The press were keen to give him a big welcome, so Keable was lucky to have Major Putnam to look after him. He later confirmed the Major had been 'absolutely splendid', protecting him from the press and handling the 'film people'. In all, he spent a week in New York, telling Sadler that it was 'likely to afford material for nightmares for the rest of [his] natural existence'. The only formal engagements were a private dinner at the Coffee House Club with the film people – Abe Warner, SM Warner and a scriptwriter, Pearl

Keating – and an evening at the theatre to see 'the most incredible and awful production' of *Simon Called Peter*.

With no lectures or other public engagements, Keable gave just one formal interview, which led to a short but kind profile in *Time* magazine. The journalist was intrigued by how a quiet English clergyman had become the author of a sensational bestseller:

> He does not impress one as a radical gentleman. There is nothing to suggest the resigned clergyman, author of books marked by their sex frankness and melodrama. In fact his scholarly bearing and gentleness mark him rather as a country curate, who should be acting as a character in a novel by May Sinclair and passing out crumpets to maiden ladies in a decorous drawing room instead of writing of Tahitian damsels as he has done in his new novel, *Numerous Treasure*... Keable is a pleasing person. He is something of a poet. It is my belief that many a popular novelist is really a poet at heart.

As if to reinforce this impression, a cartoon of Keable published in the *New York Times* by Robert James Malone depicted him in a raincoat leaning across a café table with a pipe in one hand and a cup of coffee in the other, talking earnestly like an overgrown schoolboy.

Financially, the week in New York was very rewarding. Keable signed

Robert James Malone's caricature of Robert Keable

a new book deal with Putnam's, with a £1,500 advance on the next novel – *Lighten Our Darkness* – and sold the option to film and stage *Numerous Treasure*. The intention had been for *Numerous Treasure* to follow *Recompense* as a Hollywood movie. Grace Sanderson Michie, who had written two films, *Defying Destiny* and *Pagan Passions*, was commissioned to write the script. However, the film wasn't made, and another effort in 1935 – when the film rights were assigned to the Harry Edington agency – also came to nothing.

Despite the months of planning, the visit to Hollywood did not transpire, though the reason for this is not clear. Instead, discussions with Warner Brothers took place in New York, where Keable was shown photos of the leading actors and stills from *Recompense*. Warner Brothers declared that Keable's 'suggestions for picturizing his sensational sequel… proved invaluable and were incorporated in the film'.

Keable was not happy with the studio's treatment of his novel. He wrote to Sadler after he had seen the photos:

> that unfortunate novel emerges from the sausage machine as a tenth-rate melodrama ending with marriage bells. Peter fights Stenhouse with cowhide whips, barrels, tins of bully beef and ultimately revolvers. Mosheshoe is a kind of Uncle Tom and Christian martyr. Julie marries Peter because the principal man will not consent not to marry her.

He assured Sadler that he had made soothing comments to the producers since 'it is a good principle to spoil the Egyptians' – referring to Roman leaders charming Cleopatra.

Accordingly, an article in the *Seattle Star* reported:

> Mr Keable said Warner Brothers had made the atmospheric background of his story startlingly accurate, and after looking over the various still pictures of Marie Prevost as Julie he paid her a neat compliment. 'Miss Prevost seems to be absolutely in the mental attitude of Julie' he stated. 'She seems to have studied the character from the book and absorbed the woman's psychology.'

He particularly disliked the happy ending that Warner Brothers had insisted upon. He was quoted in Ohio's *Mansfield News*:

While I appreciate the public demand at present for happy endings and realize that producers must live up to that demand, I feel the day will come when life can be shown on the screen as it really is… [in ten years] the public will be so educated that it will not be necessary for a wedding at the end to satisfy the taste of the audience.

The film of *Recompense* was released in April 1925. Unfortunately, prints of the film have not survived and all that remains are stills, newspaper adverts and reviews. In one advertisement, *Recompense* was described as 'The story that startled two continents' and 'Robert Keable's sensational sequel to *Simon Called Peter*'. The film was shown across America as the main feature for more than a year, with listings and quarter- and eighth-of-a page advertisements appearing in the local press as late as April 1926. They tried to outdo each other with their sensational headlines:

Love endured even across the vast stretches of the veldt.
The price they paid for a few short hours of forbidden happiness!
A strong drama where love passed into the house of lust with
devastating results.

Recompense *newspaper advertisement*

175

Warner Brothers worked hard to promote the film and placed many articles about it in the local press across the States, most of which played up the scandalous nature of the story. The reviews were mainly good. The *New York Times* commented:

> there is much to be said in favour of the picturization of Robert Keable's novel Recompense... there is a conscientious effort to obtain atmospheric accuracy, whether the scenes deal with life behind the British lines in France, glimpses of South Africa or flashes of London's Limehouse district.

The absurdities of the movie did, however, amuse the reviewer, and particularly one character, Colonel Donovan, 'who is usually immaculate in his attire, looks like a fashion plate after riding over the trail for four days'.

The two leads were Marie Prevost, a huge star at the time, and Monty Blue. The *New York Times* reviewer was not impressed by Blue's performance in *Recompense*:

> Mr Blue impersonates Peter Graham the clergyman... [but] his forte is in light comedy and with all the earnestness of his performance he does not impress one as having devoted his life to teaching the Gospel.

However, it found that Marie Prevost as the 'gay outrageous nurse', Julie, was 'well suited to the role' – 'unusually beautiful and appealing'. It added: '[her] kisses are of the usual motion picture variety – prolonged and violent'.

The end was described as 'muddled and banal', weakening the production 'due to the obvious angling for a happy ending, which has been accomplished in an obvious and stereotypical fashion'.

Recompense took twice as much at the American box office as the $129,000 it cost to make, netting Warner Brothers a good profit, with audiences of just under a million. It also had a limited release overseas, which earned Warner Brothers another $37,000. There is no record of the film being shown in the UK, but it ran at the lavish Crystal Palace cinema in Sydney, Australia, with G Harry Stone and his orchestra providing new musical numbers.

The film helped make Keable a rich man. It would have taken him more than forty years on his wartime chaplain's salary, or ten years as a teacher, to earn the money he made from selling the rights to *Recompense*. However, anxious to return to Tahiti after such a long absence, he didn't wait for the film's premiere but boarded the first ship he could back there.

CHAPTER 16

KEABLE AND THE TAHITIAN PRINCESS

On Thursday, 4th September 1913, while Keable was teaching at St Andrew's College in Old Town, Zanzibar, the American press reported that Ina Salmon, a fifteen-year-old Tahitian princess, was being held at the immigration centre at Angel Island in San Francisco Bay.

Ina Salmon had travelled to America with an eccentric American botanist, Miss Josephine Tilden, who acted as the interpreter at the Board of Special Inquiry set up at the immigration centre to look at Ina's application to enter America. Ina admitted she was past twelve, nearly thirteen, had been born in Papeete, was travelling with Tilden and Tilden's mother and was carrying $14. Tilden described Salmon's grandfather, Tati Salmon, as 'head of one of the eight tribes in Tahiti' and her father, Tauraa Salmon, as 'one of the wealthiest men in Tahiti' and 'very well known all over the Pacific'.

Tilden could also have explained that Ina Salmon was closely related to Queen Marau, the last queen consort of Tahiti. Queen Marau's husband, King Pomare V, had allowed the French to abolish the Tahitian monarchy in return for a generous pension and a title. Although by the time he had died in 1891 Queen Marau had separated from the King, she was treated with much deference by the French authorities and was made an Officer of the Order of the Legion of Honour. In the 1880s, she had been very well received in Paris, with her fashion style copied by many Parisians and, although she played no official role on the island, Queen Marau was well respected across Tahiti.

The board unanimously agreed to allow the princess to be admitted into the country and she travelled to St Paul, Minnesota, staying at first with Tilden's eighty-year-old mother, and later boarding at the Visitation Convent School. Ina Salmon only spoke French and Tahitian when she arrived in America. The plan was for her first to learn English, and then stay long enough to go to college. However, when the war broke out in 1914, her grandfather ran out of money and she returned home after only two years in America.

Ina Salmon returned to her old school in Tahiti, graduating in December 1917. The following year – after a passenger on the RMS *Tahiti* introduced Spanish flu to the island – Ina Salmon lost many of her family, including her father, grandfather and two aunts, in the space of three days.

She came from a large extended family – her great-grandparents had nine children and her grandparents eight – so, with four sisters and at least six female cousins, she was certainly not the only princess of her age on the island. However, to the English-speaking community, she was perhaps the most important one, being the eldest granddaughter of Queen Marau's favourite brother, and one of only a few who spoke perfect English, with an American accent. As soon as she was old enough, she accompanied the Queen and a select few of the Salmon clan to parties and dinners organised by Americans and Europeans who lived on the island. George Biddle, the American artist – who wrote a journal about his time on the island – noted the Dowager Queen Marau attended a party in September 1920 accompanied by two princesses, Takao and Ina.

Photographs of Ina Salmon in her youth reveal her to be tall and slim, with fair skin, large eyes, high cheekbones and a full mouth. Her long black hair, which stretched down to her waist, was usually tied up in a bun. Robert Eskridge, in his book *Manga Reva*, later dubbed her the 'Helen of Troy of Tahiti'. On a six-month visit to America in 1921, wearing elegant French dresses and pendent earrings, she attracted a lot of media attention. One newspaper suggested that she was 'wooed by a lot of eggs'. It was reported that she said she laid 'little stress' on her royal heritage and preferred to 'live a quiet and inconspicuous life as a citizen of her own country'.

When Ina Salmon returned to Tahiti, she began a relationship with Raoul Cornette de Saint Cyr, a Frenchman. They had two children, the second born in November 1924, but in 1925 he left for Morocco, never to return.

Around the time Ina Salmon was adjusting to life without the father of her children, Keable returned to Tahiti. He was still distraught about the death of Jolie Keable. A week after he arrived, he wrote:

honestly I am in no good way. Perhaps it is early days but I do not feel fit either mentally or physically. I can't rest and I can't work. And I worry. And I think I miss [Jolie] more totally every day. There are moments when she comes on me again as if here and I feel quite literally that I cannot bear her loss. Lovely as this house and situation is – and it is better even than I had hoped – that my senses do accentuate the feeling that it is empty.

There is no spot in which I do not suffer the torment of those November days over again either because of the memory of our visit in 1923 or because it is some pleasure which she did not explore or which she has been deprived. I have been within minutes of selling it all up already: I shall not be surprised in any event if I leave shortly. I think that when everything is complete, the garden laid out, the various small building additions made – I shall turn the key and walk out.

After a few more weeks back, Keable began to pull himself out of his depression. He wrote:

The house is really quite perfect from my point of view. It is dawning on me that I really can if I want to, sit still, and that there is no one to say nay to me.

It didn't take long to get the house as he wanted it. Caroline Guild, who lived on the island for seventeen years with her husband and children, wrote that Keable's house was exactly as described in *Numerous Treasure*.

In the novel, Keable described the library:

a great bay window, with a cushioned seat running around it and a desk across the arc. The centre of the room was bare. Against the nearer wall were more bookcases, a low table… and an occasional carved chest of dark native wood. In the corner between the door from the patio and the bay window stretched a wide divan, with a little table beside it and a small square window above, so that a man at his ease could look out, as through a porthole, at the garden, the sea and the mountains.

Numerous Treasure was published in the UK in January 1925, and in America the following month. The cover was based on a photograph taken by Keable from the beach in front of Gauguin's house.

It did get some good reviews on both sides of the Atlantic and in Australia, although those who did not like it suggested Keable was obsessed. Richard Ellis Roberts in the *London Daily News* thought the novel 'should be enough to destroy [Keable]', going on to say: 'Mr Keable is now much over-impressed by nudity, just as in the last book of his I read he seemed over-impressed by feminine under-garments'. He went on to ask: 'Why do novelists who rave about nudity in the tropics never mention the obvious discomforts of blowing dust and dirt?'

In America, Ida Gilbert Myers argued in her review that Keable, having been released from 'irksome restraints', now overindulged:

Now for Mr Keable the sex side of the man-and-woman question appears to have an irresistible lure. He can't keep from talking about it and writing about it… He no doubt calls his work realism. Writers are likely to when they are either specially dull or uncommonly dirty.

The Watch and Ward Society in Boston managed to place a prohibition on the novel. They did not need to prosecute a bookseller or librarian – as they had done to get *Simon Called Peter* banned – instead, a committee made up of three members of the society and three booksellers decided *Numerous Treasure* should not be sold in Boston. Bookshops, scared of expensive court cases, accepted the suggestion, as did newspapers, which agreed not to review the book. As usual, the result of the ban was that the people of Boston ended up travelling to New York to buy the book.

For the first few weeks, Keable remained in and around his house. Once he felt stronger, he started writing again, each morning, but never for more than three or four hours. Every evening, he would fix himself a cocktail, and his letters are full of references to drinking with friends. His interest in cocktails led him to write to the *New York Times* to argue, in response to an article he had read, that he did not believe they were invented by Americans, rather by the Romans and Ancient Greeks. He drew up a long list of cocktails of non-American origin, such as the 'White', the 'Sensation', the '75', the 'Luigi', the 'Angler', the 'Whiz-Bang', the 'Depth Bomb' and the 'Monkey Gland' and claimed to have invented his own one, the receipt for which he had placed at the end of his novel *Numerous Treasure*.

> *1/6 Gill GIN*
> *1/6 Gill FRENCH VERMOUTH*
> *3 dashes ABSINTHE*
> *3 dashes ORANGE BITTERS*
> *Add little Soda Water + Lemon Peel*

He ended *the New York Times* article by explaining its merits:

> The blend of gin and French Vermouth, the body of the drink is subtle upon the palate and stimulating to the stomach, while the orange bitters titillate the throat and leave it… inquiring for the after-flavour of the absinthe, which lays slow hold upon the mind and even the imagination of the drinker.

At home, Keable began to wear a traditional Tahitian *pareo*. A photograph of Keable appeared in the *San Francisco Examiner*, bare-chested, wearing the *pareo* tied round his waist and with a garland of pink blossoms crowning his rather grim bespectacled face.

Guild explained: 'It is easy to put on a *pareo*. The trick was to keep it on'. The French authorities, who wished to encourage European dress, banned anyone from wearing the *pareo* in the capital, Papeete, and Keable was one of the few Europeans who wore it constantly at home.

By June 1925, he was travelling around the island again. He had purchased a couple more properties on the island, both as an investment and also so he could rent them out to friends in need. He described a visit to one of his properties on the far side of the island at Teruaohiti, where he took a few friends:

> It is completely isolated from the tourist world, a beach on which the open sea breaks at the mouth of the exquisite valley. A wide crystal river flows out here to the sea. We bathed now in salt and now in fresh water, relaxed on the grass beneath a grove of ancient tamanu

trees, ate a lunch of fish just caught by Mauu and two nymphs in the water and drank milk of coconuts mixed in a shell with claret which requires to be tasted to be realised, the sun-shot air dispels sadness and bitterness and worry. I wish I could convey to you one half of the peace that is there, one half of the loveliness of the great ferns, the feathery bamboos, the tall palms, the deep translucent forest pools.

He explained what happened when they got back to his house that evening:

And finally we reclined on my Bokhara carpets while the not-unseemly wench I have trained, in a pareo chosen by myself to suit her, played us Chaliapin and Kreisler and Bach on my really wonderful new gramophone. The trumpet is of silk and the sound-box a new invention which really does eliminate the metallic sound of the old instruments… life is almost silly in its perfection, and I am conscious, as I write, that it truly has some flavour of a golden age so long past in England that will not quite believe me.

Though the Keables, when they had lived in Gauguin's house, had enjoyed entertaining, their house had been so small that friends rarely stayed. In Keable's new house, there were plenty of rooms for people to stay and, as it was fifty-five kilometres from Papeete, visitors tended to stay overnight and often for a week or more. Keable usually drove into Papeete once a month, when the mail boat from San Francisco docked, and would often bring home any interesting visitors to the island, such as Baron Ungern, an ADC to the Prince of Mongolia, who was on a secret mission, and Merian Cooper (later to direct Fay Wray in *King Kong*).

Keable was certainly keen to enjoy himself. It has been suggested that he became increasingly promiscuous, but the only real evidence comes from the British consul, Fred Devenish, who suggested there were 'some very wild women parties after [Keable] returned from England'.

Although Keable discussed the immorality of living in an unhappy marriage, there is no evidence that he believed in open relationships before, or after, Jolie Keable died.

Tahiti islanders had always had a reputation, begun by the stories of visitors to the island in the late eighteenth century. Bougainville had reported that he discovered in Tahiti 'an earthly paradise in which the inhabitants were naked, unashamed and amorous'; Captain Cook watched 'the sexual act [being] publicly consummated in the presence of the queen and of the lesser chiefs and ladies' and saw dances by women which he called 'too indecent and provocative to be described'; and Christian Fletcher and the mutineers on the *Bounty* were supposedly turned from sailing duties by the Tahitian women.

One has to remember, however, that according to Michael Sturma, in his article on western fantasies:

> From the beginning it is clear that the supposed 'free love' of Tahiti was far from free. Historians have generally rejected the term prostitution in describing the sexual relations between Europeans and island women, [but] early European visitors, on the other hand, had little reservation in terming the relations between seamen and Tahitian women a form of prostitution... Intercourse between Tahitian women and sailors were mainly fuelled by the islanders' desperate desire for iron, a commodity previously unknown to them... Within a couple of weeks Robertson (on the *Dolphin* with Henry Ibbot that landed in Tahiti in 1767) could report that every cleat in the ship had been drawn as every nail for hanging hammocks.

Sturma also pointed out that another feature commonly omitted in accounts of early European visits to Tahiti was the extreme youth of many of the females who engaged in sexual relations. Teha'amana, Gauguin's first Tahitian muse and lover, was only thirteen when she became his native wife.

In the 1920s, many young men did travel to Tahiti attracted by the stories of free love. Alec Waugh, who later stayed with Keable, admitted that was what was on his mind when he first visited the island. He met Tania on the bus during his first day on the island, saw her at the beach with some friends and took her back and established her in his hotel.

> This was what I had come across the world to find: and it had come, as such things do in novels but so rarely in real life, spontaneously, without planning, unpremeditated.

Keable, in his book *Tahiti, Isle of Dreams*, had been very critical of the westerners who, having arrived in Tahiti, took up with young Tahitians. Keable did, however, count a number of Tahitian women among his friends.

Keable still wanted to go travelling and he told Sadler:

Norman Hall and some American backers want the pair of us to go off together to Central Asia by way of Tokyo, Seoul, Mukden (now known as Shenyang)… I think I am attracted. It might be amusing. Hall is amusing, to start with. He was an American flying 'ace' in the war, though I confess to you that I don't actually know what an ace is, and he's very American. 'Gee, Keable, that would be great!' He has no fear, no morals and no money except what he earns en route. But he also has no pride and no delusions.

In the end, Hall decided against the trip, telling Keable that his father was ill. He had also decided to marry his girlfriend, Sarah Winchester, who had turned sixteen. So Keable offered the couple his house for their honeymoon and made plans to travel alone, hoping to visit Mongolia and research Buddhism.

Instead, a recurrence of his kidney infection confined Keable to the small hospital in Papeete with very high blood pressure and a haemorrhage. The prognosis was not good and he was advised to get on a ship to San Francisco as quickly as possible.

Arriving in America at the beginning of September 1925, Keable was rushed straight to a sanatorium. He spent a month there while doctors tried to bring his high blood pressure under control. The *Miami Daily News* reported:

Broken in health by a complication of troubles, the exact nature of which physicians did not divulge, Robert Keable, English author and playwright, was ordered to St Luke's hospital here. He would be forced to forego any labour whatsoever his physicians said, for more than a month, and it was indicated that he might be limited to dictation for a period of only one or two hours a day. Persons close to the author admitted that Mr Keable's illness was serious.

Keable reported back to Sadler:

I am installed in an apartment overlooking San Francisco Bay, a very elegant apartment wholly Americana with amazing facilities for spending money. I am in the charge of an American lady who is at once secretary, housekeeper and nurse, and a remarkably interesting person at that… Really America and Americans are incredible.

Keable stayed in the apartment for two months, with Dr Addis in charge of his care. He was prescribed a special diet as well as quiet and mental rest, and the doctor developed a special diet for him.

Once he felt better, Keable spent his last few days shopping in San Francisco. He returned to Tahiti with chickens, a cat, canaries, churns and butter utensils, an ice-cream freezer, special tinned goods, chemical apparatus for determining the quantity of salt in his urine, a large tent to go camping in, a load of books, a quantity of medicines and a nurse to care for him.

The nurse did not last long. Keable told Rita Elliott:

[The nurse] was always driving me mad by being floored if the meat didn't arrive and by wanting great quantities of staff because she didn't know and wouldn't learn how to use them. She was AWFUL… She leaves on this mail.

She was replaced by Ilonka, who came to run the house, along with her boyfriend, the Swedish artist Paul Engdahl. Keable explained:

Ilonka is perfectly wonderful – a Hungarian (in Vienna through the war) where she kept her family alive by selling off their ancestral furniture and hawking it in the streets for food. She speaks six languages, is a skilled tapestry weaver and in addition is a perfectly marvellous cook and house keeper. The war has brought out all the german excellences in that direction and after the American [nurse] she is a perfect joy.

Keable admitted:

I am living an almost ideal life. Practically no clothes at all, no Papeete, no worries. Paul Engdahl, a swedish artist, runs the place: Ilonka, his girl, a Hungarian, cooks wonderfully; Mauu, a tahitian, does the garden, Loti (Chinese) washes the plates… and your humble servant, an Englishman by birth, writes absurd books. My dogs have seven puppies, my canaries four little ones, my pidgeons more squabs then we can eat and my gold fish will consume their own eggs.

He believed the maids and other servants:

do not regard their employment as servitude and look upon me rather as a patriarch. Sometimes in the evening when I am listening to the gramophone they will steal into the room and squat on the floor to listen also.

Keable described the room to a journalist from the *Bedfordshire Times*:

The main part of the house is my music room, which has been decorated by a Swedish artist friend of mine – Paul Engdahl. The room has an eastern appearance, with oriental carpets hanging from the walls and panels in between them. The mural paintings which Paul has done in these panels are very fine. By the way this is the only sitting room on the island which can boast a fireplace. I am obliged to have one because although the island is in the tropics my house is so situated that it always gets the cool wind which blows direct from the north pole. This room is modelled on old English lines. It has a large old-fashioned chimney and in the fireplace are wrought iron fire tongs which I had made by a native blacksmith. There is also a jolly chimney corner.

He went on to explain:

In a valley I grow tropical fruits such as bananas, mangoes and limes. I keep my own chicken, pigs and cows and make my own fresh butter and it is easy to obtain all kinds of fish, with crabs, lobsters, oysters and prawns. You will see that we are practically independent. We are however obliged to import potatoes, which will not grow there owing to the heat, and flour.

Once back from San Francisco, Keable continued to entertain people with his customary generosity. When the HMS *Laburnum* weighed anchor near his house, he entertained the Commander and his officers for a few days. He reported:

> They are not likely to forget Tahiti in a hurry! Wearily they climbed abroad in the early hours, night after night in batches, raving about Tahitian maidens and rum-punches.

*

It is not clear when Keable first met Ina Salmon, nor when their love affair began, but soon after he returned from San Francisco he was clearly smitten. In April 1926, he explained in a letter to Sadler:

> Ina is a granddaughter of the Queen, who has been spending a week with me, very delightfully. Incidentally she much admired your portrait and we discussed you. It gave me a delightful five minutes to think of you, Ina and I lunching at the Café Royal. I cannot imagine what you would think of her. She is 23, was educated in America for four years, and has two illegitimate babies – who were also here – by a young Frenchman now in Morocco. She has still a perfect figure, hair to her knees and wonderful eyes. She calls me 'Bob' with an American accent, can smoke cigarettes with the maids without losing her dignity and is, with it all, 'royal'.

(The facts aren't quite accurate; she was twenty-five, a great-niece of the Queen, and had been educated in America for only two years.)

Keable related an incident to Sadler concerning Ina Salmon; his maid, Uratuwa; and his neighbour, Mauu:

> I was writing a profound work on philosophy in the study and I heard Mauu's voice in vehement native. Then Ina began to laugh, deliciously. Then Uratuwa began to cry, painfully. So I put my head out of the window and cursed them all.
>
> **Mauu** That's all very well Robert, but this girl has been sleeping with my boy.
>
> **Robert** What the devil do I care. I'm writing.

Uratuwa There! That's what I said. Robert's my master and he doesn't care whom I sleep with.

Robert So long as they don't get in through the window, I told you that.

Mauu This girl is a bad girl. She has no right to sleep with my boy last night.

Robert Why?

Mauu for long minutes in unintelligible Tahitian. So I asked Ina what he was saying.

Ina He has a feast today and he sent his boy to get shrimps now he hasn't any.

Mauu That is it. I send my boy to get shrimps and he comes and sleeps with this girl. Besides it is always the girl's fault.

Uratuwa (in bitter tears) But I didn't sleep with the boy, Robert. I wanted to sleep with you. Besides I wanted to eat shrimps. I didn't sleep with the boy, I didn't sleep with you, I don't get any shrimps and I do get scolded.

Ina Let's go and get shrimps now.

Chorus of assent and exteunt all, shrimping. I resume authorship.

Keable confided to Sadler that he was considering asking Ina Salmon to replace his Ilonka, who was ill and needed to leave the island, but he eventually decided on asking Kiki, a Czech-Slovak, to take over.

A few weeks after Ina Salmon's visit, Keable joined a trip to the nearby islands organised by two American friends who lived near him in Tautira: Knapp, who Keable had met on his first stay on the island, and Curtis, a pilot with the American forces in the First World War before coming to Tahiti. Curtis had persuaded three princesses to visit Rarotonga for the first time and convinced King Tiniaru to lend them all a house on the island. The Tahitian princesses were relations of Ina Salmon, Hotutu and her daughter, who they all called Tootsie, and Aretemoe. Tootsie was Curtis's girlfriend so, as Keable explained in a letter to Rita and Jack Elliott, there were rumours spread about him:

All Tahiti is buzzing with it to begin with. The current rumour is that I am eloping with Aretemoe. What proportions that rumour will have reached before we return, I don't know. Twins at least, I should think. So keep your eyes on the newspapers!

Seriously nothing would induce me to miss the chance, but I do think the *Daily Mirror* may get hold of something.

In the end, Keable and his party spent just over a month away. Rarotonga was two days away by boat, and they spent most of their time on the island. Keable wrote:

It is not a match on Tahiti for beauty, but more interestingly too, it is so distinctly western where Tahiti is Eastern. Tahiti has been spoiled enough, God knows, but with a different sort of spoliation. This is a bit of New Zealand; Tahiti is a bit of Indo-China, as it were. The capital of Rarotonga is a village of about ten European people's houses, Government buildings, a store or two, a rag-time cinema and perhaps 300 natives. But you should see the white ladies taking the air! Afternoon teas and cards!

Keable and Curtis did manage to spend some time travelling around some of the Cook Islands, taking canoes across the reefs to land and staying in traders' huts. Ultimately, the trip was most memorable for the amount of food and drink that he and the party consumed. Keable wrote:

One day we sat down at one o'clock at a native house to a loaded table of chicken, suckling pig, fish of all kinds, taro, kumeras, fruit and poi, and at 2.00 were informed that there was another feast as soon as we had finished in the next door house. We had to go, and it was just as plentiful! Imagine it. The others had to eat, I can always plead illness. The rest staggered home about 6.00 so full of food that they were bursting, and equally full of orange beer.

Keable wrote about the impact of prohibition on the island.

Rarotonga is dry. European men are allowed one bottle of whisky per month on the doctor's order, white ladies two bottles of wine; the natives nothing. The result is that I have never in my life seen so much drunkenness. Fact. Tahiti is nothing to it. Everybody brews beer with a terrific kick in it – which is also against the law, and everybody smuggles. So Mr A brews a beer, say 50 bottles for it is not worthwhile to brew less. Then he calls in half a dozen men to taste the brew – and they drink until it is all gone. At one party we were at, there were Curtis and I and three more men. The ladies only drank a little, I also because I am scared stiff of the stuff and its effect on me, but the other five cleared 66 bottles between midday and midnight. Curtis, who is partial to a drop, has scarcely been sober one night since we landed. And it is the same with whisky. The moment one man draws his ration, it goes at a sitting, plus the ladies' wine. In addition, it is the thing to have rum liquers, and so on, smuggled in. In Tahiti we drink a lot of rum punch and gin sling, but here they drink the rum or the gin neat in bottles-full. As for the natives, whereas in a spree in Tahiti they get a bit drunk, here, night after night, there is brewing in the bush or landing smuggled stores and drinking therefrom. The other day the skipper of a schooner got caught by a mistaken visit of the revenue officer with a bottle of rum in his cabin. He was fined five pounds, BUT he had landed the night before on the reef in canoes 50 cases. As rum sells here for 14/ a bottle – 3/ in Tahiti he did not much care.

Ina Salmon was annoyed with Keable when he returned from Rarotonga and seems to have tried to break off their relationship. Though her letter to Keable no longer exists, his reply does, kept by her son Henry Bonvalet. Keable wrote:

Ina darling and dearest,

Your letter yesterday has just arrived. It has driven me crazy. Ina you must love me. You couldn't write so if you did not. You want me, in certain moods, as companion, friend and lover. I refuse to give you up. Listen, our arrangements till the end of July shall stand… We'll see each other next Sunday, just exactly as much as we can and in all ways. You shall get to know me and I you.

What will happen? You may be bored to tears with me. I may be tired of you. If so that is life and we'll accept it. If not it will only be that I love you much and more than you me. In that case, you will come here to me when Kiki goes at the end of July and run the place for me – and run with it. Details can follow later. Then for future? Well, I shall have to go home, if well enough, next year. Your coming with me can depend on circumstances which we can talk over. But I shall certainly return. Tahiti is my home as much as yours. I love it more than you do. I want to live and die here. And I'll leave all my properties and affairs in your hands when I leave.

[Aretemoe] means nothing to me – and any other Tahiti girl. I can't help being me (and cautious) but it is you I love. I daresay I'm mad, but I love you, and you love me. You do? Really? Then please, oh please, Ina, don't look beyond. Life is too hard and short. Please love me.

So, at the beginning of August 1925, Ina Salmon moved permanently into Keable's house along with one child. (There is a photograph of her boy in Keable's car, but it seems her other child with Raoul Cornette de Saint Cyr had died.)

In *Numerous Treasure*, finished back in 1924, Keable wrote about George's decision to invite a mixed-race young woman to join his household.

It was not that she was not 'native'; he would not have liked it if she had not been native. George was far too sincere and convinced in his attitude towards civilisation... to want a wife in the European sense... If, now, he wanted Treasure, it was not merely because she was unusually good to look upon, but also because he was nearly convinced that she, and she almost alone so far as he knew... might be introduced into his establishment with success. She would not quarter her family upon him. It was quite possible that she would be reasonably faithful. It was almost certain that she had distinct taste, and more than that, he was inclined to believe that she could... learn to drive a car and mix cocktails and perhaps ultimately, order a dinner with intelligence.

There were other considerations also... He knew... what was the certain fate of Treasure if left to herself... she would be the mistress of a succession of tourists. She would ultimately become the woman of some native. She would almost certainly contract disease. George was no sentimentalist, but it seemed to him a waste.

Keable wrote this in a novel while he was living with Jolie, so it would be unfair to conclude that this was his view of Ina Salmon joining his household.

Ina Salmon was very different from the fictional *Numerous Treasure*, but she was also very different to Keable's European and American friends. A princess, but also someone who would be able to easily fit into his household, as happy to mix with both Keable's friends and with the servants, and other helpers, on the estate.

Keable was still very concerned about his health and was trying to stick to his strict diet. He explained to Jack Elliott that his trip to the islands had been an experiment to see if he was up to visiting England. He wrote:

> I have had a good deal of difficulty with my diet as I cannot get pastry cream or fresh butter and it is very hard to make up the calories, without the salt and excess proteins, from anything else. I have fallen back on figs (dried) and walnuts. But you can't eat figs or walnuts with barley porridge, and barley is far and away the best cereal there is. Still I have not exceeded the salt, though the proteins have been up. I don't know how bad protein may be for me. The result however seems to me to be that I might consider myself cured!

He decided he was strong enough to visit Europe. In July 1926, leaving Ina Salmon in charge of his house, he set off on the SS *Maunganui*, arriving in San Francisco thirteen days later. In America, local newspapers ran the story about Keable visiting the island of Rarotonga where, despite prohibition, he had seen 'more drunkenness there in a month than during a whole lifetime'. Another story, which seemed to amuse the press, was Keable's description of the favourite wife of King Tinirau Makea on Cook Island: 'as fat as sixteen pigs and she talks as much as ten American women'.

It may have been during this visit, while crossing America, that Keable met up with Alta Shaira, who lived in Brooklyn. She later wrote to Jack Elliott that she and Keable 'were close intimate friends and perhaps it is enough to say that [Keable] brought much that was beautiful into a troubled, hectic life'. Ina Salmon also wrote rather cryptically to Rita Elliott:

> By the way, what has become of the affair with a certain woman that I wrote your husband about? I have recently got a letter from a Rev Fletcher about it again. In a way I'm sorry for her but she's wicked.

Keable gave a series of talks and lectures while in America and Europe.

He was guest of honour at a dinner given by the Golden Gate Branch League of American Pen Women, where he gave a talk on 'Dressing the Heroine'. Reports suggested he 'gave personal experiences in the subject, introducing original ideas clothed with sparkling wit and scintillating humor'.

He also visited Prague, giving a talk there, and then spent a week in Glasgow in October, at the invitation of Mr McClelland, the secretary of a local literary society. The week in Glasgow had a big impact on him, as he was asked to preach a sermon for the first time since he left the priesthood seven years earlier. It was this that sparked the idea of writing a new book, later published as *The Great Galilean*, outlining his views on religion.

Keable spent Christmas 1926 with the Elliotts in Stokenchurch, paying what would be his last visit to his son, Tony. Tony was two at the time and remembered his father, whom according to the Elliotts he called 'more Daddy', coming into the nursery. Keable's present to him was toy horses.

In a letter a few months before, Keable had suggested that 'Aretemoe would be a splendid person to bring [Tony] out [to Tahiti]' as she 'was crazy over babies'. But there appears to have been no more discussion about taking Tony to Tahiti on this trip. Keable continued to send the Elliotts a quarterly cheque to pay for his son's upkeep, and he had also set up a small fund to help pay for his son's upbringing in the future. Most of his money was invested in property in Tahiti, which Tony was due to inherit.

After his return from England in February 1927, Ina Salmon quickly became pregnant. When Keable was in London, he clearly had not told Sadler that he was living with her. In a letter in March, he wrote:

> I think on the whole that things are going well here, though I am experimenting in Tahitianism as I have not done before and I can see disruptive elements on the horizon. Perhaps they will not blow up. If they do, and I feel as well as I do now, I shall just vamos.

This was the first time Keable had admitted to anyone back in England that his situation was changing. He knew that, for as long as Sybil Keable lived, he could never marry Ina Salmon. But he also knew that, if they had a child together, she would become his common-law wife. In Tahiti, that was not a problem. The French were unconcerned about mixed-race marriage, and many of Keable's friends – including Hall, Nordhoff and Stimson – had Tahitian wives.

However, elsewhere, there was huge prejudice and bigotry. In many states in America at the time, including the nearest to Tahiti – California – 'interracial' marriage was illegal. In England, many of Keable's family, friends and former acquaintances would have been scandalised. After his death, very few people discussed it and certainly his best friends, Jack and Rita Elliott – who only found out about the baby after Keable died – later did everything they could to prevent Ina Salmon having any contact with Keable's first son, Tony.

Keable wrote to Martha Smith at Constable:

As for females, you mistake. I have but one, a Tahitian princess and a dear who keeps my hands full… This morning I said to Ina at breakfast that I couldn't imagine a happier breakfast in the world. We were sitting on the patio, under masses of yellow trumpet allamanda and crimson bougainvillea, looking out at a sea streaked with every blue in the world by the rising sun, with hot rolls, glorious papaya (like big melons), loads of thick cream, home-made marmalade and wonderful home-grown coffee. Oh and fresh big eggs I had just gathered in the chicken runs. Wearing pareos, neither hot nor cold. All the day before us. Perfect.

Last week, though, we've been sitting by night in front of roaring log fires in the salon, playing chess that I've taught Ina. So comfty. A sort of Christmas tingle in the air, but of course our clothing is simple, which chiefly accounts for the fires. Moonlight. It is paradise.

Keable was pleased that the artist Robert Lee Eskridge, who came to stay, wished to paint Ina Salmon and commented that he was 'enamoured' of her. For many years the portrait was hung in pride of place in her son Henry's house in France, signed and dated: 'Eskridge, July 1927'.

Keable invited Alec Waugh, on his second trip to Tahiti, to come and stay. He described the visit in a letter to Martha:

Waugh arrived yesterday. *Entre nous*, a bit of a bore. These newcomers want so much nursing, often literally after a bit.

Waugh needed nursing because he had fallen desperately in love with a resident of Tahiti – Ruth Morris – and he was staying with Keable while he waited for news from Ruth that her husband was away.

Ina Salmon, portrait by Robert Eskridge, 1927

Ina Salmon, 1927

In 1962, Alec Waugh wrote about his stay with Keable:

He was now living in a common-law marriage with a Tahitian of a good family... his pre-war English congregation would have been astounded could they have seen him reclined among the cushions, clad only in a *pareo*, while his Tahitian princess, bare-shouldered and bare-footed, her black hair falling to her waist and a white flower behind her ear, glided negligently about the house… He talked openly about [Jolie] and how you had to go on living, even if you were broken-hearted; that you had to adjust yourself to the second best.

Whether or not Keable thought Ina Salmon was 'second-best', she certainly felt she lived in the shadow of Jolie Keable, not least because there was a large portrait of her in the main room. Ina Salmon later wrote to Rita Elliott after Keable's death:

I had always doubted his love because during our friendship he often talked to me about [Jolie Keable] and that he could never love again, and I so proudly (Rita I'm awfully proud of my race I'm sorry to confess) loved him that if he gave me time I would make him love me as he has never before in his life. I won – Rita, only too late. He confessed it in a last letter written to me – before the end.

How much did he love her? In his novel *Lighten Our Darkness*, published in 1927, Keable explained his theory of love, suggesting three types. First, 'instinctive or animal love:

none the worse for being animal… that sort of love is pure chemistry – a matter for the biological laboratory. It's just sex – something that evolved out of a volvox colony of protozoa.' Secondly, 'emotional love – human only': 'a result of civilisation. Maybe… a throw-off on the road up'. And thirdly, 'conscious love – a rare, rare thing': 'it does not love for itself; it loves for the other. It's the highest thing there is and when it comes to people the gods have smiled upon them'.

He explained his theory to Alec Waugh, who wrote:

I made no comment, but it struck me as a sentimental and false thesis of the kind that was not acceptable to the readers of glossy magazines… That was why Keable was not a better writer. He saw life in terms of magazine psychology.

Lighten Our Darkness was the only novel that Keable wrote, in its entirety, while in Tahiti. It tells the story of Richard Thurstan – a Roman Catholic missionary in South Africa after the First World War – who leaves the priesthood and returns to England. There he meets Lady Ann Carew, who has had an affair during the war and has returned to England to announce that she is leaving her husband, Lord Carew. Ann and Richard then run away together, travelling together on a trip round Europe and North Africa. After the book was published, Sadler wrote to Keable:

A misfortune… which overtook [*Lighten Our Darkness*] was that WH Smith in one of their periodic fits of prudery at the eleventh hour took exception to the bedroom scene between Ann and Richard. Of course it is out of the question to alter a thirty thousand edition just because Smith did not like one sentence, but undeniably their disfavour has harmed and is harming the book because instead of pushing its sale through all their hundreds of branches they are just sitting on their moderate initial order and dolling out copies when their customers insist on having them.

Although Sadler does not specify which section so offended WH Smith, it could have been the lines:

the fire of passion has torn through her as she had not thought possible. She had clung to him as if she could never let him go. She had lain in his arms utterly spent.

Sadler also did not mention whether WH Smith objected to the novel's cover, which depicts a naked woman standing on a beach in front of a cave, arms and face stretched upwards towards a stream of light that fills the entrance to the cave.

Further misfortune was to fall the book thanks to Keable calling the main character in the book Lady Carew. Sadler explained to Keable in March 1927:

It appears that there really is a man called Lord Carew and we had a letter from him this morning in which, not surprisingly, he takes exception to the character and behaviour of the Lord and Lady Carew in your novel. At first the situation looked dangerous because it would have been quite impossible to call in all the copies that had gone out

Cover for Lighten Our Darkness

and even to scrap the balance of the original very large edition would have meant a serious loss.

Mr Kyllmann from Constable was sent to negotiate:

> We found the gentleman to be a simple friendly little man of about 65 who was rather more distressed than angry at the possibility of his wife being confused with the heroine of *Lighten Our Darkness* and he and Kyllmann parted excellent friends. In effect I gather nothing is to be done except that it would be very well received if you were to write personally to Lord Carew to express regret that by inadvertence his name should have been used.

The Tech newspaper in America described the novel – renamed there *Ann Decides* – as 'a remarkably effective well-written book', though adding, 'Keable's books have the reputation of being a bit frank, a trifle disconcerting in the philosophy which underlies them'.

Keable had no illusions about his talent as a writer. After reading novels by Naomi Royde-Smith and Margaret Storm Jameson, he wrote:

The Housemaid and *The Three Kingdoms* left me miserable. They are so clever... I felt like having 'novelist' removed from my passport; I would if I only knew what to put instead. If you leave it blank, they write you down as a 'gentleman of means' and tax you accordingly. Once I said 'writer' and went down as 'clerk'. 'Journalist' I cannot say. I think next time I shall say 'poet'. Then nothing will be expected of me and all will be forgiven. But by the side of Storm Jameson and Miss Royde-Smith, novelist I am not.

After Keable returned from England in 1927, he enjoyed a lively few months. He continued to invite guests, including bestselling novelist Zane Grey, who in return invited Keable onto his boat so Keable could watch him fight a fish for six and a half hours. Grey had another boat rigged with a film camera and his own private operator to makes movies of his catch. For the resulting film, the cameraman got fifty dollars a foot.

Keable was also busy helping travellers who were struggling for money. Two American artists stayed for a few weeks, and he commissioned them to do some work for him.

Both of them have now been staying with me a fortnight and I expect will go on for two months. We have become great friends. One is a well-known artist, the other a young artist and woodcarver. The latter carved the posts of my bed into Tahitian gods – perfectly delightfully, the other has painted odd places on my walls.

After they left, a French couple arrived whom he described as:

A French author and a friend who have made a mistake and have got now to have a baby. They are friendless and broke so we are taking them in. Rather jolly.

By now, Keable's house was on the tourist trail and a succession of tourists and unexpected visitors came calling. He complained about three American women who turned up claiming his acquaintance, since he had once met them on the mail steamer going to San Francisco. He told Rita Elliott:

One was a mother with a daughter, for whom I think she had designs which were rudely shaken by the sight of Ina. However, having come so far, they thought they might as well get what they could out of me. But I had a mild revenge. Having fed them, I took them out in the launch – which gloriously and completely broke down. I went overboard to see what I could do (having exhausted my wits within) and the daughter followed in a pareo. The pareo came off in the water as they have a way of doing if you are not used to them and sank. I had to dive for it while the young lady waited in the costume of Eve, literally. She spoilt all her chances. She bulged with fat before and behind, especially behind, and she was pimply. However it broke the ice and I took them next day to Hitiaa, where Lili runs around the beach in an old pair of drawers and nothing else. So they had their thrills all right.

Keable also told Rita about a new maid he had employed. Ina Salmon learnt from their gardener that the maid had gonorrhoea, so Keable took her to the local doctor in Taravao. He knew that if it became officially known that she had the disease, she would be made to report for examination every fortnight at the hospital. However, at the doctor's, she refused to be examined even though Keable warned her to choose between private treatment by a doctor he knew and exposure to the authorities in town. Returning home, Keable was annoyed when she ran off to the cinema without leave, and came back at four in the morning with two men! He explained:

I sent her off to town on the truck, and she had hardly gone before the other maids discovered she had stolen fine chemises from them. I saw absolutely red. Jumped into the car, fetched the police and a warrant, and went straight off to her home, discovered the stolen property in her possession, and had her arrested. Then I informed the medical people of her condition.

Towards the end of the summer, Keable seems to have become increasingly eccentric, perhaps because his failing kidneys started to cause mental confusion. The children of Keable's neighbour, Mauu, said he was: 'going nuts and seeing tupapous [ghosts] and firing pistols off at them'.

In August 1927, Keable began dictating his final work, *The Great Galilean*, to Hall, whom he had taken on as his secretary. Keable was ill, his eyesight was failing, and he wanted to finish the book as quickly as he could. The thesis of the book is that there are two different Christs – the historical Christ – the Jesus who actually lived and about whom we know very little – and the traditional Christ – the Christ of the Church, manufactured over 2,000 years and interpreted and re-interpreted by hundreds of different Christian churches.

The book was serialised and published after Keable died. Many accepted Keable's view that we know very little of the story of the real Jesus and his teaching, but most reviewers did point out that Keable's ideas on what a common-sense Jesus must have believed are, in fact, Keable's own views. *The Times* suggested:

> The late Robert Keable had much talent and more sincerity. The posthumous book of his reminds us forcibly that there are qualities more important than talent, and that sincerity is a virtue only when combined with other virtues. *The Great Galilean* is a remarkable book, but it is remarkable chiefly for its radical incoherence and for an extraordinary sophistication… It is evidently a supreme effort to reconcile his own personal convictions with some ineradicable traces of his former Christianity. It is perfectly sincere but it is perfect humbug.

The book does, at least, give us an insight into what Keable believed at the time. He explained one reason why he had given up the priesthood was because he disliked the idea that a successful priest had to resort to extravagant preaching, which he claimed most of the congregation found belittling and pathetic. He also disliked the fact that priests had become the judge and jury of moral behaviour – in America, preaching the evils of whisky, in England, the evils of divorce and prostitution. Furthermore, he suggested priests had become glorified bureaucrats, spending their time in 'intricate organisations and committee work'. Ultimately, he admitted his biggest concern was that the ministry 'is commissioned to preach a gospel which is not [Christ's], and to administer sacraments which [Christ] did not institute'.

He also discussed his support of pacificism and the need for a fairer division of wealth. He repeated many of his well-publicised views on marriage, adultery, divorce and free love, as well as sex.

> If [Christ] was never in love with a woman himself, he was no man at all if he did not know that the average man usually is. If sex was

a secondary thing to him, he would have been a nincompoop if he had not been aware that it was a primary thing in most men's lives.

His view on birth control was equally forthright:

Nature ought to reward only a spiritual and bodily union in love with the gift of a child, but unfortunately she so equally rewards the union conceived in a drunken fit or in simple animal lust… this matter of birth control is a matter on which we have scarcely as yet dared to tackle [nature]. Common-sense men and women are increasingly coming to feel that we ought to do so, but unfortunately two lions still roar in the path of these new Christians. And what a tragedy it is that one is too often religion, and the other, often, law!

There is no suggestion in *The Great Galilean* that Keable was intending to rejoin the Church, but after his death there were rumours that he might have tried to join the Roman Catholic Church, and even that he had a death bed conversion. This seems very unlikely. Once he left the priesthood, he had gradually become an atheist, and he never showed any true signs that he was regaining his faith. In 1926, he was asked to give a donation towards a new Catholic church in Dunstable, and wrote, uncharitably:

I think it would be better for the future of the human race, that there should not be a Catholic church in the town, and on the whole I would rather for fifty Catholics remained lapsed into paganism.

When asked in 1927 by an American newspaper to choose just one book to take into exile, he elected to take the Bible, stating that he would try to put the minor prophets into English verse and that he wanted to reread 'the most beautiful historical fiction the world has ever produced'.

*

The first hint that Keable's friends in England had that he was ill again came in a letter sent in August 1927. Keable wrote: 'I am very well, only my eyes trouble me. I hope I am not going to have trouble with them'. Ironically, a month before, he had written to his father:

People are always saying how well I look, 'never better'. The Wilders...
whom I have not seen for two years and whom I have been entertaining
this month, seem to think me some sort of miracle.

By September, Keable was worried. 'My eyes have given in as last 1925, so
that I can't see to read or write at all with right eye and only a little with left'. It
is likely that high blood pressure as a result of a kidney infection had affected
the optic nerve, as had been the case in 1925. By the middle of October, he
wasn't well enough to write and had to dictate a letter to Sadler:

I am writing to you this mail because my friend Norman Hall is kindly
acting as my secretary. My eyes are no better and I have in addition a
nasty attack of some sort of influenza that is going the rounds of the
island. It went for my kidneys, which are my weak spot, and I have
been in bed nearly all month with considerable pain.

It is quite a long letter, but he did not mention that he was about to
become a father again. In November, Ina Salmon gave birth to Keable's
second son, Henry, as Keable lay ill in bed in a room next door. In a Bible,
which Henry still had nearly eighty years later, Keable wrote:

Whoever can listen to the cries of the woman he loves in childbirth
and still believes in a Father-God is devoid of imagination and
humanity like the brute beast. Tahiti 10th Nov 1927 4.00pm

Hall recalled meeting Keable with Ina Salmon in Papeete, a month later:

[I] met him that day and we had lunch together, and he seemed to
me to be in much better health and spirits than usual. He was full of
plans for a little Christmas party he meant to give to the children in
Papeari, the district where he lived, and he was expecting a box of toys
and Christmas tree ornaments he had ordered from Australia. That
was always the way with [Keable]: planning things to give pleasure to
others.

A few days later, Ina Salmon wrote to Hall to say Keable was not feeling
well and was resting in bed. Dr Cassiau, the principal doctor on the island,

contacted Hall to report that Keable's condition was serious. Hall later wrote:

> I went to Papeari at once, and Ina and I and two other friends of [Keable]'s nursed him until the end. Two physicians were in attendance and everything possible was done to help him win his battle. But he couldn't pass his urine, the poison went into his blood and from that he died.

Keable was only just forty.

His obituaries reported that he had died of Bright's disease, a chronic inflammation of the kidneys which also affected his eyesight. In the 1920s, there was little effective treatment for kidney disease. The first successful kidney transplant did not take place until the 1950s.

Hall organised the funeral and death certificate – by mistake he wrote down that Keable was forty-one when he died, the age that appeared on Keable's gravestone – and he informed Keable's family. To Keable's father, he wrote:

> Life can be horribly cruel, and so it has been in [Keable's] case, it seems to me. He had just gotten to the point where he was ready really to enjoy life; and you know, of course, of his little son born about two months ago?

He added, 'Ina has been splendid all the way through. She is heart-broken but has borne up wonderfully well...'

After Keable's death, his body was taken to Salmon's sister's house in Papeete, and after a service at the Protestant church, he was buried in Uranie Cemetery, according to Hall 'a very peaceful and well-kept burying ground in a little valley just beyond the town and opening out towards the sea'. Keable's grave was marked by a simple stone coated in white plaster which weathered so poorly that, seventy years later, one could no longer read the inscription.

*

A month before he died, Keable wrote a new will leaving all of his money and property on Tahiti to his second son, Henry. Keable's first son, Tony, who never got to see his father's house on Tahiti, was left enough money for his education, but when he was twenty-one, he was shown his father's letter, which told him, 'it is better you should hoe cabbages living by your own strength – than live in a palace on my money'. At eighteen, the capital sum providing funds for his education was transferred to Magdalene College, Cambridge, so they could begin financing scholarships for boys from Whitgift School.

Tony continued to live with the Elliotts, changing his surname to Keable-Elliott when he reached eighteen and training as a doctor, eventually taking over the practice in Stokenchurch. He became an active member of the British Medical Association, for which he was made an OBE by the Queen and received the prestigious gold medal from the BMA for his services as the association treasurer. He died in 2020, aged ninety-five.

Hugh Cecil explained what became of Keable's wife when she returned from her teaching job in South Africa:

[Sybil Keable] lived on, her religion increasingly important to her. She stayed at first at her brother's house, but kind and tolerant though he was, he found her personally too strong at close quarters and had to ask her to leave. Thereafter she lodged in Catholic convents until she died in 1970 at St. Mary's Abbey, Mill Hill.

After Keable's death, Ina Salmon stayed on in the house along with two of her sisters. According to a neighbour, Star Mauu, who had been four at the time, Salmon continued to entertain in the style that Keable had over the years, with loud music throughout the night and crates of champagne supplied by *le truck*, the island's delivery service. Nine months after Keable's death, Salmon married Cyril (Bill) Wainwright, a thirty-year-old Englishman. They had a daughter, Elizabeth, but divorced soon after and Ina Salmon married Albert Bonvalet in 1933. In 1935, she left Tahiti with her husband, Henry Keable and another boy, Albert Bonvalet. The couple settled in Lyon, where they lived until her husband died.

Surprisingly for Tahiti, where regular cyclones and fast weathering have destroyed most houses of that time, Keable's bungalow, designed with three sides part enclosing a small courtyard, still stands. For many years, Ina Salmon rented out the house. Fred Devenish remembered among others a beekeeper called Sechrist; a pilot called Alex Cross; and a relation of Rupert Brooke, Peter Brooke, who tried to turn it into a restaurant and hotel in

Robert Keable's renovated grave

the early 1950s. A French pilot nicknamed the 'French Lindeberg', Andre Jupy, bought the house from Ina Salmon after the Second World War and renovated it, removing the central pond and fountain, knocking through some of the rooms and roofing over the courtyard. Perhaps fittingly, an Englishman, Roger Gowen – who was shipwrecked on a reef off Tahiti during a round-the-world voyage – bought the house in the 1960s, and he and his wife, Juliette, have looked after it with great care ever since. The original flooring and roof tiles, imported from California, are still in place, although the fireplace and chimney, which Keable claimed was the first one on the island, have gone. Many of Keable's books – of the 3,000 he claimed, in 1927, to have in his library – are still in the house, each with Keable's distinctive bookplate, designed by Sidney Hunt, featuring hermits in contemplation, with the line, 'My sonne seeke wisdome from thy youth up'. (Taken from the Ecclesiasticus verse: 'My son, gather instruction from thy youth up: so shalt thou find wisdom till thine old age'.)

The Gowens and their daughter, Lee Moy, recently renovated Keable's burial plot in Uranie Cemetery, replacing the gravestone so that one can read the inscription again. Ina's ashes were buried beside Keable's grave, marked by a small plaque that still leans up against Keable's gravestone, stating simply:

'In memory of Mamy Salmon Ina 1900–1978'

CHAPTER 17

SIMON CALLED PETER FROM THE GREAT GATSBY
TO TODAY

By coincidence, Ina Salmon, the Tahitian princess – who was Keable's partner at the end of his life – lived and was educated in St Paul, Minnesota, when she first stayed in America, the same town where F Scott Fitzgerald, who so disliked *Simon Called Peter*, was born, spent much of his early life and wrote his novel *The Beautiful and Damned*.

Fitzgerald began writing *The Great Gatsby* in June 1922, a few months after *Simon Called Peter* was published in America. He had just returned from a three-month holiday in France with his wife, Zelda. A few months later, they moved to New York where he continued with his masterpiece, before finally completing it – many drafts later – on a trip to the French Riviera during the summer of 1924. The novel was finally published in April 1925.

When Fitzgerald first read *Simon Called Peter*, he did not publicly comment on it. Then in early March 1923, in his *New York Herald* review of another book, *Of Many Marriages* by Sherwood Anderson, he wrote:

> There is a recent piece of trash entitled *Simon Called Peter* which seems to me utterly immoral, because the characters move in a continued labyrinth of mild sexual stimulation. Over this stimulation play the coloured lights of romantic Christianity.

Calling a novel 'utterly immoral' is quite a charge, and Fitzgerald repeated the 'immoral' claim in June that year when, in a piece for *The Literary Digest*, where he was commenting on Supreme Court Justice Ford's campaign against unclean books, he wrote that *Simon Called Peter* was 'really immoral'.

When Fitzgerald submitted *The Great Gatsby* manuscript to his publisher Maxwell Perkins, he asked: 'in Chapter II of my book when Tom and Myrtle go into the bedroom while Carraway reads *Simon Called Peter* – is that raw? Let me know. I think it's pretty necessary'.

Fitzgerald references *Simon Called Peter* twice in *The Great Gatsby*. A description of the living room in Myrtle Wilson's apartment includes the sentence:

> Several old copies of *Town Tattle* lay on the same table together with a copy of *Simon Called Peter*, and some of the small scandal magazines of Broadway.

In the next paragraph, after the narrator, Nick Carraway, has left the apartment to buy cigarettes, he says:

> When I came back they had both disappeared, so I sat down discreetly in the living-room and read a chapter of *Simon Called Peter* – either it was terrible stuff or the whisky distorted things, because it didn't make any sense to me.

Fitzgerald was referencing a very well-known novel. In the 1920s, very few people read Fitzgerald's novel and indeed, by the time of his death in 1940, *The Great Gatsby* had sold only 25,000 copies. In comparison, within five years of its publication, *Simon Called Peter* had sold twenty times that many. In America, Fitzgerald's *The Beautiful and Damned* came out at the same time as *Simon Called Peter* and was also outsold. Fitzgerald would have found it galling to see Keable's novel have so much more success than his own.

Fitzgerald may have also known that Keable was seen as a serious author. In the short period after *Simon Called Peter* was published, he became a literary star. He was invited to submit short stories to Volumes 3 and 4 of the *New Decameron*, which included stories by DH Lawrence, Vita Sackville-West, JD Beresford and Compton Mackenzie. He was also commissioned to write an article for a book on censorship called *Nonsenseorship* alongside, among others, Dorothy Parker, Wallace Irwin and Ben Hecht.

Sarah Churchwell, in *Careless People: Murder, Mayhem and the Invention of The Great Gatsby*, suggests that mentioning *Simon Called Peter* in the early scene in the book would remove any doubts about the adulterous activities of Tom Buchanan and his mistress, Myrtle Wilson, since 'for men like John Sumner (the executive secretary of the New York Society for the Suppression of Vice), merely reading *Simon Called Peter* was to be caught *in flagrante delicto*'. The scene itself is discreetly described. There is no mention of Tom and Myrtle going to the bedroom, simply that when Carraway returned from the drug store 'they had both disappeared', and after Carraway had read a chapter of *Simon Called Peter*, 'Tom and Myrtle… reappeared'.

But there were other reasons Fitzgerald referenced *Simon Called Peter*. For a start, having Nick think *Simon Called Peter*'s 'terrible stuff', which 'didn't make any sense', would have been seen by contemporary readers as an attack on Keable, and on his novel.

Fitzgerald also wanted to add to his portrait of Myrtle Wilson, Tom Buchanan's mistress, by suggesting she was the sort of woman who read gossip magazines and trashy novels. Fitzgerald chose his words, and references, very carefully. He could have chosen any gossip magazine to place on Myrtle's table, but as Sharon Hamilton explained in her article for the *F Scott Fitzgerald Review*, contemporary readers would have known *Town Tattle* was referring to the magazine *Town Topics*, which gossiped about wealthy Long Islanders and had mentioned Scott and Zelda as 'drunks' in one copy. Similarly, he could have chosen a different 'trashy' novel, but *Simon Called Peter* was notorious. Notorious thanks to the gruesome murders of Hall and Mills that had fascinated Americans throughout the autumn of 1922, while Fitzgerald was working on *The Great Gatsby* at his home in New York. *Simon Called Peter* had been much cited in the coverage that followed the murders.

Sarah Churchwell suggests that not only was Fitzgerald fully aware of the Hall and Mills murders but that he developed the key themes of class warfare, forbidden passion and murderous jealousy from the double murder case. So, another reason for mentioning *Simon Called Peter* in *The Great Gatsby* was that it allowed Fitzgerald to draw his contemporary readers to the Hall–Mills case and, in doing so, prewarn them of the deaths of Myrtle, Gatsby and George at the end of his novel.

*

Throughout his life, *Simon Called Peter* sold well, and when Keable died at the end of 1927 it allowed his obituary writers a chance to reassess the novel.

Sadler, his publisher, was not surprisingly the most generous. He wrote in *The Times*:

> Many were offended by *Simon Called Peter* but very few were bored by it. And indeed boredom must melt before the flames of life-love and of burning indignation which blazed through those often strident pages. With all its crudities *Simon Called Peter* is a great novel, because it was written from the heart of a man who had both intellect and passion who loved religion and loved life equally, and could not endure an interpretation of the former which denied the latter.

The obituary in *The Truth* suggested the novel was 'one of the few really moving works of fiction that the war inspired... It was daring but not erotic', while the *Western Mail* stated that the novel had been 'described by all the critics of the time as the most vivid picture of life behind the firing line in the Great War', and suggested it made Keable 'famous wherever English is read, and secured for him a host of affectionate admirers'.

The *Newcastle Daily Chronicle* believed that *Simon Called Peter* would 'long keep [Keable] in remembrance', but Father Bede Jarrett in his obituary in *Blackfriars Magazine* disagreed, writing:

> We are sorry to think his books will not live. For all his vigour, they suffer from the trail of mire over them. They seem to have been fleshy for the sake of being fleshy, they seem to be frank for the mere sake of saying what does not gain by being said.

In Australia, news of Keable's death was covered in many papers, with journalists commenting on *Simon Called Peter*, including the *Sydney Daily Telegraph*:

> Everyone said it was 'daring'. Some used a stronger word. At any rate, it made Keable, who had been a very hard-up young clergyman, a literary world-figure.

In *The Australian*, it was suggested that the novel had been a bestseller because Keable had taken 'a certain freedom in choice of material and in treatment' but concluded it had 'small literary value'.

Sales of *Simon Called Peter* peaked in the 1920s, but the novel continued to sell steadily throughout the 1930s. Hurst and Blackett took over the rights in 1931. Over that decade, they sold 215,000 copies of a cheap 9d edition, as well as 34,000 copies of a 2/- edition, and 9,000 of a 2s/6d edition.

In Australia, it was still being discussed in the papers as an important novel. In 1934, Walter Hutchinson was reported as saying the greatest regret of his publishing life had been taking a day off from the office on the very day that *Simon Called Peter* was offered to his firm. He said that his father Sir George Thompson Hutchinson's decision to reject it was 'one of the quickest and most unfortunate decisions ever made by a publisher'. In an attempt to put things right, when Hutchinson launched their 'Pocket Library' in 1935, in response to the success of Penguin books, *Simon Called Peter* was chosen as the twelfth book in the series. On the title page, they suggested that over 500,000 copies of the book had already been sold.

In 1939, Constable took back the rights and continued to sell copies throughout the war. Dutton renewed their rights for *Simon Called Peter* in America in 1948, but by then sales were very low.

Dr Douglas, in the late 1950s, was the first serious biographer to re-examine the work of Keable. He believed *Simon Called Peter* was an important novel because of its 'courage, vitality and immense sincerity'. He also praised the novel for presenting 'soldiers as they really were' and for writing 'a love story of a Padre who sacrificed career and vows to the principle of comradeship, and to the recklessness of human passion'.

Claud Cockburn, the journalist and author, examined the novel in his book *Bestsellers*, published in 1972. He argued that the novel had been a success because it offered women readers the opportunity for both identification and anti-identification. The inadequacy and lack of understanding of Peter's fiancée, Hilda – who Cockburn called a 'coarse-grained bitch' – allowed for anti-identification, while readers could identify with Julie since she:

> not only gives [Peter] a wonderful time in bed but in the end agonizedly refuses to marry him because his love for her is going to interfere with his love of God.

Cockburn mocked both the plot and the main characters, suggesting that

Peter, 'after a lot of soul-searching and acute women trouble, comes up with approximately the same explanation of everything!'

At the end of 1977, the copyright on *Simon Called Peter* expired in the UK and today the book is now freely available online and in cheap print copies. Versions are advertised with anachronistic cover pictures – including one with a girl in an eighteenth-century bonnet, and a second with four Roman soldiers – as well as overblown claims: 'an astounding novel, the most delicate, the most beautiful, and the most outspoken love story of modern fiction'.

Hugh Cecil reassessed *Simon Called Peter* in *The Flower of Battle*, his book on British fiction writers of the First World War, published in 1995. He explained *Simon Called Peter*'s popularity:

> Firstly it was vividly written and fast-moving. Secondly albeit moral in its way, it took a tilt at Victorian sexual hypocrisy and conventional English religion, both contemporary targets for attack; but it also stresses hope and self-realisation... Thirdly... it was... an absolutely authentic account of a padre's experience.

In 2005, the American academic J Gregory Brister suggested that *Simon Called Peter* was one of the first important modernist novels, though he has since argued that many post-war novels had modernist passages, not only *Simon Called Peter*. What is certain is that the character of Julie was seen by many, in 1922, as very modern – portrayed as she was as fun-loving and free from guilt.

Sara Haslam disputed any modernist claims for the novel, arguing that it lacked originality and presented war as an opportunity for personal and moral development, which she saw as a 'far cry from the modernists' dazzling and deafening "equinoctial storm"'.

George Simmers, who wrote his PhD on the fiction of the Great War, believed that what was most interesting about *Simon Called Peter* was that it was a war novel with no fighting. So 'while it belongs to a standard genre – man goes to war and discovers the realities of life – his discoveries are not the usual ones, but all about sex'. Simmers was intrigued by the background of the book with the 'descriptions of officers with their Kirschner pin-ups and their whisky, and their liaisons with French girls'. His conclusion was that the novel was both cleverly written and artless.

There is no doubt that *Simon Called Peter* is a book of its time, and some readers today struggle with the style of writing. Written in just three weeks, it lacks the craft and subtlety of a great novel. It is, however, an important novel, especially for anyone seeking a truthful picture of life in France during the First World War from someone who was there. Keable would perhaps have preferred to be remembered for his work in Africa or his time in Tahiti, but few are allowed the luxury of deciding that, and he will always be remembered as the author of *Simon Called Peter*.

A note on sources

Michael Sadler, Robert Keable's friend and publisher, changed his surname to Sadlier, so as not to be confused with his father, but I have called him Sadler throughout.

Below is a list of the archives, libraries and the books and articles I have consulted, so that the interested reader will be able to locate the material on which I have drawn.

Robert Keable's books

The Perpetual Sacrifice (Nisbet & Co, 1912)

Darkness or Light (UMCA, 1912)

A City of the Dawn (Nisbet & Co, 1915)

The Adventures of Paul Kangai (UMCA, 1918)

The Loneliness of Christ (Nisbet & Co, 1915)

This Same Jesus: Meditations on the Manifestations of Christ To-day (Nisbet & Co, 1918)

Standing By: War-time Reflections in France and Flanders (Nisbet & Co, 1919)

The Drift of Pinions (Skeffington and Son, 1918)

Missionary Stories: African Scout Stories (SPCK, 1919)

Pilgrim Papers, from the Writings of Francis Thomas Wilfrid, Priest (Christophers, 1920)

Simon Called Peter (Constable & Co Ltd, 1921)

The Mother of All Living (Constable & Co Ltd, 1922)

Peradventure or The Silence of God (Constable & Co Ltd, 1922)

Recompense (Constable & Co Ltd, 1924)

Numerous Treasure (Constable & Co Ltd, 1925)

Tahiti, Isle of Dreams (Hutchinson & Co, 1925)

Lighten Our Darkness (Constable & Co, 1927), also known as *Ann Decides* (GP
   Putnam's, 1927)

The Madness of Monty (Nisbet & Co, 1928), also known as *Though This Be
   Madness* (GP Putnam's, 1928)

The Great Galilean (Cassell & Co, 1928)

ROBERT KEABLE'S ARTICLES AND SHORT STORIES

'A Wanderer on Wireless', *Radio Times*, 27 June 1924, p 2

'African Priests in France', *The East & the West: A Quarterly Review for the Study
   of Missionary Problems*, January 1918

'Bohemian and Rebel in the World's Garden' *Asia*, November 1924

'Denies Cocktail is American', *The New York Times*, 21 June 1925, p 14

'From Known to Unknown', *Atlantic Monthly*, April 1928, pp 435–436

'From the House of Gauguin', *Century Magazine*, 1923, pp 765–772

'New trumpets and old uncertainties', *Blackfriars*, April 1921, pp 15–24

'Of the Universities' Mission to Central Africa, Sermon Preached at St Barnabas,
   Pimlico on the Feast of St Luke', *Church Times*, 23 October 1914

'Participating in the Great Adventure', *Atlantic Monthly*, March 1926, pp 310–
   319

'Peace… Where There Is No Peace', *Blackfriars*, May 1921, pp 67–75

'A People of Dreams', *Hibbert Journal*, 1920, pp 522–531

'The Priest's Tale, Pere Etienne', *The New Decameron, 3rd Volume* (Basil Blackwell,
   1922)

'The Late Extra', *The New Decameron, 4th Volume* (Basil Blackwell, 1925)

'Slave, Serf, Citizen and the Way Back', *Blackfriars*, December 1920, pp 503–564

'Sword of Pizzaro', *Blackfriars*, January 1920, pp 585–590)

'Tahitian Visitors', *Asia*, 1926, pp 422–427, 455–457

'The Censorship of Truth', *Nonsenseorship* (GP Putnam's Sons, 1922)

'The Worth of an African', *International Review of Mission*, 1918, pp 319–332

ROBERT KEABLE'S PRIVATE LETTERS AND OTHER PRIVATE PAPERS

Buck, William Stucley Beresford, letter to his daughters Anne and Pamela, 14
   December 1955 (private collection of author)

Dean, Basil, letters to Robert Keable, December 1919 (Rylands Library,
   Manchester University)

Douglas, Dr JD, letters from friends and relatives of Robert Keable, 1959–1961 (private collection of author)

Dutton, EP, letters written to and from Robert Keable and private papers relating to Robert Keable's works (EP Dutton and Co records, Special Collections Research Center, Syracuse University Libraries, Box 44, six folders)

Keable, Robert, letters written to Rita Elliott (private collection of author)

Keable, Robert, letter written to his son Tony Keable-Elliott (private collection of author)

Keable, Robert, letter to Mr McClelland, 24 October 1926 (private collection of author)

Keable, Robert, letter to Arthur Grimble, 27 September 1921 (private collection of author)

Sadler, Michael, letters to and from Robert Keable 1921–1927 and papers relating to Robert Keable's works' (Constable & Co records, Special Collections Research Centre, Temple University Libraries, Series 1. Correspondence, Box 8, Folders 34 & 35)

Watts, AP, Robert Keable letters to and from AP Watt and papers relating to Robert Keable's works' (AP Watts records, 1888–1982 (#11036), Rare Book Literacy and Historical papers, Louis Round Wilson Special Collections Library, the University of North Carolina at Chapel Hill, 46 folders in boxes ranging from Box 170 to Box 453)

SOURCES OF NEWSPAPER ARTICLES

Allen's Indian Mail, November 1858, https://newspaperarchive.com

Canadian Soldiers.com, https://www.canadiansoldiers.com/corpsbranches/forestrycorps.htm

Hindustan Times, Ghosts of Beresford family, 6 January 2008

Historic American newspapers, https://chroniclingamerica.loc.gov

Ilanga Lase, Letter by NATIVE, 10 May 1918

Leeze Zabaatsaadu, 'Letter from Archbishop of Capetown', 2 July 1918

New York Times archives, https://www.nytimes.com/search

Tablet, 'Review of *Blackfriars*', 11 December 1920, p 787

Church Times, articles and letter from 1904 to 1927, https://www.churchtimes.co.uk/archive

Books and Articles Used in the Writing
of This Book

Anderson, Warwick, *Hybridity, Race and Science, the Voyage of the Zaca, 1934–1935* (University of Chicago Press, June 2012)

Beinart, William (and Bundy, Colin), *Hidden Struggles in Rural South Africa: Politics and Popular Movements in the Transkei and Eastern Cape, 1890–1930* (North America: University of California Press, 1997)

Bell, Mandy J, 'A Historical Overview of Preeclampsia-Eclampsia', *J Obstet Gynecol Neonatal Nurs*, September 2010, pp 510–518

Biddle, George, *Tahitian Journal* (University of Minnesota Press, 1968)

Briand, Paul L Jr, *In Search of Paradise, The Nordhoff–Hall Story* (Mutual Publishing, 2007)

Brister, J Gregory, 'It Didn't Make Sense to Me: Robert Keable's Simon Called Peter and Popular Modernism', paper presented in a symposium on Pulp Modernism: Print Culture and the Avant-Garde. Modernist Studies Association Conference, November 2005

Brown, Alison M, 'Army Chaplains in the First World War', PhD thesis, University of St Andrews, 1996

Bruccoli, Matthew, Baughman, Judith S (editors), *A Life in Letters by F Scott Fitzgerald (Author)* (Scribner, July 1994)

Carter, David, 'The Conditions of Fame, Literary Celebrity in Australia between the Wars', *Journal of Modern Literature*, Vol. 39, 2015, pp 170–187

Casado, Carmelo Medina, 'Sifting through Censorship: The British Home Office "Ulysses" Files (1922–1936)', *James Joyce Quarterly*, Vol. 37, no. 3/4, University of Tulsa, 2000, pp 479–508, http://www.jstor.org/stable/25477754

Cecil, Hugh, *The Flower of Battle, British Fiction Writers of the First World War* (Secker and Warburg, 1995)

Chamberlain, Geoffrey 'British Maternal Mortality in the 19th and early 20th Centuries', *J R Soc Med*, November 2006, pp 559–563

Churton, Tobias, *Aleister Crowley: The Beast in Berlin: Art, Sex, and Magick in the Weimar Republic* (Simon & Schuster, 2014)

Churchwell, Sarah, *Careless People: Murder, Mayhem and the Invention of The Great Gatsby* (Virago, 2013)

Clayton, Joseph, 'Robert Keable: Some Personal Recollections', *The Bookman*, February 1928

Clothier, Norman, *Black Valour: The South African Native Labour Contingent 1916–1918 and the Sinking of the Mendi* (Pietermaritzburg University of Natal Press, 1987)

Cockburn, Claud, *Bestseller. The Books that Everyone Read 1900–1939* (Penguin, 1975)

Colonial Report No 1016 for Basutoland 1918–1919 (His Majesty's Stationery Office, 1919)

Cretney, Stephen, *Family Law in the Twentieth Century: A History* (Oxford University Press, 2004)

Dawson, Sandra Trudgen, 'Downton Abbey, Maternal Death and the Crisis of Childbirth in Britain', *Nursing Clio*, 5 February 2013, https://nursingclio.org

Dean, Basil, *Seven Ages: An Autobiography, 1888–1927* (Hutchinson, 1970)

Demm, Eberhard, *Censorship* (International Encyclopaedia of the First World War Online)

Dietrich, John H, 'Has Jesus a Message for Today?' *The Humanist Pulpit* (The First Unitarian Society, 1932)

Dove, Canon R, *Anglican Pioneers in Lesotho Some Account of the Dioceses of Lesotho 1876–1930* (Maseru, 1975)

Dunstable School magazine 1921–1922, extracts

Eade, Philip, *Evelyn Waugh: A Life Revisited* (Weidenfeld and Nicholson, 2016)

Edgar, Robert, 'Lesotho and the First World War: Recruiting, Resistance and the South African Native Labour Contingent', *Mohlomi: Journal of Southern Africa Historical Studies*, Vols. iii/iv/v, 1979–81

Elliot, Rosemary Elizabeth, 'Destructive but Sweet': Cigarette Smoking among Women 1890–1990', PhD dissertation, University of Glasgow, 2001

Eskridge, Robert Lee, *Manga Reva, The Forgotten Islands* (The Bobbs-Merrill Co, 1931)

Field, Louise Maunsell, 'Eve in South Africa, Review of The Mother of All Living' (*The New York Times*, 13 August 1922)

Fitzgerald, F Scott, *The Great Gatsby* (Charles Scribner's Sons, 1925)

Fox, Kate, *Watching the English* (Hodder and Stoughton, 2004)

Gerhart M, Karis T (editors), *From Protest to Challenge: A Documentary History of African Politics in South Africa: 1882–1964*, Political Profiles 1882–1964, Vol. 4 (Hoover Institution Press: Stanford University, 1977)

Gossler, Claus, 'The Social and Economic Fall of the Salmon/Brander Clan of Tahiti', *The Journal of Pacific History*, September 2005, pp 193–212

Grimble, Sir Arthur, *Migrations, Myth and Magic from the Gilbert Islands: Early Writings of Sir Arthur Grimble* (Routledge & Kegan Paul, 1972)

Grundlingh, Albert, *Fighting Their Own War: South African Blacks and the First World War* (Ravan Press, 1987)

Grundlingh, Albert, *War and Society: Participation and Remembrance. South African Black and Coloured Troops in the First World War, 1914–1918* (Sun Press, 2014)

Guild, Caroline, *Rainbow in Tahiti* (Hammond, Hammond and Co Ltd, 1951)

Hall, James Norman, *My Island Home* (Little Brown and Company, 1952)

Hall, James Norman, *The Forgotten One and Other True Tales of the South Seas* (Commemorative Edition Mutual Publishing)

Hamilton, Sharon, 'The New York Gossip Magazine in The Great Gatsby', *The F. Scott Fitzgerald Review*, September 2010, pp 34–56

Hardiman, David (editor), *Healing Bodies, Saving Souls: Medical Missions in Asia and Africa* (Rodopi, 2006)

Hart's Annual Army List, Militia List and Yeomanry Cavalry List for 1902 (John Murray, 1902)

Haslam, Sara '"The Moaning of the World" and the "Words That Bring Me Peace" Modernism and the First World War' in Piette, Adam, Rawlinson, Mark (editors), *The Edinburgh Companion to British and American War Literature* (Edinburgh University Press, 2012), pp 47–57)

Hastings, Selina, *The Red Earl: The Extraordinary Life of the 16th Earl of Huntingdon* (Bloomsbury, 2014)

Herbert, AP, *The Secret Battle* (Methuen & Co, Ltd 1919)

Hertslet, Lewis, *The Native Problem* (The State Library, 1969)

Jerrold, Douglas William, *The Lie about the War, a Note on Some Contemporary War Books* (Faber and Faber, 1930)

Jones, Rev James, 'Reminiscences: Benson, Keable and Mallory 1906–1910', *Magdalene College Magazine*, October 2000, pp 63–70

Jones, Nigel, *Rupert Brooke, Life, Death and Myth* (Richard Cohen Books, 1999)

Keating, Jenny, 'Government Policy towards Secondary Schools and History Teaching 1900–1910', https://archives.history.ac.uk/history-in-education/sites

Levine, Philippa, *Amateur and the Professionals, Antiquarians, Historians and Archaeologists in Victorian Britain 1838–1886* (Cambridge University Press, 1986)

Levy, Robert, *Tahitians: Mind and Experience in the Society Islands* (University of Chicago, 1973)

Lincoln, Jackson Steward, *The Dream in Native American and Other Primitive Cultures* (Dover Publications, 2003)

Long Trail, https://www.longlongtrail.co.uk/battlefields

Loudon, I, *Death in Childbirth. An International Study of Maternal Care and Maternal Mortality 1800–1950* (Clarendon Press, 1992)

Lubbock, Percy (editor), The *Diary of Arthur Christopher Benson* (Hutchinson and Co Ltd, 1926)

Machobane, LBBJ, *Government and Change in Lesotho, 1800–1966* (Macmillan Press, 1990)

Madigan, Edward, *The Clergy in Khaki: New Perspectives on British Army Chaplaincy in the First World War*, Ashgate Studies in First World War History (Routledge, 2013)

Makepeace, Clare, 'Sex and the Trenches', *The First World War Story*, (BBC History Magazine, 2016)

Maltby, Richard, 'To Prevent the Prevalent Type of Book: Censorship and Adaptation in Hollywood, 1924–1934', *American Quarterly*, Vol. 44, no. 4, Special Issue: Hollywood, Censorship, and American Culture, December 1992, pp 554–583

Manning, Anita, 'What it Was Like Being Pregnant in 1915?' https://next. voxcreative.com

Manwaring, Randle, 'From Controversy to Co-Existence: Evangelicals in the Church of England, 1914–1980', *Church History*, Vol. 55, September 1986

Mason, Walter, 'An Appreciation of EF Benson, His Life and Times', *The Newtown Review of Books*, June 2013, http://newtownreviewofbooks. com.au

McKibbin, Ross, *Classes and Cultures: England 1918–1951* (Oxford University Press, 1998)

Meredith, Martin, *Diamonds, Gold and War: The British, the Boers, and the Making of South Africa* (Public Affairs, 2007), p 157

Metcalfe, HG, *That Summer in Tahiti* (General Store Pub. House, 1999)

Minturn, Robert B Jr, *From New York To Delhi By Way Of Rio De Janeiro, Australia and China* (D Appleton & Co, 1858)

'Missionary's letter', *Magdalene College Magazine*, 8 April 1916

Molteno family, *Chronicle of the Molteno Family magazine (1913–20)* The section covering the travels of Kathleen and Margaret, https://www.

moltenofamily.net/stories-and-history/chronicle-of-the-family

Mordaunt, Elinor, *The Venture Book* (John Lane, The Bodley Head, 1926)

Motsamai, Edward, *Mehla ea Malimo (The Times of the Cannibals)* (Morija-Lesotho: Morija Sesuto Book Depot, 1980)

Neame, Sylvia, 'The ICU and British Imperialism', *Societies for Southern Africa Seminar Papers*, 1970

Newbury, Colin W, *Tahiti Nui: Change and Survival in French Polynesia, 1767–1945* (University of Hawaii Press, 1980)

O'Brien, Frederick, *Mystic Isles of the South Seas* (Hodder and Stoughton, 1921)

Ollard, SL, *A Short History of the Oxford Movement* (AR Mowbray & Co, 1915)

O'Shea, May, *Bloomie: Memoirs of the Twenties* (Don Nelson, 1977)

Parker, Linda Mary, 'Shell-shocked Prophets: The Influence of Former Anglican Army Chaplains on the Church of England and British Society in the Interwar Years', PhD thesis, University of Birmingham, 2013

Phillips, Howard, *In a Time of Plague: Memories of the 'Spanish' Flu Epidemic of 1918 in South Africa* (Van Riebeeck Society for the Publication of Southern African Historical Documents, 2018)

Piette, Adam, *Edinburgh Companion to Twentieth Century British and American War Literature* (Edinburgh University Press, 2012)

Putnam GG and Others, *Nonsenseorship, Sundry Observations Concerning Prohibitions Inhibitions and Illegalities,* incl. Keable, Robert, *The Censorship of Truth* (GP Putnam's, 1922)

Ross, Robert, Mager, Anne Kelk, Nasson, Bill, (editors), *The Cambridge History of South Africa: Volume 2, 1885–1994* (Cambridge University Press, 2011)

Simmers, George, 'Robert Keable', *Great War Fiction Plus*, https://greatwarfiction.wordpress.com/2006/06/11/robert-keable/

Smith, H Maynard, *Frank, Bishop of Zanzibar* (SPCK, 1926), Chapter XIV, http://anglicanhistory.org/weston/frank14.html

Smith, Preserved, *A History of Modern Culture* (George Routledge and Sons, 1934)

Snedegar, Keith, *Mission, Science, and Race in South Africa: A. W. Roberts of Lovedale, 1883–1938* (Lexington Books, 2015)

South Africa War Graves Project, http://www.southafricawargraves.org

Sterling, John, Lee, Ivor, *No Labour, No Battle: Military Labour during the*

First World War (Military Historical Society, 2014)

Steiner, Zara S, *The Foreign Office and Foreign Policy, 1898–1914* (Cambridge University Press, 1969)

Sturma, Michael, *South Sea Maidens: Western Fantasy and Sexual Politics in the South Pacific* (Greenwood Press, 2002)

Tietjens, Eunice, *The World at My Shoulder* (MacMillan Company, 1938)

The First Troops, https://cms.scouts.org.uk/media/12898/the-first-troops.pdf

Thompson, John Handby, 'The Free Church Army Chaplain 1830–1930', PhD thesis, University of Sheffield, 1990

Van Niekerk, Sybrand Gerhardus, *The History, Role and Influence of the South African Military Chaplaincy 1914–2002* (University of South Africa, 2002)

Waten, Judah, Carter, David (editors), *Fiction, Memoirs, Criticism* (University of Queensland, 1998)

Waugh, Alec, *The Early Years of Alec Waugh* (Cassell, 1962)

Wearing JP, *The London Stage 1920–1929: A Calendar of Productions, Performers, and Personnel* (Rowman and Littlefield, 2014)

Wessex Archaeology, *SS Mendi Archaeological Desk-based Assessment* (English Heritage, April 2007)

WHM, 'How a Young Man Finds Himself – and a Wife, A Review of Peradventure' *Daily Mail*, 19 September 1922

Willan, BP, 'The South African Native Labour Contingent 1916–1918', *The Journal of African History*, Vol. 19, no. 1, 1978, pp 61–86

Wilson, GH, *The History of the Universities' Mission to Central Africa* (Garden City Press Limited, 1936)

Winegard, Timothy C, *Indigenous Peoples of the British Dominions and the First World War* (Cambridge, November 2011)

Wyndham, Diana, *Norman Haire and the Study of Sex* (Sydney University Press, 2012)

Youé, Christopher P, *Robert Thorne Coryndon: Proconsular Imperialism in Southern and Eastern Africa 1897–1925* (Wilfrid Laurier University Press, 1986)

INDEX